Christians and the State

Christians and the State

John Duddington

GRACEWING

First published in 2016

Gracewing
2 Southern Avenue, Leominster
Herefordshire HR6 0QF

ISBN 978 085244 829 8

Typeset by
Action Publishing Technology Ltd, Gloucester GL1 5SR

Contents

Dedication and Acknowledgements   vii
Foreword   ix

Introduction   1

Chapter 1   Christians and the State: A Historical
             Perspective   5
Chapter 2   Church and State in the World Today   23
Chapter 3   Is English Law Based on Christianity?   44
Chapter 4   Faith and Reason   56
Chapter 5   Natural Law   65
Chapter 6   Christians, Conscience and the Law   85
Chapter 7   Law and Justice   98
Chapter 8   The State and Morality   110
Chapter 9   Religion and Public Debate   123
Chapter 10   Christianity, Equality and Human Rights   140
Chapter 11   Christians and Religious Liberty   164
Chapter 12   Christians and the Law   177
Chapter 13   Conclusion: A Future for Religion in
             Public Life?   203

Bibliography   209
Index of Cases   219
Index of Statutes   221
Index   222

Dedication and Acknowledgements

In all my writings I think of my late father, Walter Duddington, who first encouraged me to become a lawyer and who still inspires me. My thanks go to my wife Anne, for her constant support, loyalty and technical expertise over many years and without which my books would never begin to be written; to my daughter Mary, for her seemingly faultless proofreading and sense of fun which keeps me going, and to my son Christopher for just being himself.

I would also like to thank my colleagues on the editorial board of *Law and Justice* and *The Newman,* the journal of the Newman Association, for their stimulating companionship and friendship. I have, in writing this, benefited enormously from their ideas. Special thanks go to two members: Frank Cranmer, a member of the editorial board of *Law and Justice* and a Fellow of the Centre for Law and Religion at Cardiff University, very kindly commented on some chapters and made some percipient comments from a non-Catholic perspective which have added greatly to the value of this book. In addition, the case notes which he contributes to *Law and Justice* have proved absolutely indispensable in keeping up with the flow of litigation in this area. Secondly, Fr Robert Ombres, OP, of Blackfriars, Oxford, has commented on two chapters to their great benefit. Not only this but over many years of friendship he and Dr Javier Oliva of Manchester University have been the source of wise ideas many of which have, I hope, found their way into the pages of this book. I would also like to thank Paul Barber, Director of the Catholic Education Service, for some extremely helpful guidance on recent developments. Needless to say, none of them are responsible for what appears in these pages.

Some of the thoughts contained in this book originally appeared in articles, essays and booklets published by the *Catholic Herald,* the Catholic Truth Society, Theos and *The Newman,* and I am grateful to the respective editors and publishers, Luke Coppen, Fergal Martin, Nick Spencer and Barry Riley, for allowing me the space to develop my ideas. In addition grateful thanks go to Tom Longford, Managing Director of Gracewing Publishing and Rev. Dr Paul Haffner, Editorial Director, who have supported me so much during the writing and the production process. I would also like to give special thanks to Sr Mary Joseph, OSB, who has not only been an eagle-eyed copy editor but who has suggested a number of amendments to the text which have greatly improved its flow and readability.

Finally, I am enormously grateful to Lord Mackay of Clashfern, Lord Chancellor from 1987–1997, for so generously contributing a Foreword. He remains an inspiration to all Christian lawyers.

Although I have been able to make some amendments during the publishing process, the bulk of this book was completed on the anniversary of what was, by any standard, a low date in Church-State relations. It is in the hope that, by contrast, today Christians and the State can work together for the common good that this book has been written.

John Duddington
Feast of St Thomas Becket
29 December 2015

Foreword

Lord Mackay of Clashfern,
Lord Chancellor of Great Britain, 1987–1997

John Duddington has a wide experience as a lawyer and as editor of *Law and Justice*, which is a journal with a Christian background that deals with subjects of many kinds that fall under the headings of its title.

In this book he deals with the important question, very much in issue today, of the extent, if any, to which it is open to resort to Christian views in political debate. This is part of the larger question. Does religion have a part to play in the political process and in the formulation of our laws?

This is sometimes answered in the negative on the ground that if my religion forbids a certain course of action why should I be allowed to argue that it should not be allowed to those who do not share my religion.

To deal with these challenges the author surveys the history of the relationship between Church and State and then the state of this relationship in the world at the present time. He then pauses to examine in detail many of the specific areas where this question arises.

In reading these chapters, I have found particular interest in the many examples he gives of the way in which this subject has arisen and how it has been treated. Sufficient background is given to enable the reader to appreciate the way in which the examples relate to the topic without the necessity of recourse to the original sources.

Finally the author draws his conclusion that action is desirable to protect the right of Christians to have their voices heard in discussion of public affairs today.

Although this book is written from a Christian viewpoint, the topic is of importance to people of any religion and to those who have no religion. Why should an atheist have a right to have his voice heard in public debate if that is denied to a Christian?

I commend this book therefore to any who are interested in the conduct of public debate today. Here they will find careful well-informed help to increase their knowledge of the subject.

Mackay of Clashfern

Introduction

The genesis of this book lies in the address which Pope Benedict
XVI gave to both Houses of the United Kingdom Parliament in
September 2010 in which he spoke of the contribution which
religion can and indeed should make to political debate. Various
parts of this address will be referred to throughout this book but
the central part seemed to me to be as follows:

> The central question at issue, then, is this: where is the ethical foun-
> dation for political choices to be found? The Catholic tradition
> maintains that the objective norms governing right action are acces-
> sible to reason, prescinding from the content of revelation.
> According to this understanding, the role of religion in political
> debate is not so much to supply these norms, as if they could not be
> known by non-believers – still less to propose concrete political
> solutions, which would lie altogether outside the competence of
> religion – but rather to help purify and shed light upon the appli-
> cation of reason to the discovery of objective moral principles.[1]

Later on in his address in Westminster Hall he observed that
'Religion ... is not a problem for legislators to solve, but a vital
contribution to the national conversation'.

It seemed to me that these words needed a response which
looked in detail at the relationship between Christians and the
State today and addressed both the question of how religion could
and should contribute to political debate in this country and also
the challenges which it faces. This book, then, is my response to
Pope Benedict's words on that September evening. For, make no
mistake, there is a substantial body of opinion which would
confine religion merely to private belief and would deny religious
views of any denomination the right to be heard in public debate.
Take, for instance, the words of Baroness Warnock when the

Catholic Bishops opposed the 2008 Human Fertilisation and Embryology Bill. She said in the *New Statesman* that Roman Catholic MPs would 'have no business' opposing the 2008 Human Fertilisation and Embryology Bill on the basis of their faith. They should not oppose it 'unless they could find other reasons than their own religious convictions on which to base their opposition'. It is my contention that this view is wrong and that a public life and a political debate that fails to accord weight to religious views will be greatly impoverished.

Where there can be no argument is that the theme of Christians and the State is both urgent and highly topical. When I was preparing this book, I thought that I would select at random one week and see what issues made the news. I selected one newspaper, the *Daily Telegraph*, in this case, as I wanted to assess the extent of one newspaper's coverage, and the week ran from Monday 7 October to Friday 11 October 2013. I also wanted to see how many of the issues dealt with were real examples of threats by the State to religious beliefs and which were not threats at all but had, in fact, been misinterpreted as such by religious believers.

Monday's story was entitled 'Church opposes proposal to drop Bible in court' and dealt with a proposal to be debated by the Magistrates' Association that the practice of witnesses swearing on oath on the Bible should be dropped and replaced by a promise to tell the truth 'sincerely'. The proposal was in fact rejected. Nevertheless Andrea Minichiello, the Chief Executive of Christian Concern, saw the proposal as 'stamping secularisation at the heart of the legal system'. This comment shows how the religion v. secular debate had penetrated into public debate in that even this proposal, which would have been supported by many Christian lawyers who see the oath as simply encouragement to witnesses to commit perjury or blasphemy, was seen in the light of the religion v. secular clash. Was this helpful? I think not.

On Wednesday the story concerned Peter and Hazelmary Bull, who had refused a double room in their bed and breakfast house to a couple who were in a same-sex relationship and were now taking their case to the Supreme Court. As we shall see, they lost. Thursday's story was about the sending home from school of two bearded Muslim pupils from Mount Carmel High School in Accrington, on the basis that the wearing of beards contravened the school's dress code. The wearing of religious dress and the display of religious symbols are considered in detail in Chapter 12 but for now we can mention that it ended by the school allowing one boy back into school, the head teacher reportedly[2] saying that the school would comply with the European Convention on Human Rights, which insists schools must make 'reasonable' adjustments to uniform policy if students object on religious grounds.

Added to this, abortion on the ground of gender selection featured as a news item that week. Although this is not a book about abortion as such, the divergent views of some Churches at least, and the law on this issue, deserve analysis as an example of the relationship (or lack of it) between some religions and the State. On Monday 7 October the story was the alleged failure of the Attorney-General to prosecute doctors who had carried out abortions on this ground, and this simmered throughout the week, with the paper reporting on Wednesday 9 October that Lord Steel who, as David Steel, had piloted what became the Abortion Act 1967 through Parliament, saying that 'Terminating a foetus on gender grounds is wholly repugnant'.

This, I hope, justifies the need for a book which, if it does not aim to provide all the answers, does aim to stimulate debate and offer some ideas on a way forward, particularly in the final section. Moreover my perspective is not that of the academic philosopher but that of a lawyer who, as editor of the *Christian Law Review* for over twenty years, has watched and monitored these developments.

A word is needed about the sub-title of this book: 'A Catholic perspective for the 21st century'. Why 'Catholic' and why not 'Christian'? The answer is that whilst I hope that most if not all of what I say is within mainstream Christian thought about the relationship between the Christian believer and the civil powers, some of the thinking behind it comes from the Catholic tradition. For example, my view of the nature of conscience is a Catholic one and so is my belief in the relationship between faith and reason, albeit shared by some non-Catholics. Moreover, Catholic thought accords a primacy to natural law in a way that not all non-Catholics would, although a growing number are recognising its significance. Not only this, but it is my belief that, in spite of protestations to the contrary by some liberal thinkers, it is in fact impossible to be neutral in one's beliefs about the part played by religion or indeed any other system of belief or thought in political life. Any view presupposes a particular set of ideas on which that view is based. That being so, it would be wrong of me to hide my own Christian faith, as represented by the Catholic tradition, as that is what underpins my view of the topics in this book. However, it is my hope that all Christians, and indeed those of other religions or none, will find much to agree with in these pages.

Notes

1   The whole of his address can be found in Peter Jennings (ed.), *Benedict XVI and Blessed John Henry Newman, The State Visit September 2010, The Official Record* (London: CTS, 2010), pp. 102–106. I should mention that just before this book went to press, I was able to make use of a fascinating presentation of Pope Benedict's thought: M. Carbatia and A. Simoncini (eds), *Pope Benedict's Legal Thought* (Cambridge: Cambridge University Press, 2015).

2   www.huffingtonpost.co.uk/.../banned-muslim-student-beard-**school**-lanc Accessed 30/12/2013.

Chapter 1

Christians and the State: A Historical Perspective

'Jesus is Lord' *1 Cor 12:3*

Introduction

It is the Christian conviction that Jesus is Lord of all creation, but how is this to be worked out in practice, especially as there is also an ancient tradition that there are two spheres: the spiritual, belonging to the Church, and the temporal, belonging to the State? Yet the two must not be sundered for, if they are, the Christian message is not heard in the political world and it is one of the main contentions of this book that that is precisely where it must be heard.

This is not a book on the detailed history of Church-State relationships. Indeed for much of history the notion of Church and State would have made no sense at all as the two were seen as interlinked or even as one. Instead the focus of this inquiry is the present day. However, it is impossible to understand the tensions and challenges which arise today in the relationship without some historical perspective. Two instances will suffice. In Protestant countries, the theory of Luther that there are two kingdoms, one the spiritual and one the secular, was arguably influential in the attitude of many Germans to Hitler[1] and, in the United Kingdom, the Monarch is still, by Act of Parliament passed in 1558, 'Defender of the Faith'.[2]

Anyone who investigates the relationship between religion on the one hand and politics on the other must constantly steer clear of two rocks, the Scylla and the Charybdis of this topic. On the one hand, if one adopts a completely other-worldly view, there is the danger of steering so far from this world that one ignores the challenges and dangers which beset Christians in it. On the other hand, if one adopts a standpoint which engages too much with the concerns of this world, then one may steer so far away from the world to come that the Kingdom of God becomes one of this world and not the next. In his recent book, *Freedom and Order*,[3] Nick Spencer describes the Labour Church, founded in 1891, which focused on 'Jesus the radical, on human brotherhood, on the earthly reality of the Kingdom of God and on the sense that God was immanent in the whole world'.[4] As Spencer puts it:

> The Labour Church was an extreme example of the perils that awaited (some) Christian politics in the twentieth century. Identify the kingdom of God too closely with worldly politics and you would risk losing it altogether. Equate it with the coming socialist order and you might end up being doubly disappointed.[5]

The Early Christians and the State

The modern idea of Church and State as opposites would not have meant a great deal to the medieval mind, despite the apparent juxtaposition of God and Caesar by Christ (see below). Instead Church and State would have been seen as part of one pattern of authority in the community. However, what is important is to trace the attitude of Christians to the State throughout the ages.

The early Christian view of the relationship of Christians to the civil authorities was expressed long ago in the Epistle to Diognetus, written probably in the early second century, where it is expressed thus: '... though they are residents there at home in their own country their behaviour is more like transients; they take their full part as citizens, but they also submit to anything and everything as if they were aliens'.[6]

However, one must not overstate the extent to which disengagement with the civil authorities was urged on Christians. Moreover, the Epistle to Diognetus was written when many Christians believed that the Lord would soon return and so there was little necessity for engagement with the concerns of this world. A slightly more robust view was, however, expressed by Clement in his First Epistle to the Corinthians who, whilst recognising that political institutions are legitimate, also urged that: 'in peace and mildness they may put to godly use the authority thou hast given them ...'[7] A theme is starting to emerge: Christians recognise the civil powers, and give them obedience, but Christians also insist that those civil powers are, like them, under the Lordship of Christ. At the same time Christians are wary of upsetting the authorities.

Thus in 1 Pt 2:13–17, we find that: 'For the sake of the Lord, accept the authority of every social institution: the emperor as supreme authority, and the governors as commissioned by him to punish criminals and praise good citizenship'. This could be read as advocating that Christians should adopt a subservient attitude to governments. But St Paul (Rm 13:1–3), whilst expressing the same thought as St Peter, has a slightly different but significant slant: 'You must obey all the governing authorities. Since all government comes from God, the civil authorities were appointed by God and anyone who resists authority is rebelling against God's decision, and such an act is bound to be punished'. Thus although St Paul does indeed advocate obedience to the authorities, he points out very clearly that 'all government comes from God'. Similarly, St Peter begins: 'For the sake of the Lord'. It is clear that although neither Peter nor Paul wished Christians to needlessly upset the ruling powers, and indeed the Pax Romana enforced by the Romans enabled both of them to journey to Rome, they wished to emphasise that the authority of governments comes ultimately from God and so governments are ultimately accountable to Him.

The point that Christ is the Lord of all Creation is clearly brought out in the dialogue between Jesus and Pilate (Jn 19:10–11). Pilate lets Jesus know of the extent of the civil power to which Jesus is subject: 'Do you not know that I have power to release you, and power to crucify you?' Jesus' answer is unequivocal: 'You would have no power over me unless it had been given you from above.' This, as Tom Wright expresses it, 'does not mean that Jesus' kingdom is a mere spiritual one, a gnostic dream of escape that has nothing to do with the present world … Jesus' kingdom does not *derive from* the world, but it is *designed for* the world'. As he says: 'it is the kingdom of the wise Creator God who longs to heal the world'.[8]

The passages in the letters of Peter and Paul quoted above both see a dual role for government and therefore law. They regard law as being necessary to deal with behaviour which is contrary to justice but in addition they regard law as having a positive force in promoting what is good. Thus St Peter says in the same sentence that governors have powers 'to punish criminals and praise good citizenship'. Again St Paul, later in the same passage at 13:4, points out that: 'The state is there to serve God for your benefit'. The Christian duty not only to avoid evil but also to promote good is also the duty of lawmakers.[9]

When arrested, St Paul does not hesitate to use Roman law

procedures to safeguard his rights and appeals to Caesar,[10] yet he also criticises the Christians at Corinth for having recourse to the civil courts to settle disputes with each other instead of allowing the community to settle them.[11] The early Christian community did not question the authority of the State in general but would not comply when its requirements ran contrary to the demands of divine law and thus in conscience it could not be obeyed. This was, of course, why Christians refused to offer sacrifice as required to the Roman gods and so suffered death. When Christians today resist a law on the grounds that it is contrary to deeply held conscientious beliefs, they are following in the footsteps of these early Christians.[12]

The Laws of God and the Laws of Society: Church and State

There is a distinction in the New Testament between the law of God and the laws of civil society. This is most clearly seen in the celebrated, if all too often misunderstood, encounter between Jesus and the Pharisees when Jesus is questioned about whether it is lawful to pay taxes to Caesar (Lk 20:20–26; Mk 12:13–17; Mt 22:15–22). The dialogue can only be understood if we remember that the Jews objected to heads on coins as it violated their law against images. So the Romans minted copper coins without the Emperor's head for internal circulation inside Palestine. (This, incidentally, is a good example of secular law taking account of religious beliefs and is a precedent which modern legislatures might follow.) However, what was in effect a poll tax paid to the Roman Emperor had to be paid in silver coin with the Emperor's head on it and it was this coin which led to Jesus' reply, in Mark's version: 'Give back to Caesar what belongs to Caesar – and to God what belongs to God'. This does not mean that the secular and the sacred belong to two separate compartments of our existence. What it does mean is that God sometimes deals with us directly and sometimes through the civil authorities and, provided that Caesar and all civil authorities perform their task, under God, of promoting the common good, then they are entitled to what is due to them. This can be the payment of taxes and, more broadly, obedience to the secular law. Thus the God and Caesar dialogue is not authority for saying that there are two worlds, the sacred and the secular, and God is only concerned with the sacred. It is in fact quite the opposite: there is one world, over which Christ has dominion.

There is yet more to this distinction drawn by Jesus between God and Caesar. As Pope Benedict XVI has pointed out, 'In his teaching and in his whole ministry Jesus had inaugurated a non-political Messianic kingdom and had begun to detach these two hitherto inseparable realities (i.e. religion and politics) from one another'.[13] It is worth pausing to note just how radical, especially in the context of his time, this teaching of Jesus was. We think of Roman gods and Greek gods and, of course, the Jewish God of the Old Testament, but here Jesus refused to recognise any connection between nationality and religion. Thus, as Aidan Nichols has pointed out, Pope Benedict sees Jesus' distinction between God and Caesar 'as the end of the automatic assumption that politics is holy'.[14] It is instructive too, in the context of German nationalism and the attitude of some German Christians to the Nazi party, to note how Pope Benedict regards the notion of fatherland as being replaced by the Church, in contrast to the views of some Protestant theologians such as Paul Althaus with their theology of the *Volk* and their belief that God did not only create individuals but also their *Volk*.[15] Such dangerous teaching is countered by the Christian view that the State no longer has a religious authority but instead, as Nichols puts it, the State points 'for its final ethical authority to an institution beyond itself.' This is, of course, the Church and so I would argue that whilst in one sense the Church stands outside politics, yet in another sense it is deeply involved in politics as the Church claims to set out the fundamental truths by which politicians should be guided.

What is of the utmost significance is that, before these words of Jesus, no one had attempted to draw any distinction at all between religion and politics and so the title of this book could not have been 'Christians and the State' but 'Christians as the State'. Yet if we have an identification between Church and State this means that the State itself claims a right to make fundamental ethical judgements and to impose these on us. If this is so, then that is the end of any true freedom. A separation between Church and State thus becomes of critical importance for Christians and indeed all of us.[16]

Church and State in the Era of Constantine and Beyond

With the end of persecution of Christians following the Edict of Milan in 312, we come to an era in which the relationship between Christians and the State undergoes a subtle change and we begin

to see the start of the kind of see-saw tension which has characterised the interplay between Christians, on the one hand, and the
State and the Law on the other, ever since. At times the Church
was felt by the State to be too powerful and was accused of attempting to interfere in the secular sphere, and at others the State was
seen by the Church to be encroaching on what rightfully belonged
to the spiritual.

First, however, it is important to emphasise the extent to which
the adoption of Christian beliefs made a dramatic difference in
society, a point too often missed not only by the critics of
Christianity but by Christians themselves. Alvin Schmidt has
pointed out[17] how, during the century following the end of persecution of Christianity, branding the faces of criminals was ended in
315, the segregation of male and female prisoners was instituted in
361, child abortion and abandonment in the Roman Empire was
outlawed in 374 and battles to the death between gladiators were
outlawed in 401. These are but instances of many ways in which the
law was made more humane through Christian influence, another
being the granting of property rights and protections to women.
Not only this but note the cruel way in which writers of the pre-
Christian era wrote about the treatment of children, especially
those who were born disabled. Thus Aristotle says that: 'let there
be a law that no deformed child shall live'.[18] Plato wrote that
children who were born after their parents were 'past the age for
breeding' must be 'disposed of as a creature that must not be
reared'.[19] As David Jones points out,[20] not only was abortion not
regarded as morally objectionable but neither was infanticide, and
so the abandonment of new-born children judged unfit to live was
thought of as a moral duty. This link between abortion and infanticide is one that needs to be stressed today. Contrast this with
some of the earliest Christian teaching from the sub-Apostolic age
where in *The Didache*,[21] dating from around 100 AD, it is stated that
both abortion and infanticide are forbidden.

We will deal with developments in the relation between Church
and State as this chapter progresses but before we do so it is worth
noting a striking occasion when the Church called a ruler to
account for, in effect, a breach of fundamental principles of
natural law. In 390, the citizens of Thessalonica killed the captain
of the imperial army garrison. There had apparently been resent-
ment over the billeting of soldiers and matters had come to a head
when the captain imprisoned the most popular charioteer in the
city. At all events, a terrible retribution was exacted by the

Emperor Theodosius I who ordered the army to reassert its authority in whatever way it sought fit to do so. Taking him at his word, the soldiers slaughtered 7,000 of the citizens when they were gathered for the games.[22]

Ambrose, Bishop of Milan, where the Imperial Court was based, was outraged and held Theodosius responsible even though the Emperor seems to have regretted having given the order and tried to countermand it. Ambrose told him that he could not receive the Eucharist until he had performed public penance, which Theodosius did. He appeared bareheaded and dressed in sackcloth in Milan Cathedral to beg forgiveness.

This is one of the first, and certainly the first noteworthy occasion when the Church spoke 'Truth to Power' and called the State to account for a breach of fundamental principles of what we would now term natural law. As Owen Chadwick puts it, Ambrose 'enforced the point that the concern of the church extends to actions contrary to natural law and repugnant to humanity, not merely to its private interests'.[23] As such his action stands as an inspiration to us all down the ages when confronted with either laws or breaches of the law, which are contrary to the law of God.

Not long after this episode, St Augustine wrote *The City of God*, distinguishing between the city of this world, the city of the Roman authorities and the pagans, and the City of God. Some attempts have been made to construct a theory of Church and State from this, but the effort is clearly mistaken. The City of God is identified with the love of God and consequent contempt of oneself, and the city of this world is the opposite.[24] As David Knowles points out in his Introduction: 'The two cities are therefore two loves. And these are an inward and spiritual, not outward and political, distinction'.[25]

The 'Gelasian Dyarchy'

The climate changed in the fifth century. There were occasions when the Roman Emperors were seen by the Popes as supporters of heresy and at the same time the divide between Rome and the Churches in the East was becoming more apparent. Thus, in 484 the Patriarch Acacius of Constantinople adopted a pro-Monophysite theology and was supported by the Emperor Zeno. The result was that Rome and Constantinople broke off communion with each other and the divide between the Church, as represented by the Pope, and State, as represented by the Emperor, deepened. It was time to define the relations between them. As Duffy puts it: 'In practice ... the emperors were suspect, supporters of heresy. This suspicion led the popes to make an increasingly sharp distinction between the secular and the sacred, and to resist imperial claims to authority over the Church.' [26] Thus it was that in 492 Pope Gelasius I wrote to the Emperor Anastasius that although he was 'a Roman born, I love, respect and honour the Roman Emperor' there was, as it were, another side to the coin: ' ... there are two powers by which the earth is chiefly ruled: the sacred authority of bishops and the royal power. Of these the priestly power is much more important, because it has to render account for the kings of men themselves at the judgement seat of God'.[27]

It is doubtful whether Pope Gelasius ever intended that these words would be taken as a fundamental text on the relationship between Church and State, but so they have been, because the 'Gelasian Dyarchy' expresses a fundamental truth: there are indeed two powers, the sacred (the Church) and the secular (the State); both respect each other but the sacred claims ultimate authority. If it did not, then it would be abandoning much of human activity to any Christian, and indeed any religious influence whatsoever. The claim made by Pope Gelasius is one still made by Christians today.[28]

However, before we look at what lessons the further development of Church and State relations holds for us today, we must note how they fared in the Eastern Roman Empire.

Church and State in the Eastern Roman Empire

The relations between Church and State in the Eastern Roman Empire took a different turn from that in the West and gave rise to what became known as 'Caesaropapism' and a much closer relationship between Church and State was envisaged.[29]

The origin of this was the violent controversies which raged in the East over the Person of Christ and in particular over the decrees of the Council of Chalcedon in 451 that Christ had two natures, the human and the divine, although in his own Person he is both God and man. The Monophysite heresy taught that Christ had only one nature,[30] and by the time of the accession of the Emperor Justinian this position was held by two of the major

Eastern centers of power, Antioch and Alexandria. This was of political importance as bishops, and especially those of two such major centres, were expected to play a major part in keeping the Empire united. Thus Church divisions became of State importance too. To our eyes such violent and bitter disputes over matters of doctrine seems strange but in fact the conflicting movements were animated as much by social and nationalistic ideas as by religious ones and it is important to keep this in mind.

Thus it was that the Emperor Justinian took an active interest in ecclesiastical matters and on 17 April 535 issued an edict which became known as the Sixth Novella, the object of which was to 'ensure the implementation of God's law in public life and the protection of the faith'.[31] So the preamble stated that:

> There are two greatest gifts which God, in his love for man, has granted from on high: the priesthood and the imperial dignity. The first serves divine things, while the latter directs and administers church affairs ... Hence nothing should be such a source of care to the emperors as the dignity of the priests, since it is for their imperial welfare that they constantly implore God.

There then followed legislation on such matters as the marital status of the clergy, church property and clergy selection and residence.[32]

In some ways this is no different to the involvement of the Holy Roman Emperors in the affairs of the Catholic Church at various junctures, for example at the Synod of Pavia in 1022 the Emperor Henry II and Pope Benedict VIII agreed on a series of decrees which prohibited marriage among the clergy and reduced the children of clerics to serfdom. However, in the Eastern Church this involvement of the Emperor was part of the continuing fabric of society where the State made legal regulations for the Church in what became known, misleadingly, as Caesaropapism. The term is misleading in that the Eastern Churches did not recognise the Papacy in the Western sense as a supreme religious power and the Emperors were not involved in 'the actual content of the faith.'[33] Instead there was what is often called a symphony between Church and State in the East. Thus, as Ware points out[34] 'it was the Emperor's task to summon councils and to carry their decrees into effect, but it lay beyond his powers to dictate the content of those decrees ...' So Ware argues that 'in Byzantine history Church and State were closely interdependent, but neither was subordinate to the other'.

A close relationship between Church and State in the East has persisted to this day and this is bolstered by the fact that Orthodox churches tend to be organised on national lines. Moreover, it is argued that the links between the present day Russian Orthodox Church and the Russian Government are too close. This was seen in the so-called 'Pussy Riot Case' where members of a punk band were convicted after performing an obscenity-laced song called Punk Prayer in Moscow's Christ the Saviour cathedral in February 2012. The song was heavily critical of the Orthodox Church's support for the president, calling on the Virgin Mary to 'throw Putin out'. Against this supposition in the West of too close a relationship, even a cosy one, between Church and State, Patriarch Kirill of Moscow and All Russia has written strongly on human rights and personal dignity[35] and has drawn attention to how Church-State relations have developed in Russia. He points out how 'real national tragedies have come about whenever the one side has sought to bring the other side under its thumb'. Patriarch Kirill instances both the attempts of Ivan the Terrible (1547–1584) to subjugate the Church to the State and Patriarch Nikon in the seventeenth century who worked to remove the Church from secular authority whilst at the same time elevating, as Patriarch Kirill puts it: 'the role of the church and its primate in public life to excessive levels.' As he says, both the paths pursued by Ivan Terrible and Patriarch Nikon were disastrous for the Church.

The present view of Church-State relations in Russia is set out in the 'Basis of the Social Concept of the Russian Orthodox Church'.[36] This broadly follows the view of the Western churches set out above but includes this statement: 'The Church should not assume the prerogatives of the State, such as use of temporal authoritative powers and assumption of the governmental functions which presuppose coercion or restriction.' This is straightforward, but it then adds: 'At the same time, the Church may request or urge the government to exercise power in particular cases, yet the decision rests with the State.' This is an interesting view and shows that there is still evidence of a closer relationship between Church and State in Russia than elsewhere.[37]

Church and State in the West in the Middle Ages

Let us return to the instances given by Patriarch Kirill above of where the relationship between Church and State has gone wrong: one where the secular exercises too great a power over the sacred, in the case of Ivan the Terrible, and the contrary situation where the sacred has seemed to usurp sacred functions in the case of Patriarch Nikon. This really encapsulates the whole story of Church-State relations.

It would serve no purpose for this enquiry, which is aimed at Christians and the State today, to give a detailed history of Church-State relations in the West but we can give some instances of where relations have veered too much towards domination by the one over the other and which serve as a warning for today.

For much of the Middle Ages there was a close involvement between Church and State, highlighted by the practice of appointing the leading German ruler as Holy Roman Emperor from 962 onwards. Given that the State was avowedly Christian, this was not objectionable and some rulers had a positively beneficent influence on the Church, for instance the young emperor Otto III (996–1002) who, in a dark era for the papacy itself, appointed two excellent candidates of his own, Popes Gregory V and Sylvester II. On a local level close collaboration worked too. Thus in Anglo-Saxon times it was the practice for court cases involving the clergy, as well of course as the laity, to be heard in the hundred courts,[38] one of the secular courts, and indeed local bishops acted as judges in these courts. It was William I who, at a council in 1076, gave royal sanction to the establishment of a system of ecclesiastical courts at which point one assumes that cases involving the clergy were transferred to these. If we look at Carolingian France we find that, as David Knowles puts it: 'the regiment of the church would be a loose confederacy of bishops controlled externally by the ruler, but recognising the spiritual unity of their body in terms of union with the See of Peter as the ultimate source of doctrine and jurisdiction'.[39]

Nevertheless this close relationship could, and did, spill over into conflict when one side or the other overplayed their hand, as it were. In the eleventh century the papacy made high claims for its authority. As St Bernard of Clairvaux observed, although there are indeed two powers, as Pope Gelasius had pointed out, the spiritual and the temporal, both of these belonged to Peter and his successors: 'the one to be unsheathed at his nod, the other by his hand'.[40] This is really an argument for a theocratic state in which all authority comes from the Church, even in secular matters, with the result that the secular is explicitly subordinate to the religious and the pope even has the authority to depose secular rulers. This was the position adopted at the very high-water mark of papal claims in the papacy of Gregory VII (Hildebrand) (1073–1085). One flashpoint was the question of investiture: should bishops be invested with ring and staff by the temporal ruler? If so, then the implication was that they were his bishops. Yet in some ways bishops were indeed the King's men as they were often powerful feudal princes as well as spiritual rulers of their dioceses. Gregory and the German King Henry IV quarrelled over this and other matters with the result that Henry actually pronounced sentence of deposition on the Pope. Here Henry went too far and Pope Gregory forced a memorable submission over him by making him stand in the snow outside the castle of Canossa for three days in January 1077 before granting him an audience and then absolution.

Yet the quarrel continued until the investiture controversy was eventually settled by a compromise at the Concordat of Worms in 1122: new bishops swore fealty to the temporal ruler for the temporalities of their sees, but the ruler made it clear that this involved no claim by him to spiritual jurisdiction and so he did not invest them with ring and staff.

The investiture controversy was among many conflicts between Church and State in the Middle Ages. Amongst many instances was the celebrated quarrel between Henry II of England and Thomas Becket, Archbishop of Canterbury, which ended with the Archbishop's martyrdom in 1170. It concerned the particular issue of the application of the criminal law to the clergy but was in fact about a deeper issue: who controlled the Church in England?

What we will not find in the medieval period is any clear division between Church and State. It is true that Magna Carta (1215) said: 'that the English Church shall be free'; but this meant little in practice, and when Thomas More tried to raise this at his trial against the Act of Supremacy declaring Henry VIII Head of the Church, he was roughly brushed aside. Medieval governments did often cooperate with the Church to suppress heresy, but this can often be explained on the basis that heretics were seen as a threat to the established order rather than by religious zeal on the part of the authorities. An obvious illustration is the statute *De Heretico Comburendo*, passed by the English Parliament in 1401, which was designed to combat heresy. It provided that heretics were to be brought before Church courts. Those who would not recant beliefs contrary to Church teaching would be found guilty of heresy by those courts, and then turned over to the secular authority to be burned at the stake.

One could easily multiply such instances, but if we seek illumination of present-day issues by lessons from the past, then it is more profitable to turn to two great figures of the Reformation, Luther and Calvin, for their ideas, and especially those of the former, which still have an influence today.

The Reformation

Luther's contribution to what we can now term 'political theology' was through his celebrated and often misunderstood doctrine of the 'two kingdoms'. In *Temporal Authority: To What Extent It Can Be Obeyed*, written in 1523, Luther argued that:

> For God has established two kinds of government among men. The one is spiritual: it has no sword, but it has the word ... The other kind is worldly government, which works through the sword so that those who do not want to be good and righteous to eternal life may be forced to become good and righteous in the eyes of the world.[41]

This has been taken as advocating a dualism between the secular and the sacred and, by contrast with Pope Gelasius' two powers where the secular was nevertheless subject to the sacred, Luther seems to be implying a separation between the two. Thus, as Kirwan points out: 'The inherent danger and instability of the 'Two Kingdoms' position is that a separation of two realms, the religious and the political, results too easily in an other-worldly form of piety on the one hand and an unbridled nationalism on the other.'[42] Thus it has been argued that this theory was one reason why some German Protestants did not oppose Hitler and indeed set up the German Christian Church.[43]

In fact, too much can be made of Luther's theory and its subsequent influence. Writing primarily as a historian rather a theologian, Diarmaid MacCulloch[44] points to the actual circumstances in which Luther enunciated this theory. By 1522 no prince had declared for his reform but by contrast it was facing fierce opposition from some of them, notably Prince Georg of Saxony. It

was in this context that Luther set out to preserve what he saw as
the true freedom of the Church against what he saw as misguided
rulers like Prince Georg and so his emphasis was that it was not
appropriate for secular rulers to exercise rule over the Church just
as the Church should not exercise worldly rule. As MacCulloch
says:

> two contradictory impulses ran through Luther's thinking on
> authority and he never really resolved them. On the one hand, he
> wanted desperately to secure the support of the princes, and on the
> other he was concerned to ensure that godly reformation was not
> threatened by unsympathetic princes.[45]

This is seen when by 1525 Luther had secured the support of
some princes and so the famous doctrine: *Cuius regio, eius religio*
('whose realm, his religion') which meant that the religion of the
ruler dictated the religion of the ruled, was adopted, although it
did not become finally established as a political principle until
the Peace of Westphalia in 1648. This made perfect sense as a
means of ensuring that particular princes who had embraced
Protestantism were protected from interference from the Holy
Roman Emperor, who of course remained Catholic, but it cut
right across the 'Two Kingdoms' theory as it inevitably meant that
sovereigns would assume a much larger role in religious affairs
and it did become a characteristic feature of Lutheran states that
the State played a dominant role in Church affairs. For example,
to this day in the Lutheran Church of Denmark, its dignitaries
are appointed by the Crown on the recommendation of the
Minister of Church Affairs, and because the Church has no
system of synodical government, its canons are still promulgated
by Parliament.[46]

Thus although Luther never proposed a thorough-going separation of the sacred from the secular, there is no doubt that
Protestantism has seen Church and State as distinct and separate
parts of the world and that, as Protestantism has, in Europe,
become the National Church in many Northern European
countries, it has led to a subservience of Church to State. Even in
England, where many members of the Anglican National Church
would reject the label 'Protestant', there is seen a reluctance to
stand up to the State and to secular trends within it. For example,
when in 2012 the Church of England voted against the ordination
of women as bishops Archbishop Rowan Williams said: 'Whatever

the motivation for voting yesterday, whatever the theological principle on which people acted or spoke,' dissenters had to understand that their objection to women bishops 'is not intelligible to wider society. Worse than that, it seems as if we are willfully blind to some of the trends and priorities of wider society.' It is in fact precisely that attitude in itself which is completely unintelligible to many Christians.[47]

Another way in which the thought of Luther has permeated to the present day is in its emphasis on the individual and the individual will. For in his theology he spoke of the individual's unmediated relationship before God and this, as Kirwan says: 'both challenges the Church's claim to be a mediator of salvation, and leans in the direction of individualism and democracy'.[48] We shall examine the part that this has played in Church-State relations in subsequent chapters but now it is time to turn to that other great figure of the Reformation, John Calvin.

Calvin's thought differed from Luther in that he emphasised the 'Lordship of Christ'. In *The Institutes of the Christian Religion*[49] he argues that: 'The end of secular government, however, while we remain in this world, is to foster and protect the external worship of God, defend pure doctrine and the good condition of the church ...' Carried out to its fullest extent, this leaves the way open for theocracy, where the State is subordinated to the Church. MacCulloch[50] argues that in fact this did not take place in Geneva, Calvin's stronghold, but instead there occurred a graphic illustration of Luther's two kingdoms theory as there was a divide between the civil and Church systems of government where the Church 'stood alongside the civil authority and felt a God-given right to criticize it if necessary, whilst still aspiring to minister to the entire population'.[51] On this basis there were continual disputes over who had the power to excommunicate, which would have consequences in civil law: was it the civil authority or the Church, with Calvin naturally insisting that it belonged to the Church. Even when things did not go this far, it is clear that Calvin adopted a much more robust attitude to State power than did the Lutherans and did not see a strong divide between human and divine justice. Thus he argued that: 'the Christian does not live in two different worlds; he or she lives in one encompassing lordship of Christ in various relationships in this world',[52] a view which is much nearer the classic view of the relation of the Christian to the State than that of Luther.

This blurring of jurisdiction between civil and ecclesiastical authorities which we noted in pre-Reformation times continued after the Reformation: in Scotland, for instance, the kirk sessions set up under the Presbyterian system established in 1559 heard cases where the moral standards and doctrinal teaching of the Church could be enforced. These included not only what might be thought of as Church matters such as allegations of adultery and profanation of the Sabbath, but also those of a more strictly civil character such as quarrelling and assault.[53] Not only this, but local magistrates sat in these Kirk session courts and, in the Scottish Parliament, recognised the jurisdiction of the Kirk in the 'correction of manners', and breach of the Sabbath was made a statutory offence. This mirrored the practice of Calvin in Geneva where he created a tribunal called the *consistoire* to 'interrogate all who fell from doctrinal and moral purity'.[54]

It would be possible to multiply these examples of close collaboration between Church and State but the point is simply that, in spite of Christ's command to separate religion (God) and politics (Caesar), until modern times this distinction was so completely blurred as often to be invisible. The question now becomes the relation of Christians to the State in the modern era and it is to that which we must now turn.

Notes

1   See K. Scholder, *A Requiem for Hitler and Other New Perspectives on the German Church Struggle* (London and Philadelphia: SCM Press, 1989). See also Ch. 2 for a particular instance of the attitude of Cardinal Bertram, the President of the German Bishops Conference.

2   The precise implications of this title will be explored in Chapter 3.

3   N. Spencer, *Freedom and Order* (London: Hodder and Stoughton, 2011).

4   Ibid., p. 258.

5   Ibid., p. 259.

6   Letter to Diognetus (trans. M. Staniforth), *Early Christian Writings: the Apostolic Fathers* (London: Penguin Books, 1968), p. 176.

7   *Early Christian Writings*, see especially pp. 55–56. See also the commentary on Clement by Pope Benedict XVI in *The Fathers of the Church* (London: CTS, 2008).

8   In 'Government and the New Testament' an essay in N. Spencer and J. Chaplin, (eds.), *God and Government* (London: SPCK, 2009), p. 65. Author's italics.

9   This point is well brought out by A. Nichols in *The Realm: An Unfashionable Essay on the Conversion of England* (Oxford: Family Publications, 2008), pp. 41–42.

10 Acts 25:6–12.

11 1 Cor. 6:1–6.
12 Law and Conscience is considered in detail in Chapter 7.
13 See *Jesus of Nazareth* (San Francisco: Ignatius Press, 2011), p. 170.
14 Aidan Nichols, *The Thought of Benedict XVI, An Introduction to the Theology of Joseph Ratzinger* (London: Burns and Oates, 2007), p. 184.
15 Ibid., p. 104.
16 It could be argued that this lack of separation of religion from politics also has the consequence that whereas Christians see some matters outside the competence of religion altogether, non-Christian religions do not. This then leads to quite different attitudes on, for example, the proper place of law in society and the desire of non-Christian religions to set up systems of adjudication that parallel those of the state, as we shall see in chapter 3.
17 In *How Christianity Changed the World* (Grand Rapids: Zondervan, 2004), pp. 51–66. See also the discussion of this topic in W. Grudem, *Politics According to the Bible* (Grand Rapids: Zondervan, 2010), pp. 49–51.
18 Aristotle, *Politics*, trans. B. Jowett (Oxford: Oxford University Press, 1905), 7.14. But have things changed? Look for a moment at s. 1 (1) (d) of the Abortion Act 1967 permitting abortions up to term where 'there is a substantial risk that if the child were born it would suffer from such physical or mental abnormalities as to be seriously handicapped'.
19 Plato, *Republic*, trans. H.D.P. Lee (Harmondsworth: Penguin Classics, 1955), 5.461c.
20 D. Jones, *The Soul of the Embryo* (London: Continuum, 2004), pp. 33–34. His whole discussion of this topic in pp. 33–42 is most valuable.
21 In *Early Christian Writings*, (trans. Staniforth), p. 228.
22 I have here followed the account in J. Norwich, *A Short History of Byzantium* (London: Penguin Books, 1988), pp. 33–34.
23 In *The Early Church*, Vol. 1 of the Penguin History of the Church (London: Penguin Books, 1967), p. 168.
24 *The City of God* (London: Penguin Books, 1972), Bk xiv, 28.
25 Introduction to *The City of God*, p. xvii.
26 See E. Duffy, *Saints and Sinners, A History of the Popes* (New Haven and London: Yale University Press, 1997), p. 38. The Monophysite heresy is explained below.
27 Ibid.
28 Although largely forgotten, Gelasius was in fact a distinguished Pope and is described by Kelly as 'next to Leo I, the most distinguished pope of the fifth century.' J.N.D. Kelly, *Dictionary of the Popes* (Oxford: Oxford University Press, 1986), p. 49.
29 I have relied here principally on J. Meyendorf, *The Byzantine Legacy and the Orthodox Church* (New York: SVS Press, 2001) which has the advantage of being written from a present-day Orthodox standpoint. Chapter II (Church and State) is especially useful. I have also used the stimulating essay by A.H. Armstrong, 'Church and State in the East' in *Under God and the Law, Papers read to the Thomas More Society*, edited by Richard O'Sullivan (Oxford: Basil Blackwell, 1949). An excellent modern account of the position of the Russian Orthodox Church on Human Rights is by Patriarch Kirill of Moscow, *Freedom and Responsibility* (London: Darton Longman and Todd, 2011).
30 This was eventually condemned at the Sixth Ecumenical Council in 680–681.
31 Kirill, *Freedom and Responsibility*, p. 45.

32 Meyendorf, The *Byzantine Legacy and the Orthodox Church,* pp. 48–49.
33 Ibid., p. 50.
34 T. Ware (Bishop Kallistos of Diokleia), *The Orthodox Church* (London: Penguin Books, 1997), p. 41.
35 In Kirill, *Freedom and Responsibility,* especially Chapter 4: 'God's plan for Man and Free Will', pp. 39–50.
36 See https://mospat.ru/en/documents/social-concepts/ (accessed 15 February 2014).
37 Note the apparent clear support given by the Russian Orthodox Church to the Russian Government in the current conflict in the Ukraine. This attitude can only be understood in the context of the different Orthodox national churches in this area.
38 See F.M. Stenton, *Anglo-Saxon England* (Oxford: Clarendon Press, 1943), p. 661. This paragraph relies largely on Chapter XVIII, 'The Reorganisation of the English Church'.
39 In his Introduction to *The City of God,* p. xxi.
40 Quoted in Duffy, *Saints and Sinners, A History of the Popes,* p. 106.
41 Quoted in M. Kirwan, *Political Theology* (London: Darton, Longman and Todd, 2008), p. 74.
42 Ibid., p. 75.
43 The notion of two swords was ultimately derived from the remark of Christ when presented by the disciples with two swords: 'It is enough'. (Lk 22:38)
44 In D. MacCulloch, *Reformation, Europe's House Divided* (London: Penguin Books, 2004), see especially p. 157 and pp. 164–65. See also W.D.J. Cargill Thompson, *The Political Thought of Martin Luther* (Brighton: Sussex: The Harvester Press, 1984), pp. 36–61.
45 D. MacCulloch, *Reformation, Europe's House Divided,* p. 157.
46 Article 66 of the Constitution: 'The constitution of the Established Church shall be laid down by statute'.
47 Against this, we must note the resurrection in the study of political theology among many Christians, which aims to recover a distinctive Christian response to politics. See, for example, the excellent collection of essays: J. Chaplin and N. Spencer, (eds), *God and Government* (London: SPCK, 2009).
48 Kirwan, *Political Theology,* p. 73.
49 Bk IV, ch. 20.
50 MacCulloch, *Reformation, Europe's House Divided,* p. 240.
51 Ibid.
52 *Kirwan, Political Theology,* p. 77, quoting the German theologian Jürgen Moltmann.
53 G. Parker, *Empire, War and Faith in Early Modern Empire* (London: Penguin, 2002), see Ch.10, 'The Kirk by Law Established'.
54 Ibid., p. 258.

Chapter 2

Church and State in the World Today

'For here there is no eternal city for us in this life but we
look for one in the life to come'.

(Heb 13:14)

Introduction

The passage from Hebrews that is at the head of this chapter sets
out what is a dilemma for many Christians: our home is in Heaven
and it is to there that we direct our steps but at the same time we
must engage with the secular world around us. To what extent
then can the Christian Churches fulfil their mission in a world
where the prevailing ethos is secular?

In the previous chapter we looked at how Christianity and the
State had related to each other in history. In this chapter we take
a present-day perspective and look not only at the position in the
United Kingdom but in other countries also. In doing so we look
at the various methods of structuring Church-State relationships
and, in particular, at the idea of a National Church and ask: if a
Church is indeed the Church of a particular nation, does this
impede its witness to Christ or does it provide an added means of
fulfilling it?

Terminology: Secular and Secularisation

Relations between Church and State are classified in different ways
and sometimes the terminology used leads to confusion. One
commonly used term in this area is 'secular' together with the term
'secularisation'. I shall argue later in this chapter that this is too
board-brush a distinction and that a more nuanced categorisation
of Church-State relations is preferable, but it will serve to open this
discussion.

What does it mean to say that a State is secular and does this pose
any threat to Christianity and, indeed, other religions? My under-

standing of the term 'secular State' is simply that the State, as such, does not espouse any form of religion or religious belief, and this is the sense in which the term is used in this chapter. This seems to me to reflect the teachings of Jesus in his discourse on God and Caesar, as well as the thought of Pope Benedict XVI discussed in Chapter 1, that the State does not have a religious authority. What 'secular' should not mean is that religion is altogether excluded from public debate and is pushed into the realm of private belief. Instead, as we shall see in the following chapters, we can make a case that a State, whilst avowedly secular, can and should be influenced by Christian principles in how it operates.

We will shortly look at the extent to which we can say that the United Kingdom is a secular State in the context of the Church of England as the established Church, but for now we can contrast a secular State with one where the actual constitution, or other founding document, of a State expressly confers a special status on a particular Church. For example, in Malta, reflecting the fact that the overwhelming majority of the population is Roman Catholic, the Constitution establishes Roman Catholicism as the state religion by providing in Article 2 that:

> The religion of Malta is the Roman Catholic Apostolic Religion; the authorities of the Roman Catholic Apostolic Church have the duty and the right to teach which principles are right and which are wrong; Religious teaching of the Roman Catholic Apostolic faith shall be provided in all state schools as part of compulsory education.

Malta serves as a good example, however, of how difficult it is to classify a State as secular or as confessional in the full sense that the State actually enforces a particular religion on its subjects. The Maltese law on annulment and divorce is an example. The Marriage Law Amendment Act 1995 provides that the Republic of Malta recognizes, for all civil effects, marriages celebrated in Malta according to the canonical norms of the Catholic Church together with the judgments of nullity and the decrees of ratification of nullity of marriage given by the Ecclesiastical Tribunals. Although this recognition of Catholic marriages is in itself no different from that in other countries, such as Spain and Portugal, and in England marriages celebrated according to the rites of the Church of England are valid in English civil law,[1] the difference in Malta was that divorce was not permitted, and so the only means of ending a marriage for Catholics was by a decree of nullity granted by the Ecclesiastical Tribunals. This was, however, changed as a result of a referendum in 2011, after which divorce was legalised, and so this close Church-State relationship, in a country where over 90% of the population are Roman Catholics, was weakened, although the Marriage Law Amendment Act 1995 remains in force.

The same difficulty of categorisation applies to Church-State relations in Ireland following the adoption of the 1937 Constitution which, by Article 44.1.2, provided that: 'The State recognises the special position of the Holy Catholic Apostolic and Roman Church as the guardian of the Faith professed by the great majority of the citizens'. Art. 44.1.3. then provided that:

> The State also recognises the Church of Ireland, the Presbyterian Church in Ireland, the Methodist Church in Ireland, the Religious Society of Friends in Ireland, as well as the Jewish Congregations and the other religious denominations existing in Ireland at the date of the coming into operation of this Constitution.

If we examine this closely, it does not establish Roman Catholicism as the State Religion in Ireland but only gives it a 'special place' which is never defined. It was removed, following a referendum, in 1973.

It could be argued that the provisions of the Constitution of Ireland gave the Church some semblance of authority over the State. By contrast, the *Erastian* system allows the secular authorities to exercise supremacy over religion which, historically, was a common model in Europe. One could say that the Henrician Reformation in England brought about such a system, and we shall examine this later when we look at the position of the Church of England.

The most striking modern example of a religious body that is at least *quasi-Erastian* is the Church of Denmark.[2] Its dignitaries are appointed by the Crown on the recommendation of the Minister of Church Affairs; moreover, because the Church has no system of synodical government, its canons are still promulgated by Parliament.[3] Denmark is certainly not *Erastian* in the classical sense that everyone is obliged to belong to a single State-controlled Church: on the contrary, freedom of religion is guaranteed by the Constitutional Act of 1953.[4] However, there is still a strong body of opinion among Danes that the Government holds the ring between competing theological views in a way that the National Church itself cannot – an opinion shared by Queen Margrethe herself who, it is reported, told her biographer that she was afraid that disestablishment would only serve to marginalise religious belief. Her views are worth quoting, especially in the context of the call for the Church of England to be disestablished: 'I am not fond of the free congregations that are so fine and feel they are the genuine Christians ... What about all of us? Where do we belong? There is one entrance, baptism, and that is enough. I am afraid that if you separate Church and State then we will for real get a de-Christianisation of the country'.[5]

An extreme instance of the exact opposite to a secular state is a theocracy, where the secular authorities are subordinate to the religious. This was the *de facto* situation in Geneva during Calvin's ascendancy. Though there is no obvious current example in a Christian context (leaving aside the Vatican and Mount Athos, which are special cases), Iran under Ayatollah Khomeini looked remarkably like a theocracy, while several Islamic states have introduced overtly religious elements such as the *sharia* into their legal and political systems.

The danger of having a constitutional link between Church and State is, I think, threefold: first, the Church is dragged into the secular sphere; second, the Church is so identified with the State that a defeat for the State is seen as a defeat for the Church; and, third, that the Church is so allied to the State that it cannot act as a prophetic voice in opposing the Government when needed. This does not mean that the Church should divorce itself from the secular sphere in the words of that silly phrase: 'religion has nothing to do with politics'. I would contend, on the contrary, that it has everything to do with politics. But the Church, in order to speak to the political world, must not be part of that world.

It would be easy to multiply instances of where the Church has got too close to the State. One could instance Ireland in the years from 1922 until towards the end of the century. But what I think is the most striking instance is from the dying days of the Second World War when Cardinal Bertram, at that time the President of the German Bishops' Conference, who had been a bishop since 1906, actually drafted a letter to his clergy, amidst the awful chaos and horror of the collapse of the Third Reich, ordering them to say a Requiem Mass 'in memory of the Führer'. There were other intentions too, in particular the future of the Catholic Church in Germany, but this order to offer a Requiem for Hitler strikes one, to put it mildly, as strange. Bertram was, in fact, no Nazi and had consistently used private means of communication to Hitler to tenaciously defend the Church. However, he saw Hitler as the Head of a State with clear ties to the Catholic Church and he held fast to, in the words of Scholder: 'the close bond of German Catholics with Führer and Volk, army and fatherland'[6] so that, at the last, he could not see beyond. One notes incidentally that his wishes were never carried out and a line was struck through this letter. Bertram himself died a month later.

I would therefore argue that there is nothing to stop religions flourishing in a secular climate and that this is healthier than a narrow confessional State or even those without express constitutional links between Church and State, but where, even so, Church and State have become too close. On the other hand, the term 'secularisation' presents, I suggest, dangers to Christianity and to all religions, as what lies behind it is precisely what it says: that public life should be secular and that religion should have no place in it.[7]

The former Archbishop of Canterbury, Rowan William, has distinguished between 'procedural secularism 'and 'programmatic secularism'.[8] Procedural secularism, he suggests, is found in the State that 'defines its role as one of overseeing a variety of communities of religious conviction and, where necessary, assisting them to keep the peace together'. In short, it exists where the State adopts a principle of neutrality between religious groups and is thus a secular State in itself. But, at the same time, the word 'procedural', as Lord Harris of Pentregarth (the former Bishop of Oxford) said: 'refers to a set of procedures, arrangements and rules of discourse that enable rational debate to take place and decisions to be made with everyone participating on an equal basis'.[9] This, he feels, is acceptable. Programmatic secularism, corresponding to my term secularisation, by contrast, relegates religious belief to the private sphere in the way rejected by both Pope Benedict and Pope Francis, so that only one loyalty counts in public debate, loyalty to what he calls 'public orthodoxy'.

In fact the complexity of the modern State can, I would argue, require a more nuanced approach than to simply distinguish between secular and secularisation, and Jonathan Chaplin distinguishes between four varieties:[10]

    (a) A State may be called secular if it is officially committed to a secularist worldview (such as atheism or materialism or secular

humanism) and to propagating it through state action. Most
Communist States have been secular in this sense. This he
terms 'militant secularism'.

(b) A State may be called secular if, while upholding religious
liberty, it strives to keep the influence of religious faith out of
public debate and public institutions, and especially out of the
legislative realm. This he terms 'exclusivist secularism' and is
what many secularists advocate for the UK today.

(c) A state may be called secular if it refrains from officially
endorsing any one religious faith and seeks to adopt a stance of
impartiality towards the different religions represented among
its population. Such a secular State would be contrasted with a
'confessional' State – one which explicitly recognises one
religious faith in its constitution (e.g., Ireland for much of its
independent history). This third category turns out to be very
wide, since States as diverse as the USA, France, Turkey[11] and
India all claim to be officially secular in this sense. This he
terms 'impartial secularism'.

(d) Fourth, a State may be called secular if it refrains from present-
ing religious justifications for its law or policies, offering only
those reasons which will be acknowledged as legitimate policy
reasons by most of its citizens; such reasons may then be
defined as 'secular' or 'public'. Most western liberal democra-
cies regard themselves as secular in this more specific sense.
This he terms 'justificatory secularism'.

The advantage of this categorisation is that it allows one to see how
a State may slide, as it were, from a very hostile attitude to religion,
as evidenced by militant secularism, through the different types
which gradually become more favourable to religion, until we
reach the most favourable – 'impartial' and 'justificatory secularism'. In fact, as Chaplin notes, most contemporary liberal
democratic States exemplify (or claim to exemplify) both impartial
secularism and justificatory secularism. Not only do they refrain
from privileging one religious faith, they also refrain from offering
religious reasons when justifying their official decisions to their
citizens.[12]

Chaplin also points out that 'Sometimes, critics of one or other
variant of secularism allege that one particular variant inevitably
leads to another.' He gives the example of exclusivist secularism
where some allege that this leads almost invariably (perhaps even
necessarily) to militant secularism. Those who adopt this argument
would then assert that, on this point, the difference between the
Soviet Union and France or Turkey is only one of degree.

We shall examine in Chapter 9 how recently in public debate there have been calls from those promoting secularisation for religion to be merely a matter of private belief and how Christians might respond to this.

What Does Separation Between Church and State Actually Mean?

Clearly a State that is secular, and even more one which adopts the principle of secularisation, will have a separation between Church and State, but what will this actually mean? One cannot say that separation will mean in effect that the two will take no notice of each other because even the most extreme secularist does not argue for the actual prohibition of any public expression of religious belief so that, as in some Communist countries, the churches are driven underground. Thus we need to establish principle(s) under which Church and State can establish a *modus vivendi*. Sandberg and Doe posit the principle of neutrality but in an active sense:

> Separation requires neutrality from the State but this is not a passive obligation: in its pursuit of religious freedom, liberty and equality, the State actively seeks to remove all existing boundaries and often seeks to provide the means whereby all citizens – regardless of their religious convictions – enjoy the equal right to manifest their religiosity throughout their everyday life ...[13]

However, we need to probe further. Separation requires neutrality from the State but what Sandberg and Doe seem to be saying is that separation means that the State holds the ring, as it were, between religions. We could sum this up by saying that in those terms separation means that the State has a duty to behave impartially between itself and religion as a whole and impartially between different religions. Nevertheless, as Sandberg and Doe would themselves agree, we need to ask how this neutrality is to be exercised in actual situations. Take the case of Lilian Ladele who, as a registrar of Births, Marriages and Deaths, was called on to perform civil partnership ceremonies, and this conflicted with her religious beliefs.[14] Here there was a clear conflict: how was it to be resolved?

Ian Leigh makes the valuable point that: 'Beyond impartiality, however, conceptual controversy begins'.[15] He then identifies four other variants:

(a) The equi-distance of the State from all religions, which is often taken to imply separation of the Church from the State, although it does not necessarily mean this.

(b) Strict equality of treatment by the State of all religions, which would rule out, for example, the Establishment of the Church of England.

(c) Equal respect for all religions. The distinction from equality of treatment is that here the state recognises local religious diversity. This is a broader and more nuanced principle than simply equal treatment.

(d) Objectivity, which can be considered as the treatment by the State of all religions as subjective belief systems so that, in Leigh's words: 'at best, the state is indifferent towards them or, at worst, they are seen as irrelevant or misguided'. There is an echo of this last attitude in the words of Lord Justice Laws in the case of Gary McFarlane that 'religious faith is necessarily subjective'.[16]

Which of these principles to adopt? Leigh points out that the European Court of Justice, when interpreting and applying the European Convention on Human Rights, has adopted the principle of neutrality in the sense of both equi-distance and strict equality of treatment. This applies when, for example, it adjudicates on disputes between different religious groups. However , it also apples the principle of equal respect as in the *Lautsi* case, where it took into account the strong religious character of the Italian State in accepting that the display of crucifixes in school classrooms in Italy did not infringe the European Convention of Human Rights.[17] My own view is that Christians should argue for the principle of equal respect for all religions as this recognises that the State should not simply stand aside and say with regard to all religions: 'We are neutral'. Instead it should respect not only religion as a whole but different strands of religious belief as enriching the national culture.

State Impartiality in Practice: The Employment Status of the Clergy

Touron points out that State impartiality must be based on the incompetence of the State to judge the truth or falsity of religious doctrines and, more generally, to have any judgment on strictly religious issues.[18] Is this so under UK law? In the case of *R v. Chief*

Rabbi ex. p. Wachman (1993) there seemed to be a recognition of such a principle when the court refused an application for judicial review of a decision by a Chief Rabbi, following an inquiry, that Wachman was no longer morally and religiously fit to hold rabbinical office. This principle does not, however, apply where there is a dispute not involving doctrinal matters but instead a civil dispute between members of the religious body over, for example, church property. Here under the principle established in the case of *Forbes v. Eden* (1867) the court may intervene on the basis of a contract between all the members of the church to enforce the rules of the church.

However, the principle in *Wachman* can be difficult to apply as seen in the later case of *Shergill & others v. Khaira & others* (2014) which concerned the question of whether a particular person was the spiritual leader of the Nirmal Sikh community, with the consequent power to remove and appoint trustees of two gurdwaras (places of worship) used by members of that community. This inevitably involved the determination of religious issues and the Supreme Court accepted that there was a general principle that the courts would not adjudicate on the truth of religious beliefs or on the validity of particular rites in themselves. However, where a claimant, as here, sought the enforcement of private rights and obligations that depended on religious issues, a court might have to determine such religious issues as were capable of objective assessment.

An area for potential conflict between Church and State in the UK lies in the increasing number of cases where the clergy have claimed the status of employees and thus the protection of civil laws protecting them from dismissal and discrimination, to take two obvious examples. In one case, that of *Percy v. Church of Scotland Board of National Mission* (2005) where a minister of the Church of Scotland claimed sex discrimination, the issue of whether the courts have any business at all to hear cases of this kind involved consideration of the Church of Scotland Act 1921. This declared the exclusive jurisdiction of the Church in certain matters, the relevant words being in Article IV of the Constitution of the Church. These provide that the Church has the power 'to adjudicate finally in all matters of doctrine, worship, government, and discipline in the Church, including the right to determine all questions concerning membership and office in the Church'. Despite these strong words their Lordships were unanimous in holding that they were intended to deal with spiritual matters and did not therefore exclude the jurisdiction of the courts and tribunals in contractual disputes.[19]

In two recent cases in this area the courts reached different conclusions on the facts. In *President of the Methodist Conference v. Preston* (2013), a Methodist minister was held not to be an employee, but an Anglican priest, Kevin Sharpe, was held to be an employee by the Employment Appeal Tribunal in *Sharpe v. Worcester Diocesan Board of Finance Ltd and The Bishop of Worcester* (2013), but this was reversed by the Court of Appeal. Mr. Sharpe alleged bullying and harassment by his parishioners which in effect drove him from his parish.

The problem is that if employment status is conferred on the clergy it could lead to the courts inevitably being drawn into doctrinal matters. For example, in 1994 Anthony Freeman was deprived of his licence by his bishop (the Bishop of Chichester) following publication of his book '*God in Us: The Case for Christian Humanism*' which appeared to deny the divinity of Christ. Suppose that he had alleged that his dismissal from the ministry amounted to unfair dismissal. There is a tendency in dismissal cases for different issues to be intermingled and it is easy to see how here a court could become embroiled in looking at the doctrine of the Anglican Church to see if his dismissal was justified.[20]

The Idea of a National Church

Although there may be or may not be a separation between Church and State, a particular Church may be recognised as a National Church. Richard Hooker[21] saw this link as the essential identity of the people as a political society and the Church as a spiritual assembly, and it was this that motivated his insistence on Church and State as being two interdependent sectors of the same commonwealth, and on each National Church having the right to regulate its own external forms of worship and government. 'Church and Commonwealth are names which import things really different. But those things are accidents, and such accidents should always dwell lovingly together in one subject'.

What does the idea of a National Church mean for us today? Norman Doe has identified eight characteristics of a National Church:[22] these may be summarised as one where the Church is recognised as a National Church by both civil and canon law; it

participates directly in the public events of the nation; whose
ministry is linked explicitly to the spiritual and temporal concerns
of the nation; and where the Church has a national ministry owed
by its officers to the nation and its citizens.

We shall look at the position of the Church of England shortly
but one matter is, I suggest, of especial concern: as the prevailing
mores of society have drifted away from traditional Christian
belief, as with the widespread acceptance of abortion as lawful and
the similar acceptance of same-sex marriage, will the fact that a
Church is national mean that it sees itself as being required to
reflect those prevailing mores rather than to preach the Gospel of
Christ? For instance, when the Church of England voted not to
ordain women as bishops in 2012,[23] Sir Tony Baldry, MP, the
Second Church Estates Commissioner said: 'The Church of
England now stands to be left behind by the society it seeks to
serve, looking outdated, irrelevant, and frankly eccentric by this
decision'. There may be excellent reasons for ordaining bishops
but this, I suggest, is not one of them! Moreover, following this, a
number of MPs spoke of putting pressure on the Church of
England to ordain women bishops, which would have been
unimaginable had the Church of England not been established.
When supporters of establishment, of which I count myself, speak
of its value to the nation, we ought also to answer honestly whether
we agree with this kind of secular interference.

The Church of England as the Established Church

It is fairly clear that the Church of England does satisfy Doe's
criteria of being a National Church even though the bonds
between Church and State seem to be progressively weakening.
Thus, in 2007, the Prime Minister surrendered his role in the
choice of bishops for the Church of England.[24]

What does cause difficulty is the term 'established' Church
which is used in relation to the Church of England. An argument
is often heard that Christianity does have a special place in
England, as the Church of England is the established Church in
England and the Church of Scotland is likewise the established
Church in Scotland. (In Wales and Northern Ireland there is no
established Church.) But what does this actually mean?

The problem is that the term 'established' is not really clear.
Originally it meant no more than that the Church of England had

been established by the 'Elizabethan settlement' when Queen
Elizabeth I finally established it as the religion of England and
Wales following all the changes in the reigns of Henry VIII, Edward
VI and Mary. What is clear is that the Church of England is not a
State Church in the way that, for example, the Church of Denmark
is, where, as explained above, there is no autonomous decision-
making body such as the Synod of the Church of England, and its
canons (i.e., its internal laws) are made by the government. The
Church of England does indeed enjoy a special status in the constitutional arrangements of this country. For example, twenty-six of
its bishops are members of the House of Lords, and it is routinely
the Church most often consulted by governments on religious
questions. This is because a Measure of the Church of England
counts as legislation. Once approved by the General Synod, it
passes to Parliament and if both Houses pass a resolution agreeing
to the measure, on receiving royal assent it becomes a law.[25]

Normally Parliamentary approval is a foregone conclusion but
this was not so with the celebrated Prayer Book Measure of 1927
which sought to update the 1662 Prayer Book. This was rejected by
Parliament in 1928 apparently on the grounds that it allowed the
reservation of the sacrament for the first time. The position in this
case would be different today by virtue of the Church of England
(Worship and Doctrine) Measure 1974, which gives the Church
power by Canon to alter the Worship of the Church if the doctrine
of the Church is not adversely affected, and thus, in the case of a
proposed revision of the Prayer Book, Parliamentary approval
would not be needed, as the clear implication is that the Church
itself is the judge of whether the doctrinal condition is breached.

The idea of Establishment is seen at its most potent at the
Coronation, when the Monarch takes the Coronation Oath. Part of
the oath sworn by the present Queen on June 2, 1953 was 'to the
utmost of your power maintain in the United Kingdom the
Protestant Reformed Religion established by law.' This, as Aidan
Nichols points out is 'an explicit denial of the secularity of the
United Kingdom'.[26] However, it may well be that the oath sworn by
the next monarch will be different. Aidan Nichols has analysed the
1953 Coronation[27] and notes that when: 'the Queen rose from
praying at the "Chair of Estate" all power in the realm had been
given for one moment into the keeping of the Church'. Thus,
quoting the *Times* for June 3, 1953: 'having the plenitude of power
in his possession the Archbishop could make terms for its
disposal'. So he required of her to make the ancient promises to

govern her peoples with justice and mercy, to maintain the profession of the Gospel and the Protestant reformed religion. Here then is the link between Church and State in action. If the Church of England was to be disestablished, then this ceremony would go. It is mere symbolism and does it reflect a deeper Christian message? One assumes that this part of the ceremony will be unchanged at the next coronation as the Church of England will presumably still be the Established Church.

Moreover, by an Act of Parliament of 1558 the sovereign is styled 'Defender of the Faith', a title originally conferred on Henry VIII by Pope Leo X in 1521. The Prince of Wales has however, spoken of his desire to be 'Defender of Faiths', although this would seem to require a new Act of Parliament and the agreement of all Commonwealth states which still accept the British monarch as Head of State.

Lord Mackay, speaking as a former Lord Chancellor, sees the Church of England, through its position as the established Church, as having a duty to protect all faiths, a point also made by the Queen in a speech at Lambeth Palace during her Diamond Jubilee celebrations when she said that:

> The concept of our established Church is occasionally misunderstood and, I believe, commonly under-appreciated. Its role is not to defend Anglicanism to the exclusion of other religions. Instead the Church has a duty to protect the free practice of all faiths in this country.

Lord Mackay also mentioned the view of the former Chief Rabbi, Lord Jonathan Sacks, that one benefit of Establishment is that 'it keeps religion at the forefront of the nation.'[28] If this is the correct view, and I believe that it is, then it is the duty of all Christians, including Catholics, to defend Establishment especially from the attacks of the secularists who would undoubtedly see the end of Establishment as a victory for them and a setback for Christianity.

The Position in Scotland

The former Lord Chancellor, Lord Mackay, himself a leading Scottish lawyer, said in a lecture in 2013 that: 'I think it can be said that the relationship of the State to the Church of Scotland is one of recognition with a degree of support. As Professor Frank Lyall has said, "All that establishment means is that the civil authority has recognised the Church's self-imposed task to bring the ordinances of religion to all Scotland, and looks to the Church on suitable ceremonial occasions."'[29] Thus the arrangement is much less formal than that in England, although the Queen appoints a representative, known as the Lord High Commissioner, to the General Assembly of the Church of Scotland and he attends daily business as an observer.

Where the Church Voluntarily Places Itself under Legislative Control

In some instances a Church may decide to place some or all of its functions under secular legislative control.[30] The Salvation Army did this by the Salvation Army Act 1931. The background to this was that, following the death of its first general and founder, William Booth, leadership passed to his daughter, Bramwell Booth. However, by 1928 a number of prominent Salvation Army officers considered Bramwell Booth no longer to be fit to serve as leader, and she was removed. Nevertheless it was thought desirable that the whole matter of the election of a leader and the holding of the assets of The Salvation Army should be formalised, and this was done by the Salvation Army Act of 1931, which limited the leader's powers by providing for the future election of the General by High Council elections, and transferring Salvation Army assets, held in the name of the General, to The Salvation Army Trustee Company. Again when the three main strands of Methodism (the Wesleyans, the United Methodists and the Primitives) came together in 1932 to form the modern Methodist Church, the terms of the union were those set out in the Methodist Church Union Act 1929. Section 8 (2) of that Act provided that the doctrinal standards of the united Church would be those subscribed in a Deed of Union that was to be adopted by the first Conference of the united Church and that, thereafter, those standards were not to be varied without further legislation. When, in the 1970s, the Church decided that it wished to assume responsibility for doctrinal matters, it had to seek a further Act: the Methodist Church Act 1976. So, as Oliva and Cranmer remark: 'leaving aside religious considerations, in strictly legal terms the modern Methodist Church of Great Britain is wholly a creature of statute.'[31]

Thus statutory regulation does not lead to State control of the religion in question as the State is acting more as a facilitator. It is arguable that it can lead to almost the opposite result with the religion regarding itself as an 'island of exclusivity'[32] where the religion regards its own activities as outside the scope of the general civil law. This may be one reason why The Salvation Army argued in *Rogers v. Booth* (1937) that its officers should not have the status of employees.

Separation Between Church and State: The American Experience and Prayers at Council Meetings

The First Amendment to the US Constitution provides *inter alia* that 'Congress shall make no law respecting an establishment of religion, or prohibiting the free exercise thereof' and, in principle, the secular and the religious are completely divorced from one another.[33]

There have been many instances of the US Supreme Court deciding cases on the basis of a strict separation between Church and State. For example, in 1962, in the case of *Engel v. Vitale,* it declared unconstitutional an official 'school prayer' at a public school in New York, and in the case of *School District of Abington Township v. Schempp* in 1963, it forbad the recitation of the Lord's Prayer and Bible-readings in the public schools of Pennsylvania.

However, it would be wrong to say that the Supreme Court has always come down on the side of strict separation. One interesting example is that of prayers at local council meetings. In the case of *Marsh v. Chambers* in 1983, the Court had upheld the Nebraska Legislature's funding of a chaplain who delivered daily prayers. Chief Justice Warren Burger ruled that such prayers were 'part of the fabric of our society.' The effect of this decision was to prohibit only those prayers that take sides by advancing or disparaging a particular religion. Thus the recitation of the Lord's Prayer would be lawful but not one said, for example, by Catholics, which disparaged Protestantism. This decision was extended in March 2014 in *Town of Greece v. Galloway* where the US Supreme Court held that prayers before council meetings in the town of Greece in New York State were lawful, provided that there was no attempt to intimidate, coerce or convert non-believers. Two residents, one Jewish, and one atheist, said that the practice of prayers made them uncomfortable, but Justice Kennedy held that 'offense . . . does not equate to coercion.' However, in *Mouvement laïque québécois v. Saguenay*

(City) (2015), the Canadian Supreme Court has held that the practice of offering a Christian prayer at the start of council meetings was in breach of the Quebec Charter of Human Rights and Freedoms and the Canadian Charter of Rights and Freedoms. It held that the evolution of Canadian society had given rise to a concept of neutrality according to which the state must not interfere in religion and beliefs. Moreover, if the state adheres to a form of religious expression under the guise of cultural or historical reality or heritage, it breaches its duty of neutrality.

One can contrast this with the position in the UK where, without a strict separation between Church and State, the High Court declared, in a case promoted by the Secular Society, that the saying of prayers before meetings of the Town Council at Bideford in Devon was not lawful. It is interesting to contrast the different ways in which the USA and UK courts approached the matter. By contrast to the broad approach of the USA courts, the UK court applied Section 111 of the Local Government Act 1972 that provides that a local authority, such as Bideford Town Council, can do anything which is calculated to facilitate or is incidental to the discharge of its functions. Did the saying of prayers, in effect, assist the council to carry out its functions towards the people of Bideford? The judge thought not and declined, as he put it, to rule on 'divine guidance' being available to the Bideford councillors through their prayers.[34] Subsequently, Parliament passed the Local Government (Religious etc. Observances) Act 2015 which provides that business at a meeting of a local authority in England may include time for prayers or other religious observances, or observances connected with a religious or philosophical belief.

One could also view these two cases through a wider prism. Whilst in the UK the courts have been concerned, perhaps overconcerned, to say that religious views do not have a special place in public life, in the USA we have seen the reverse trend. President Barack Obama, a Democrat, supported the saying of prayers before meetings and, from the other side, Kentucky Republican Mitch McConnell, the minority leader in the U.S. Senate, said that the court had 'reaffirmed the strong constitutional footing of this important American tradition.' Contrast this with the statement of John Kennedy when running for President in 1960. On September 12 he spoke in Houston, Texas, and declared that: 'I believe in a president whose religious views are his own private affair'. He then went on to say that: 'Whatever issue may come before me as president – on birth-control, divorce, censorship, gambling, or any other subject – I will make my decision … in accordance with what my conscience tells me to be the national interest, and without regard to outside religious pressure or dictates.' The language of US politicians today is strikingly different and President Obama, for instance, has referred to: 'the role my faith has in guiding my own values and my beliefs'.[35]

Strict Separation: The French and Turkish Experience

In France, the term used is *laïcité* which denotes a strict separation between Church and State so that neither involve themselves in the affairs of the other. There is no complete separation, although *laïcité* is clearly nearer to secularisation than to secular in the sense that we have used these terms.

This principle is enshrined by the *Loi de la Séparation* of 9 December 1905 so that, for example, unless contracted abroad, a religious marriage is not recognised as valid in French law and must be validated by a civil wedding. However, as we saw with the USA, separation is not as strict as it seems. Roman Catholic churches built before 1905 are owned and maintained by the Republic rather than by the Church and the *Loi Debré* of 1959 reinstated a degree of State support for religious education under which schools run by religious organisations can enter into contracts with the State provided that they agree not to impose any religious test on admissions.[36] On the other hand, more recently, under the *Loi* n° 2004–228 of 15 March 2004, France banned the wearing of ostentatious religious symbols in schools. This was challenged in the case of *Dogru v. France* in 2008, where the expulsion of a secondary school pupil who refused to remove her Islamic headscarf during physical education classes was found not to violate Article 9 of the European Convention on Human Rights, which provides for freedom of thought, conscience and religion.

Nevertheless odd corners remain. Although the Concordat with the Vatican concluded by Napoleon in 1801 was abrogated in 1905, the President of the Republic is still consulted about the appointment of Roman Catholic bishops. Moreover, because they were part of the German Empire when the concordat was abrogated, the Concordat is still largely in force in Alsace and Lorraine. Thus clergy whose offices are recognised by the Concordat are paid from public funds and the President has a role in appointments to the more important ecclesiastical offices. Lutheran superintendents are appointed subject to his approval, while he and the Pope jointly appoint the Archbishop of Strasbourg and the Bishop of Metz.

Turkey has perhaps the most extreme version of *laïcité*. Paragraph 5 of the Preamble to the Constitution declares that 'as required by the principle of secularism, there shall be no interference whatsoever by sacred religious feelings in state affairs and politics' and Article 2 states that Turkey 'is a democratic, secular and social state governed by the rule of law'.[37] Thus in 1998 Turkey's Constitutional Court ordered the Welfare Party [*Refah Partisi*] to close on the grounds that it was 'a centre of activities against the principle of secularism'. The ban was subsequently upheld by the Grand Chamber of the European Court of Human Rights.[38]

Conclusion

As Cranmer and Oliva put it,

> The relationship between faith and society in Western Europe has come under increasing scrutiny as the latter has become more multi-cultural and multi-faith. While commentators such as Grace Davie have written widely on the secularisation of Western Europe and the phenomenon of 'believing without belonging',[39] those who still maintain some kind of religious belief probably hold to it more tenaciously now than in the recent past.[40]

On this basis Christians cannot, of course, argue for any relationship with the State that in any way is exclusive to Christianity or indeed exclusive to religion in general. I suggest that the best way to describe the current model of Church-State relations, both in the UK and in many other countries, is that of 'pluralism-cooperation'. In a regime of pluralism-cooperation, religious organisations are free to operate as voluntary associations. The secular authorities may not regard religious institutions as being different from other voluntary bodies and thus religious bodies do not have any special status as religious bodies, but the State gives a measure of financial support to some of their social and educational activities. Moreover, in this spirit of co-operation, they recognise the work done by religious bodies in such fields as education and social services, and they accept the right of religious bodies to contribute as such to national debate. If we argue that this is the model for the UK, then what does it mean for the notion of Establishment? The easy answer would be that it is relegated to the ceremonial and the symbolic. But for the Christian, that can never be right and if that is what Establishment is to mean in the future, then frankly we would be better off without it.

If Establishment is to remain, then I suggest that we need to keep in mind the words of both the present Queen and those of Lord Sachs,[41] who both see it as having a value in keeping religious values at the forefront of the nation. Paul Avis puts it well:

> On the basis of the mission imperative, the Church of England, the Nonconformist churches and the Roman Catholic Church (so far as that is possible) should embark in a greater partnership in the national mission, grounded of course in solid theological agreement, and involving the sharing and strengthening of the pastoral and prophetic opportunities provided by the Church of England's unique position in the nation.[42]

To which one could add that wherever possible non-Christian religions should be invited to make this journey too.

Notes

1 For a full survey of this subject, see N. Doe, *Law and Religion in Europe* (Oxford University Press, 2011), pp. 214–236.

2 I owe this information to F. Cranmer and J. Oliva, 'Church-State Relationships: An Overview' in *Law and Justice*, 162 (2009), pp. 4–17. In addition, the assistance of this article in the writing of this whole chapter is gratefully acknowledged.

3 Article 66 of the Constitution provides that: 'The constitution of the Established Church shall be laid down by statute'.

4 Article 67: 'Citizens shall be at liberty to form congregations for the worship of God in a manner according with their convictions, provided that nothing contrary to good morals or public order shall be taught or done'.

5 Council on International Relations of the Evangelical Lutheran Church in Denmark: 'Queen prefers Church & State', in *Church News from Denmark*, June 2005:3/6, quoted in Cranmer and Oliva's article above.

6 K. Scholder, *A Requiem for Hitler and Other New Perspectives on the German Church Struggle*, especially Chapter 9. The quotation in the text is on p. 164.

7 See the interesting remarks on this by the Archbishop of Birmingham, Bernard Longley, 'Secularism can help spread of the Gospel, says Archbishop', *The Tablet*, 11 February 2012, p. 33.

8 R. Williams, *Faith in the Public Square* (London: Bloomsbury Publishing, 2012), see especially pp. 1–2.

9 In a debate which he initiated in the House of Lords on November 27, 2014 on Religion and Belief. British Public Life. Hansard columns, 1004–1007.

10 J. Chaplin, 'In the Place of Religious Arguments for Law Reform in a Secular State', *Law and Justice*, 162 (2009), pp. 18–35.

11 Church-State relations in the USA, France and Italy are noted in more detail later in this chapter. For an account of Church-State relations in the USA, UK and Germany, seen from a USA perspective, see E. Eberle, *Church and State in Western Europe* (Aldershot: Ashgate, 2011).

12 The issue of the extent to which religious reasons can and should be put forward in public debate is explored in Chapter 9.

13 R. Sandberg and N. Doe, 'Church-State Relations in Europe', *Religion Compass*, 1/5 (2007), pp. 561–578.

14 This case is considered further in Chapter 12.

15 I. Leigh, 'The European Court of Human Rights and Religious Neutrality', in D. D'Costa, M. Evans, T. Modood, J. Rivers, (eds), *Religion in a Liberal State* (Cambridge: Cambridge University Press, 2013), pp. 38–66. The quotation is on p. 38.

16 This case also is considered further in Chapter 12.

17 This case is considered further in Chapter 4 and the operation of the European Convention is considered in Chapter 12.

18 J. Martinez-Touron, 'Institutional Religious Symbols, State Neutrality and Protection of Minorities in Europe' in *Law and Justice*, 171 (2013), pp. 21–51.

19 See the discussion of this case in J. Duddington, 'God, Caesar and the Employment Status of Ministers of Religion' in *Law and Justice*, 159 (2007), pp. 129–135.

20 The issue of ministers of religion and employment law is discussed in J. Duddington, 'The Employment Status of the Clergy: Preston Starts to Unravel' in *Law and Justice*, 171 (2013), pp. 79–94.

21 R. Hooker, *Of the Lawes of Ecclesiasticall Politie*, Folger edition, Book VIII, 1.5.

22 N. Doe, 'The Notion of a National Church: A Juridical Framework' *Law and Justice*, 149 (2002), pp. 77–91.

23 A decision, of course, subsequently reversed in 2014.

24 HM Government, *The Governance of Britain*, Cm 7170 (London: TSO, 2007), para. 63.

25 Church of England Assembly (Powers) Act 1919 s. 4 – but once enacted, they are part of the general law of England and are bound in the statute-book for the year in question.

26 In *The Realm* (Oxford: Family Publications, 2008), p. 48.

27 Ibid., pp. 42–49. The quotation is on p. 45.

28 J. Mackay (Lord Mackay), 'Does Establishment have a Future?' in *Law and Justice*, 170 (2013), pp. 7–18.

29 In 'Does Establishment have a Future?' *Law and Justice*, 170 (2013), p. 13.

30 See Rivers, *The Law of Organised Religions* (Oxford: Oxford University Press, 2010), pp. 85–88.

31 In 'Church State Relationships: An Overview', *Law and Justice* (2009) at p. 16.

32 This phrase comes from the title of an article by A. Esau, 'Islands of Exclusivity: Religious Organisations and Employment Discrimination' in 33 *UBC L Rev* (2000), pp. 719–827.

33 For a valuable account of separation in the USA not only in a particular context but in general see J. Waltman, *Religious Free Exercise and Contemporary American Politics* (London and New York: Continuum, 2011).

34 The Bideford case is known as *National Secular Society v. Bideford Town Council* (2012).

35 I owe the foregoing references to the statements of John Kennedy and Barack Obama to M. Sandel, *Justice: What's the Right Thing to Do?* (London: Penguin, 2010), pp. 244–245.

36 For an official analysis, see <http://education.assemblee-nationale.fr/site-jeunes/laicite/fiche-dates/fiche-1959/fiche.pdf> (accessed 15 February 2014).

37 Constitution of the Republic of Turkey, as amended 17 October 2001.

38 *Refah Partisi & Others v. Turkey* [2003].

39 This comes from the title of her book, *Religion in Britain since 1945: Believing without Belonging* (Oxford: Blackwell, 1994).

40 In 'Church-State Relationships: An Overview', *Law and Justice* (2009), p. 17.

41 Quoted above.

42 P. Avis, *Church, State and Establishment* (London: SPCK, 2001).

Chapter 3

Is English Law Based on Christianity?

*Although historically this country is part of the Christian
west and, although it has an established church which is
Christian, we sit as secular judges serving a
multi-cultural community of many faiths, sworn
to do justice 'to all manner of people'.*

(Sir James Munby)

Introduction

Sir James Munby, a senior judge who is President of the Family
Division, gave a speech to the Law Society's Family Law Annual
Conference on 29 October 2013[1] which made the headlines. Mail
Online reported that: 'British courts are "no longer Christian" says
top judge to reflect modern multicultural society'[2] which, to the
paper, was apparently something new. In fact, what Sir James said
was more nuanced but, nevertheless, he did stress that Christianity,
and values associated with it, no longer had a special place in
English law.[3] Is this true? Is it a sudden development, and should
we as Christians be concerned about it? We shall now explore these
issues.

What is Meant by the Statement that English Law
is Based on Christianity?

There are in fact three issues which are often confused, not least
when someone like Sir James Munby speaks in this way:

(a) Is English law influenced by the basic principles of Christianity?
This question leads on to another issue which will be considered in the next three chapters: to what extent can and should

Christianity influence public debate on the shape and content of law today?

(b) Does Christianity enjoy a special place in English law? If the answer to this question is yes, then it amounts to saying that Christianity not only has a special place in the legal system of this country but also has a special relationship to the State. This is often put more loosely by saying that the question is whether the United Kingdom is still a Christian country. Many people would say that of course Christianity does have a special place as the Church of England is the Established Church but, as we saw in the previous chapter, the whole concept of Establishment needs careful analysis and does not by itself give Christianity a special place in this country.

(c) Do the courts enforce moral precepts as such? This is what occupied a great deal of Sir James Munby's lecture but it is, of course, a different issue, although linked to the present enquiry, and is considered in Chapter 8.

Is English Law Influenced by the Principles of Christianity?

Nick Spencer begins his book *Freedom and Order*[4] with the story of the assembly of the Kentish men at Bearsted near Maidstone in 695 AD, led by Brithwold, the Archbishop of Canterbury where, according to the Venerable Bede, the kingdom's leading men devised twenty-eight laws which were to be added to the existing laws of the Kentish people. What is significant is the first one: 'The Church [is to be free] from all taxation. And the king is to be prayed for, and they are to honour him of their own free will without compulsion'. As Spencer says: 'It would be hard to frame more succinctly the intimate and symbolic relationship between Christianity and political life that would dominate national life for the next 1,300 years.'

Over the centuries examples could be multiplied of the close link between English law (and the English state) and Christianity. However, my enquiry is different as I am interested in the extent to which the principles of Christianity have influenced English law rather than the question of the relationship between the English state and Christianity.

It is in fact clear that English law was, from the start, influenced by basic Christian principles. It is important to remember that it was not until much later that statute law acquired the importance which it has today and thus the law was made by the King's judges

and became known as the 'common law'. This term 'common law'
itself came from the notion of the 'ius commune' which was, in the
early Middle Ages, the name given to that body of law common to
Western Europe which was heavily influenced by the law of the
Church: Canon Law. Thus the first of our law books, the *Tractatus
de legibus et consuetudinibus regni Angliae* of Glanvil, a Royal Justice in
the time of Henry II, was heavily influenced by Roman Law and
also by Canon Law. This particular period saw a tremendous
flowering of English law, for slightly later Henry Bracton wrote
another treatise: *De Legibus et Consuetudinibus Angliae* (On the Laws
and Customs of England). Here we find the basic principle of any
legal system which is influenced by Christianity: *Rex non debet esse
sub homine sed sub deo et sub lege* (the King is not under men but is
under God and the law).

It is worth pondering the implications of this: that the King of
England is not an absolute ruler but is governed both by the law
and by God. Indeed Bracton went on to take this point further:
'the King', he said, is 'no King when will and not law is the
principle of his rule'. Thus, in Christian terms, law is not the
expression of the will of the sovereign: instead law is the rule of
reason and not the command of a superior. We shall explore in the
following chapters (4 and 5) how a Christian view of law might
operate today through reason enlightened by faith leading us to a
knowledge of the natural law, but for now we need to trace the
effect of Bracton's principle through the formative stages in the
development of English Law.[5]

For the effect of Bracton's words was that the King was subject to
a higher law, which we would call natural law, and by which he
could be judged. These words of Bracton were quoted by Robert
Jackson, Chief Counsel for the United States, in his opening
speech at the Nuremburg War Crimes Trials in 1945: 'The Charter
of this Tribunal evidences a faith that the law is not only to govern
the conduct of little men, but that even rulers are, as under God
and the law.'[6]

Richard O'Sullivan points out, 'By virtue of his nature, that is,
according to a principle of natural law and justice, Everyman is a
free man. And Everyman is deemed to be a good man until the
contrary is proved by lawful evidence'.[7] From this, O'Sullivan
argued that from Christian principles the common law derived the
great principle of the free and lawful man: *liber et legalis homo*. What
does this mean for us today? First, as O'Sullivan maintained, it
means that, by virtue of their nature, men and women are free.

Secondly, through this concept the common law created a system aimed at strengthening the bonds of society by administering equal justice to all its members.

This is clearly evidenced by Magna Carta, in which an Archbishop of Canterbury, Stephen Langton, was a moving spirit, and in which Article 39, still in force today by a statute of 1297, sets out principles of Christian justice by providing that:

> NO Freeman shall be taken or imprisoned, or be disseised of his Freehold, or Liberties, or free Customs, or be outlawed, or exiled, or any other wise destroyed; nor will We not pass upon him, nor condemn him, but by lawful judgment of his Peers, or by the Law of the Land. We will sell to no man, we will not deny or defer to any man either Justice or Right.

This is still a vital guiding principle: in Chapter 7 we shall see how access to justice can be blocked by the lack of means to pay for legal advice and representation. Not only this, but the very idea of a free person is expressed in the presumption of innocence until proved guilty. It is a bedrock of our legal system and we must be wary of attempts by governments to change it in particular cases by reversing the burden of proof.

In his *Doctor and Student*[8] published in 1518, Nicholas St. German wrote of the 'law of nature of reasonable creatures or the law of reason as it is commonly called by those that are learned in the laws of England'. This book was enormously influential in putting forward a Christian theory of law and indeed Pollock argued[9] on the basis of this that the use of the words 'reason' in the law of nature and 'reasonable' in the common law showed that 'there is a real link between the medieval doctrine of the law of nature and the principles of the Common Law.' I would be reluctant to go so far as this as, in natural law as understood in the Christian sense, there is a connection to faith whereas ultimately the common law concept of the reasonable man came to depend on the man on the Clapham Omnibus, but in any event matters were soon to take a different turn.

For the so-called Reformation Parliament of 1529–1536 dealt a heavy blow to the notion that, above and beyond the letter of the law, there is a greater principle that we call natural law. The actual process of what is called the Reformation in England was very much a legal construct, brought into effect by Statute Law: Acts of Parliament. This had two consequences, both disastrous for the

Christian concept of natural law. First, it enhanced a principle that had been growing steadily in importance, that of the Supremacy of Statute Law as a source of law. Secondly, the very act of the Reformation by which Henry VIII claimed supremacy over both Church and State, was an affront to the principle of Bracton that that the King was under God and the Law.

The opening words of the Act in Restraint of Appeals in 1532, forbidding appeals to Rome, make this clear:

> Where by divers sundry old authentic histories and chronicles, it is manifestly declared and expressed that this realm of England is an Empire, and so hath been accepted in the world, governed by one Supreme Head and King having the dignity and royal estate of the imperial Crown of the same ...

Thus the claim that England is an empire, although not in fact borne out ' by divers sundry old authentic histories and chronicles' meant that within England there was no source of authority save the Sovereign, whose will must prevail.

Thomas More saw this clearly. When he had been convicted of treason on 7 May 1535 and was about to be sentenced, he claimed the right of every defendant to address the court and in doing so he went directly to the issue:

> Forasmuch, my lord, as this indictment is grounded upon an act of Parliament directly repugnant to the laws of God and his holy church, the supreme government of which, or of any part thereof, may no temporal prince presume by any law to take upon him, as rightfully belonging to the See of Rome, a spiritual pre-eminence by the mouth of our Saviour himself, personally present upon the earth, to Saint Peter and his successors, bishops of the same see, by special prerogative granted; it is therefore in law amongst Christian men, insufficient to charge any Christian man ...[10]

Thus for More, as for many Christians, the ultimate source of law is in Reason leading to Natural Law and not in the will of the sovereign.

This declaration by Henry VIII that he was the Head of an Empire which encompassed both Church and State was one of the great turning points in English history. Often the date of 1485 is taken as a watershed in English history with the defeat of Richard III at Bosworth and the accession of Henry VIII's father Henry VII. In fact the real watershed was not then but in the 1530s when the independence of the Church from the State ended and instead the Church was placed in a position of subordination.

Although the notion of natural law did not disappear from the language of philosophers, it came to be understood in the sense of natural rights, which takes us to the modern doctrine of human rights which is considered in Chapter 10, but for now we must stay with the legal development of the notion of sovereignty.

From the assertion of the supremacy of Statute Law in making the Reformation there developed the doctrine of Parliamentary Sovereignty, which, as defined by the jurist Dicey, provides that: 'Parliament has, under the English Constitution, the right to make or unmake any law whatever; and further, that no person or body is recognised by the law of England as having a right to override or set aside the legislation of our Parliament'.[11] Thus in 1935, Sir Wilfrid Greene, KC, argued in court that Parliament 'could pass an Act tomorrow that all persons under the age of one year should be put to death'. No one suggests that the UK Parliament, on a day-to-day basis, exercises tyrannical power, but under this classic doctrine it is there, untrammelled by any considerations of fundamental principles of natural law.

The Place of Equity in English Law

Before we examine the subject of Christianity and the law today, we must note one area of law, directly stemming from Christian principles, which still has vigour. This is known as Equity. In the Middle Ages the King's Chancellor, who had a much more prominent role than the holder of that office does today,[12] came to hear cases where it was alleged that the judges of the common law courts had failed to do justice. This basis of their jurisdiction, which came to be known as 'Equity' was a concern for moderating the strict letter of the law[13] with a focus on personal conscience. The point for us is that the Chancellors were ecclesiastics and, thus, trained in Canon Law, and the idea of 'conscience' which they used was not conscience in any subjective sense, but conscience in the Christian sense, as an objective standard of conduct. This jurisdiction survives in full vigour today with an emphasis on providing a remedy for unconscionable conduct. Thus here is a special instance of where Christian principles are indeed part of the law today.

Does Christianity Enjoy a Special Place in English Law Today?

Judges and others frequently state that 'Christianity is not part of the law of England'. As long ago as 1917, in the case of *Bowman v. Secular Society*, the courts rejected the view that 'it is part of the law of the land that all must believe in the fundamental doctrines of Christianity' and indeed this had been the case long before then.

More recently, in *McFarlane v. Relate Avon Limited* (2010), Lord Justice Laws made the position clear and his words are worth quoting in full:

> The Judeo- Christian tradition, stretching over many centuries, has no doubt exerted a profound influence upon the judgment of law-makers as to the objective merits of this or that social policy, and the liturgy and practice of the established church are to some extent prescribed by law. But the conferment of any legal protection or preference upon a particular substantive moral position on the ground only that it is espoused by the adherents of a particular faith, however long its tradition, however rich its culture, is deeply unprincipled; it imposes compulsory law not to advance the general good on objective grounds, but to give effect to the force of subjective opinion. This must be so, since, in the eye of everyone save the believer, religious faith is necessarily subjective.

What the judges really mean is that Christianity as an institution has no privileged status in the law and constitution of this country. That is probably obvious to most people. But there is another issue: does the State, and through it the law, give any special protection to the expression of Christian beliefs? Take this example: Suppose that I, as a Christian with strong beliefs against nuclear weapons, try to enter a base where these weapons are held and am then charged with a criminal offence. What I cannot do is to argue that my Christian beliefs give me the right to do this. That is probably obvious to most people. What is important is to bear in mind that the courts have distinguished between the law's protection of the right to hold and express a belief and the law's protection of that belief's substance or content. In the latter case this amounts to arguing for a special status for that belief, such as a Christian belief, and this, as Lord Justice Laws pointed out above, is what the courts will not allow.

Nevertheless there does seem to be a determination by the judges, many of whom are practising Christians themselves, to almost over-emphasise the point that Christianity no longer has any special place in our society, and here I would part company with them. For I would say that the basic precepts of Christianity are still relevant in our legal system. In particular, the idea that law is not just the expression of the will of the sovereign, and that there is a touchstone against which laws are judged which we call natural law, are two Christian principles that are still valid today. What is interesting is that these ideas have now become part of the legal system with the passage of the Human Rights Act 1998, which has entrenched into our legal system some fundamental human rights. The result is that it is no longer true to say, as Dicey did, that Parliament has absolute power and thus law is no more than the expression of the sovereign will.

Should Religions Claim That They and Their Followers Should be Subject to a Special Law?

There is another issue which has surfaced recently: Should religions claim a kind of enclave for them and their followers, whereby special laws apply to them rather than the general law of the land? This topic was raised by the then Archbishop of Canterbury, Rowan Williams, in a lecture on 7 February 2008 entitled 'Law in England: a religious perspective', at the Royal Courts of Justice.[14] Here he said that:

> an increased legal recognition of communal religious identities can be met if we are prepared to think about the basic ground rules that might organise the relationship between jurisdictions, making sure that we do not collude with unexamined systems that have oppressive effect or allow shared public liberties to be decisively taken away by a supplementary jurisdiction.

All this seems somewhat obscure, to say the least, but what Dr Williams was saying was that, in some cases, religions might have this kind of private law to which we referred above. In an interview on BBC Radio 4's *The World at One*, the Archbishop mentioned explicitly the recognition of Sharia Law. He said that:

> as a matter of fact, certain conditions of Sharia are already recognised in our society and under our law, so it is not as if we are bringing in an alien and rival system. We already have in this country a number of situations in which the internal law of religious

communities is recognised by the law of the land as justifying conscientious objections in certain circumstances. There are ways of
looking at marital disputes, for example, which provide an alternative to the divorce courts as we understand them.

The problem was that the very mention of Sharia Law by the
Archbishop led to a rush on all sides to say that this was wrong
without looking at the underlying issues. So the then Prime
Minister, Gordon Brown, said that 'Sharia Law could not be used
as a justification for committing breaches of British law, nor could
the principles of Sharia Law be applied in a civil court in reaching
a decision on a contractual dispute under British law'.

What Dr Williams did not advocate was the wholesale adoption
of Sharia Law into the legal system of this country but instead
argued for a debate on the extent to which it was possible for there
to be what is sometimes called 'transformative accommodation'
between the laws of particular religions and the laws of the State.

There is undoubtedly a case to be made for religious believers to
opt out of certain legal provisions: for example, some Roman
Catholic adoption agencies were forced to close because of the
Equality Act (Sexual Orientation) Regulations 2007[15] which
compelled them to offer their adoption services to same-sex
couples. I would certainly argue that there should have been an
exemption in this instance. Moreover the Treasury and HM
Revenue and Customs have spent considerable time and effort
over the past few years in helping the financial services industry to
devise legitimate investment vehicles that are also Sharia-
compliant, in order to circumvent the Koranic inhibition on usury.

However, these are very specific cases applying in defined situations. What I suggest is dangerous, is for religions of any kind to set
up systems of law which run contrary to those that apply to the rest
of society. This does happen using the provisions of the Arbitration
Act 1996 which allows the parties to in effect bypass the courts and
submit their dispute to arbitration. So s. 1 of this Act provides that:
'the parties should be free to agree how their disputes are resolved,
subject only to such safeguards as are necessary in the public
interest'. This is frequently used by members of the Jewish
community to enable them to use the Beth Din (literally 'house of
judgment') which has rights under Jewish law to determine
disputes in religious matters. Similarly, members of the Muslim
community have used the Arbitration Act to enable Sharia councils
to apply Sharia legal principles.

The problem is that, by contrast with Christians, the religious principles of these communities spill over into areas which Christians would see as outside their religious beliefs and thus the prerogative of the civil law. This is particularly so in the areas of marriage and inheritance. Thus in the case of *Kohn v. Wagschal & Others* in 2007 the civil courts upheld an arbitration by the London Beth Din relating to the destination of shares from the estate of someone who had died intestate. More recently, on 23 March 2014, the *Sunday Telegraph* reported that the Law Society (representing the solicitors branch of the legal profession) had produced guidance enabling solicitors to compose Islamic wills that refuse women an equal share of any inheritance as well as excluding non-believers, illegitimate children and those who have been adopted from inheriting. The actual guidance[16] emphasises that 'Clients in England and Wales can legally choose to bequeath their assets according to Sharia rules, providing the will is signed in accordance with the requirements set out in the Wills Act 1837'.

Clearly these ideas cause alarm and, most importantly from our perspective, they quite simply give religion a bad name and lessen our ability to witness to our faith in public debate. Moreover, by giving the impression that, as believers, we seek a separate space for ourselves, we concede the argument of secularists that believers cannot contribute to any debate on what is for the wider public good. In fact Dr Williams, in his lecture quoted above, said that: 'Recognising a supplementary jurisdiction cannot mean recognising a liberty to exert a sort of local monopoly in some areas.' He referred to the work of the Jewish legal theorist Ayelet Shachar who 'explores the risks of any model that ends up "franchising" a non-state jurisdiction so as to reinforce its most problematic features and further disadvantage its weakest members.' She writes:

> we must be alert to the potentially injurious effects of well-meaning external protections upon different categories of group members here – effects which may unwittingly exacerbate pre-existing internal power hierarchies.[17]

There is an argument that if Sharia councils are formally recognised this could bring about greater accountability. But in a perceptive article, Samia Bano argues that, in fact, Sharia councils are reluctant to be formally recognised and moreover his study, based on first-hand research, shows the disadvantage to which Muslim women are subjected and, as he says, this itself 'undermines the Islamic principles of autonomy, choice and free will'.[18]

Thus, our society has a choice: either to prohibit any parallel systems of adjudication such as Beth Din and Sharia councils or, if they are to be allowed, to provide a detailed comprehensive regulation of them building on the provision in s. 1 of the Arbitration Act 1996 that there must be 'safeguards as are necessary in the public interest'. Although we have the overarching provisions of the Human Rights Act,[19] something more specific is needed. So far there is, though, no evidence that this is likely to happen.

Conclusion

To sum up: How do we answer the question: 'Is this still a Christian country and does Christianity have a special place in the law today? If this means that this is a country where Christianity has a special status in law, then the answer would be a clear 'No.' However, if the question is asking if Christian principles can and should influence the way in which we act, and this includes influencing the content of legislation, then I would argue that we can still answer 'Yes'. Moreover we can act as a prophetic voice in opposing unjust laws.

In Chapters 10, 11 and 12 we shall look at human rights legislation which, it can be argued, gives effect to some natural law principles, and at how it works within our legal system, but next we must turn to a more detailed examination of Natural Law preceded by a discussion of faith and reason.

Notes

1   His address was entitled: 'The sacred and the secular: religion, culture and the courts' and can be found at: www.judiciary.gov.uk/.../JCO/.../law-morality-religion-munby-2013.pd. It is this speech that is quoted at the head of this chapter.
2   See   http://www.dailymail.co.uk/news/article-2479391/Christian-values-sway-courts-says-judge.html#ixzz2q268GRGN
3   This speech is discussed in more detail in Chapter 8.
4   London: Hodder and Stoughton, 2011, p. 17.
5   The work of great judges such as Glanvil and Bracton can be traced through various standard works on English legal history. T. Plunkett's *A Concise History of the Common Law* (London: Butterworths, 1929), is still useful but a more

modern account is in J. Baker, *A History of English Law*, 4th ed. (Oxford: Oxford University Press, 2002).

6 The impact of the principles of natural law on the development of international criminal law in the twentieth century is also considered in Chapter 5.

7 In 'Natural Law and Common Law', printed in B. Wortley, (ed.), *The Spirit of the Common Law, a collection of the papers of Richard O'Sullivan* (Tenbury Wells: Fowler Wright Books, 1965).

8 This is available online at www.lonang.com/exlibris/stgermain/

9 F. Pollock, 'The History of the Law of Nature', an essay reprinted in *Jurisprudence and Legal Essays* (London: Macmillan, 1961), p. 142.

10 These famous words are to be found in many sources. One accessible source is W. Roper and N. Harpsfield (ed. E. Reynolds), *Lives of St. Thomas More* (London and New York: J.M. Dent & Sons, 1963), p. 45. This is from the life by Roper.

11 *Introduction to the Study of the Law of the Constitution*, 10th ed. (London: Macmillan, 1959).

12 Especially since it was, most regrettably, downgraded by the Constitutional Reform Act 2005.

13 See further Chapter 5.

14 The lecture, together with questions and answers to the Archbishop, was reprinted as 'Civil and Religious Law in England: A Religious Perspective' in *Ecclesiastical Law Journal*, 10 (3) (2008), pp. 262–282.

15 See Chapter 12.

16 Available at www.lawsociety.org.uk (accessed 20 April 2014).

17 'Civil and Religious Law in England: A Religious Perspective' in *Ecclesiastical Law Journal*, 10 (3) (2008), p. 270. This quotation appears in A. Shachar, *Multicultural Jurisdictions: Cultural Differences and Women's Rights* (Cambridge: Cambridge University Press, 2002).

18 'In Pursuit of Religious Diversity' in *Ecclesiastical Law Journal*, 10 (2008), p. 283–309, at p. 305.

19 See Chapter 12.

Chapter 4

Faith and Reason

Credo ut intelligam
'I believe so that I may understand'

(St Anselm of Canterbury, *Proslogion*, 1)

Introduction

In November 1793, following the abjuration of his priesthood by
Gobel, the 'bishop'[1] of Paris, and 400 priests of Paris, radicals
proceeded to turn the Cathedral of Notre Dame into a 'Temple of
Reason', and an opera singer, one Mlle Maillard, was dressed as
'the goddess of liberty', the statute of the Virgin Mary having been
dethroned. As Burleigh remarks: 'The really reasonable obviously
deplored all this'.[2] Even so, this incident stands as a vivid illustration of the eighteenth-century Enlightenment view of reason as
opposed to religion. The thinkers of the Enlightenment saw a new
Age of Reason dawning in which, as they saw it, the shackles of
religion with its antique mysticism were thrown off and all was to
be decided by the great god of reason. The view of many
Christians, however, is that faith is not an alternative to reason but
is the pre-condition of reason.[3] Moreover, it is the seeking out what
reason is saying to us that, in the words of Pope Benedict XVI,
enables us: 'to help purify and shed light upon the application of
reason to the discovery of objective moral principles'.[4]

What is the Relationship Between Faith and Reason?

The view that faith belongs to the sacred and reason to the
secular was, as mentioned above, very much a product of the
Enlightenment and, as it is a view still commonly held today, we
need to look more closely at its philosophical foundations.

The exaltation of the 'God of Reason' in the later seventeenth
and eighteenth centuries can be seen as a reaction from the

concentration on the study of academic philosophy in the late Middle Ages and, instead, a concentration on the problems of living personalities.[5] Writing towards the end of the seventeenth century, John Locke (1632–1704) said that: 'Reason must be our last guide and judge in everything,'[6] and he saw law itself as coming from the natural order of things so that it was a natural rule of reason. This theory emphasised individual will and individual reason and led to an emphasis on liberty. Rousseau's famous remark in *The Social Contract* that 'Man is born free, and everywhere he is in chains' is but one example.

There is much of this that is still with us today, with the stress always on the individual and on rights rather than duties. As Christians we must acknowledge that an emphasis on individual liberty and freedom is right and that the Enlightenment with its emphasis on this did much good. In particular, the world moved away from a situation where the sovereign power, wherever it was located, was supreme purely because it was the sovereign power to a position where rulers, ruling over those who are inherently free, need the consent of those over whom they rule. Indeed, as we saw in Chapter 3, the lawyer Richard O'Sullivan emphasised the 'free and lawful man' as a product of a Christian view of law. Where, however, the world has moved in the wrong direction is in emphasising individuals as individuals and only as individuals without locating individuals within society and arguing that it is the duty of each individual to promote the common good, a concept to which we shall return in the following chapters.

The Christian View of the Relationship Between Faith and Reason

Against the secular view of reason many Christians oppose a view of reason as an intuitive one coming from our faith.[7] Pope Benedict XVI himself writes: 'God is Logos – meaning, reason and word ... Faith in the God who is Logos is at the same time faith in the creative power of reason'.[8] In a pithy phrase, St Anselm expressed reason as 'faith seeking understanding'[9] and the First Vatican Council in *Dei Filius* put it thus: 'Even though faith is above reason, there can never be any real disagreement between faith and reason, since it is the same God who reveals the mysteries and infuses faith, and who has endowed the human mind with the light of reason ...'[10] Again St Thomas More, in one of his letters from

prison in 1534 to his daughter Margaret, spoke of his trust in
'reason with the help of faith'.[11]

So in Dante's *Purgatorio* the poet shows how, as D'Entrèves puts
it: 'Reason and faith go hand in hand but reason is the
handmaid'[12] when, on the mountain of purgatory, Virgil, having
led Dante thus far, hands him over to Beatrice with the words:

> ... What reason can see here,
> I can impart; past that, for truth of faith,
> It's Beatrice alone you must await.[13]

The leading modern exposition of faith and reason is found in
Pope John Paul II's encyclical *Fides et Ratio*.[14] In it (at 16) the Pope
speaks of the:

> profound and indissoluble unity between the knowledge of reason
> and the knowledge of faith. The world and all that happens within
> it, including history and the fate of peoples, are realities to be
> observed, analysed and assessed with all the resources of reason, but
> without faith ever being foreign to the process. Faith intervenes not
> to abolish reason's autonomy nor to reduce its scope for action, but
> solely to bring the human being to understand that in these events
> it is the God of Israel who acts. Thus the world and the events of
> history cannot be understood in depth without professing faith in
> the God who is at work in them. Faith sharpens the inner eye,
> opening the mind to discover in the flux of events the workings of
> Providence.

Later on (at 20), Pope John Paul notes that: 'human beings attain
truth by way of reason because, enlightened by faith, they discover
the deeper meaning of all things and most especially of their own
existence. Rightly, therefore, the sacred author identifies the fear
of God as the beginning of true knowledge: "The fear of the Lord
is the beginning of knowledge" (*Prov.* 1:7)'.

In his lecture at the University of Regensburg on 12 September
2006, Pope Benedict XVI emphasised this connection between
faith and reason.[15] He quoted (at para. 8) the Byzantine Emperor
Manuel II Palaeologus in dialogue with a Persian[16] in the course of
which the Pope records the Emperor as saying that God: 'is not
pleased by blood – and not acting reasonably (σὺν λόγω) is
contrary to God's nature. Faith is born of the soul, not the body.
Whoever would lead someone to faith needs the ability to speak
well and to reason properly, without violence and threats ...' As
the Pope goes on to observe: 'not to act in accordance with reason

is contrary to God's nature', and it is this fundamental principle that the Pope's lecture was intended to stress.

More than this, though, Pope Benedict saw this connection between faith and reason as coming from the encounter between early Christianity and Greek philosophy. He pointed to the vision of St Paul, who, as the Pope put it:

> saw the roads to Asia barred and in a dream saw a Macedonian man plead with him: 'Come over to Macedonia and help us!' (Acts 16:6–10) – this vision can be interpreted as a 'distillation' of the intrinsic necessity of a rapprochement between Biblical faith and Greek inquiry.'

Thus the Hellenization of Christianity took place when Christianity met Greek philosophy and came to terms with its legitimate demands, with the result that the 'critically purified Greek heritage forms an integral part of the Christian heritage'.[17]

There is a movement today toward the de-Hellenization of Christianity which is an attempt to sunder faith from reason *per se* and, as Kant and others have suggested, to anchor reason in practical reason alone. Moreover, as Aidan Nichols points out: 'If religion and reason do not mesh, reason will end up with a debased anthropology which seeks to spin whatever moral substance it can from the webs of evolutionary science, psychology, or sociology. And religion in turn will become fundamentalist'.[18]

The term 'practical reason' leads us to the distinction often drawn between speculative and practical reason. In fact, Thomas Aquinas points out that these are not different powers: speculative reason is concerned with knowledge of truth itself, whereas practical reason is concerned with the application of speculative reason to actual moral problems.[19] However, reason can of course go astray. In *Deus Caritas Est*[20] Pope Benedict pointed this out in connection with a discussion of justice: 'The State must inevitably face the question of how justice can be achieved here and now.' However, he continued: 'this presupposes an even more radical question: what is justice?' This was, he felt, a problem 'of practical reason; but if reason is to be exercised properly, it must undergo constant purification, since it can never be completely free of the danger of a certain ethical blindness caused by the dazzling effect of power and special interests.' Thus it is no good for us as Christians to constantly claim that our reason is telling us that something is right: we must always ask ourselves: is this really the voice of reason purified by faith speaking to us?

Why does this matter to Christians today? It is because we believe that our faith gives us an intuitive understanding of what is best for the human race. Reason is not just reasoning that, for instance, if we do X then Y will result, but reason, purified by our faith, gives us an insight into the divine wisdom itself. Not only this, but it is this reason which, as we shall see in subsequent chapters, gives us that knowledge of Truth that leads us to a knowledge of the natural law and guides our conscience. In his address to the Bundestag four years later, on 22 September 2011, Pope Benedict XVI emphasised the relationship between nature, reason and conscience drawing on the story of King Solomon:

> In the First Book of Kings, it is recounted that God invited the young King Solomon, on his accession to the throne, to make a request. What will the young ruler ask for at this important moment? Success – wealth – long life – destruction of his enemies? He chooses none of these things. Instead, he asks for a listening heart so that he may govern God's people, and discern between good and evil (cf. 1 Kg 3:9).[21]

In short, the young ruler asks for the gift of reason enlightened by faith.

The result is, in the words of Thomas Aquinas, that: 'The natural law is nothing else than the participation of the eternal law in a rational creature'[22] and so, as Coplestone puts it: 'For Aquinas, therefore, it is human reason which is the proximate or immediate promulgator of the natural moral law'.[23] However, before we move on to examine natural law and then conscience, we must note two contemporary points.

Christians Must Employ Their Reason in Public Debate

As we saw above, we, as Christians, although endowed with reason which is a reflection of our faith, must always be on our guard against being misled into thinking that we are being guided by reason when in fact it is not so. In particular, we must remember that reason means that our faith is reasonable and not irrational. Yet it is distressing to see Christians still making shrill statements which lead non-Christians to think that our faith is just a series of knee-jerk reactions to events. One thinks of statements such as: 'Abortion is wrong. We are Christians and so we know this.' This is, in fact, the very de-Hellenization of Christianity of which Pope Benedict spoke; our faith is divorced from our reason.

In 1985 Mr (now Lord) Dale Campbell-Savours, MP, said this in the debate on the Unborn Children (Protection) Bill introduced by Mr Enoch Powell, and which was intended to prohibit experiments on human embryos:

> A Christian need do no more than pronounce his article of faith . . . For those of us who subscribe to such views, they may be sufficient justification for supporting this Bill. But I do not believe that that approach, without the intellectual base that requires deliberation and evaluation of its merits, is sufficient to convince this House.[24]

This is precisely the point. Nor is this attitude confined to Parliament. Lucy Vickers, Professor of Law at Oxford Brookes University, points out that the Christian view that 'God has created all men in his image . . . gives no basis for non-Christians to respect human rights'.[25] What we must do as Christians is to show that our reason coming from our faith makes us believe that we are indeed created in God's image and that this then gives us a unique dignity, and it is this that gives us our commitment to human rights.

The Secular View of Reason Still Prevails

Whether it is partly the fault of Christians in making apparently unreasonable statements or not, it seems that the secular view of reason as something rational and sensible as opposed to the irrational claims of religion still prevails. This can be seen especially in the decisions of some courts in relation to the display of religious symbols. Take the case of *Lautsi v. Italy*, the Italian crucifix case, as it became known.

Mrs Soile Lautsi was a citizen of both Finland and of Italy and claimed, on behalf of herself and her children, against the School Council of a school in Abano Terme in the province of Padua, that displaying a crucifix in the school violated her right to ensure that their children's education conformed to her religious and philosophical convictions. She said that this was contrary to the European Convention on Human Rights and, in particular, she alleged that it infringed her rights under Article 2 of Protocol No. 1 of the Convention, which provides that the State shall respect the right of parents to ensure such education and teaching in conformity with their own religious and philosophical convictions, and Article 9 which protects thought, conscience and religion. The Government maintained that the crucifix was not only a religious symbol but also the 'standard of the Catholic Church' – the only Church named in the Italian Constitution – and therefore a symbol of the Italian state itself.

In the end, the display of crucifixes was held by the Grand Chamber of the European Court of Human Rights not to infringe the rights of Mrs Lautsi and her children under the Convention, but what is of interest here is the attitude of what is known as the Chamber, the first section of the Court to hear the case. This hearing, by the way, is often referred to as *Lautsi I* with the Grand Chamber hearing as *Lautsi II*.

The Court considered that the crucifix was a 'powerful' symbol with remarkable potential impact on young students, and with a primarily religious meaning. Therefore, its presence in the school premises could be emotionally disturbing for some students and restricted the parents' rights to decide the orientation of their children's education and was incompatible with the neutrality that must pervade the school environment.[26] The reference to the display of a crucifix as being 'emotionally disturbing' is significant, as underlying this is a feeling that the display of symbols such as the crucifix are, in a deep sense, irrational. As Javier Martínez-Tourón points out: 'the logical consequence of this rationale would be the removal of crucifixes from all public schools in Italy (and probably elsewhere).' And he adds: 'Implicit in that approach was a notion of neutrality as meaning the exclusion of religion from the public space, at least in the educational milieu.'[27]

Many would say that this is not neutrality at all but an example of the courts adopting a secular approach.

This is significant in the context of a discussion of faith and reason because, as Martínez-Tourón says: 'Ultimately, by making mandatory the exclusive concept of religious neutrality, *Lautsi I* axiomatically accepted a very debatable distinction between believers and non-believers, attaching non-belief to the realm of reason and belief to the realm of non-rational belief.' It then followed that religious symbols were exemplars of non-rational belief and so did not have any place in public education.

It is important to stress that this view did not prevail at the final hearing (*Lautsi II*) and this decision is considered in Chapter 11, but it is an example of the attitude of many legislators and judges today. We shall encounter further examples later in this book.

In fact, much of the rationale of *Lautsi I* follows the European Court of Human Rights' argument in the case of *Leyla Şahin v. Turkey* (2007) and others that adopt a similar approach with regard to the wearing of an Islamic headscarf or other personal clothing of religious significance. We shall examine these cases later when we look at the law on religious dress and other symbols in Chapter 11, but for now we should note that one of the reasons utilized to support restrictive policies on personal religious garments at school was that such expressions of religiosity could lead to tension or 'pressure' on other students.

Here we as Christians are at one with other religions in proclaiming that religion is not irrational, and in the idea that the display of religious symbols is not irrational but is a symbol of a faith that leads to reason. How that reason leads us to an understanding of natural law, conscience and justice, will be explored in the subsequent chapters.

Notes

1 He was never consecrated as such and his appointment was irregular: he had taken the oath of the Civil Constitution of the Clergy which gave the appointment of priests to the electoral assemblies, and was elected Archbishop of Paris. His appointment was never recognised by the Holy See.
2 See M. Burleigh, *Earthly Powers* (London: Harper Collins, 2005), p. 87.
3 Those seeking a fuller account of faith and reason should look at two excellent volumes by J.A. Malatry, *Faith Through Reason* (Leominster: Gracewing, 2006), which has a preface by the then Cardinal Ratzinger, and *When Might Becomes Human Right* (Leominster: Gracewing, 2007). Both books are infused with the thought of Cardinal Ratzinger (later Pope Benedict XVI) on this area and much else besides.
4 The whole of his address can be found in P. Jennings, ed., *Benedict XVI and Blessed John Henry Newman, The State Visit September 2010, The Official Record* (London: CTS, 2010), pp. 102–106.
5 The best discussion from the legal point of view on this area is still, I think, in C.K. Allen, *Law in the Making* (Oxford: Oxford University Press, 7th ed., 1964). See especially pp. 10–18.
6 J. Locke, *An Essay Concerning Human Understanding* (Bk 4.19.14).
7 This notion of Reason is close to that of Cicero (in *Virtute tanquam lege*, II, 4.10): 'For there was a Reason that proceeded from the nature of things, impelling to right action and deterring from wrong'.
8 'Auf der Suche nach dem Frieden', an address given on the sixtieth anniversary of the landings of the Allies in France, June 6, 2004, and published as Chapter 6, 'Searching for Peace, Tensions and Dangers' in *Values in a Time of Upheaval* (Ignatius Press: San Francisco, 2006). This whole collection of essays by Joseph Cardinal Ratzinger (Pope Benedict XVI) is strongly recommended to anyone interested in the theme of this article.

9 St Anselm, *Prosl.* prooem: PL 153. 225 quoted in *Catechism of the Catholic Church*, para. 158.

10 *Dei Filius*, 4.

11 See A. de Silva (ed.), *The Last Letters of Thomas More* (Grand Rapids, Michigan and Cambridge, UK: Eerdmans Publishing Co., 2000). This letter is at p. 99.

12 A. D'Entrèves, *Natural Law*, 2nd ed. (London: Hutchinson University Library, 1970), p. 48.

13 Dante, *Purgatorio,* xviii, 46–48; trans. A. Mandelbaum (London: Everyman's Library, 1995).

14 London: CTS, 1998.

15 For those interested in what became a celebrated lecture, and in its background, I recommend: J. V. Schnall, *The Regensburg Lecture* (South Bend, Indiana: St. Augustine's Press, 2007). This contains the text of the lecture and much else besides.

16 This was the section of his address which caused so much trouble and misunderstanding although this did not relate to the words that are quoted here but earlier in the dialogue.

17 At 31. This connection between faith and reason is explored further in the next chapter in the context of natural law.

18 A. Nichols, *From Hermes to Benedict XVI: Faith and Reason in Modern Catholic Thought* (Leominster: Gracewing, 2009), pp. 231–232. Readers are recommended in particular to study Chapter 11: From Cracow to Regensburg: Benedict XVI.

19 ST, Ia, 79,11.

20 London: CTS, 2006. The references are to para. 28.

21 www.vatican.va/.../benedict.../speeches/.../hf_ben-xvi_spe_20110922 (accessed 6 February 2014).

22 ST, Ia, IIae, 91, 2.

23 F. C. Coplestone, *Aquinas* (London: Penguin Books, 1955), p. 222.

24 Quoted in M. Warnock, *Dishonest to God: On Keeping Religion out of Politics* (London: Continuum, 2010), p. 25.

25 L. Vickers, *Religious Freedom, Religious Discrimination and the Workplace* (Portland, Oregon and Oxford: Hart Publishing, 2008), p. 32.

26 See especially *Lautsi I*, § 57.

27 J. Martínez-Tourón, 'Institutional Religious Symbols, State Neutrality and Protection of Minorities in Europe' in *Law and Justice,* 171 (2013), pp. 21–51.

Chapter 5

Natural Law

'The natural law is nothing else but a participation of
the eternal law in the minds of rational creatures.'

(Thomas Aquinas, *Summa Theologica*, Ia, IIae, 91,2)

Introduction

The term 'natural law' may seem to be a vague philosophical
concept, divorced from everyday life, but it is the aim of this
chapter to show that this is far from the case. Take this example: It
is now 2050. There is growing pressure on social services due to the
ever-increasing number of people aged 85 and over who are in
residential care and who cannot any longer afford to pay for this,
with the result that the burden is falling on the State. Euthanasia
was legalised in 2030, after a long campaign, but the law only
allows this if the person concerned has specifically requested it and
other conditions have been met. As a result, euthanasia has
become an accepted part, not quite of living, but undoubtedly of
dying. Thus in 2050 the Government, which has a large majority,
proposes a law that: 'All persons who are in residential accommodation and who have reached the age of 95 shall be conclusively
presumed to have requested that their life shall be terminated
unless a document can be produced signed by that person when
they were of sound mind specifically stating that they did not wish
this to happen'.

Put like this, it all sounds so reasonable! In fact what this law
means is that persons over the age of 95 in residential care face the
possibility of being killed. However, the Government has a large
parliamentary majority and so this monstrous proposal becomes
law. Or does it? According to a strict interpretation, indeed it does:
all the formalities were observed and this is law in the same way as
the law that provides for a 30mph speed limit. But this is where
natural law comes in.

For natural law says that in some cases a law passed by the state may so offend against basic principles of justice that it is indeed not law at all, and this is likely to be so in this case. Thus it provides a touchstone against which the validity of existing laws can be measured and it also provides a benchmark to evaluate proposals to make new law. This chapter looks at what natural law means and endeavours to give it some meaningful content so that it does not remain just a vague aspiration.

What is Meant by Natural Law?

The definition of natural law given by Aquinas at the head of this chapter is by no means the only one, as we shall see, but as we are looking at natural law from a Catholic perspective it will be used as the starting point in this chapter. John Finnis[1] looks at this phrase of Aquinas, 'the participation of the Eternal Law in the minds of rational creatures', and considers the term 'participation'. This is crucial. If we argue that natural law comes from God as the Eternal Law, then how and to what extent can mortals attain knowledge of its precepts? How can we actually participate in the Divine Mind? Finnis argues that participate means it is 'a "separate intellect" that has the power of understanding without imperfection' which 'causes in us our own power of insight, the activation of our own individual intelligence – somewhat as our power of sight activates in us our power of sight'. This 'separate intellect' which has the perfect understanding of natural law can be identified by revelation as God.[2] As Coplestone puts it:

> For although man cannot read off, as it were, the eternal law in God's mind, he can discern the fundamental tendencies and needs of his nature and by reflecting on them he can come to a knowledge of the natural law.[3]

The Second Vatican Council in *Gaudium et Spes* put it this way: 'Deep within their consciences men and women discover a law which they have laid upon themselves and which they must obey'.[4]

Thus we argue that the precepts of natural law are accessible to all. As Thomas Aquinas puts it: *Gratia non tollit naturam, sed perficit* (Grace does not destroy nature, but perfects it). The natural instincts present in every person can, by God's grace, be brought to perfection. So the *Catechism of the Catholic Church*[5] explains (at 1960): 'The precepts of natural law are not perceived by everyone clearly and immediately. In the present situation sinful man needs grace and revelation so moral and religious truths may be known "by everyone with facility, with firm certainty and with no admixture of error"'.[6] This is important as it establishes the link between faith and reason, dealt with in the previous chapter, and natural law, in that it is our reason coming from grace and revelation that enables us to discern these fundamental precepts which we term natural law. So reason and faith, and human reason and eternal values, are in harmony.

The principle of Aquinas of grace perfecting nature can be seen in operation in the way that the concept of natural law predates Christianity and was present in Greek and Roman thought. In Plato's *Theaetetus*, Socrates points out the consequences of the thesis advocated by Protagoras that each of us is the judge of what is truth and that there is no absolute standard. It means that when considering what kinds of behaviour are 'morally, legally and religiously acceptable … no community is any wiser than another'.[7] Even non-Christian religions 'testify to the existence of a patrimony of moral values common to all human beings, no matter how those values are justified within a particular world view.'[8] In the Hindu tradition, the world is regulated by an order or fundamental world view (*dharma*).[9] And in the African tradition the fundamental reality is life itself, and thus acts which 'are favourable to the opening up of life … or to increasing the vital potential of the community'[10] are considered naturally good. So we can say that an insight into natural law is given not only to Christians, nor indeed only to those with a religious faith, but that everyone, deep within them, by virtue of the reason given to them by God, has the ability to discern what is the natural law for the human race.

However, before we go further, two points need to be cleared up:

First, natural law is not the same as laws of nature, such as laws of gravitation and other laws of physics. The two are often confused but, as the discussion above made clear, natural law comes from our reason enlightened by our faith and is fundamentally about justice and the right ordering of society.

Second, although the concept of natural law is held strongly in the Roman Catholic tradition, the idea that there is a natural law is one held by other Christians too.[11] For example, coming from the Baptist tradition, David McIlroy sees a vital place for natural law in Christian thinking and writes that: 'Natural law's fundamental philosophical claim is that there is an objective moral order, that human beings are not free, on all issues, to construct whatever morality they think fit but are instead constrained by the ordering of nature. In its theological form, natural law claims that there is a God-given moral order against which human beings will be judged'.[12] Prof. John Macquarrie sees natural law in more general terms as: 'the moral awareness that belongs to man in virtue of the existentiality into which he has been created ...'.[13] But this has the danger of making natural law simply an awareness of a moral dimension to human life and, to be of value, natural law needs some content and shape.

Bishop Richard Harries, writing from an Anglican standpoint, sees a continuing place for natural law[14] and described it as: 'The concept of a natural order, or intrinsic moral order that can be grasped by rational minds.'[15] As he points out, natural law takes effect in both the law of the Church and in civil law[16] and, he suggests, contrasts with what he calls 'our meagre modern concept of law' in four ways: it originates in the Eternal mind; it has an objective reality; it is rational, designed to bring about good and avoid harm; and it 'goes wider than morality to embrace the laws of nature and aesthetics.' I would disagree with him on the last point, as this seems to confuse natural law with the laws of nature, but the other three ways in which he sees natural law as operating seem to me to be both valid and an excellent framework for looking further into how natural law actually operates in the world today.

The notion of natural law as having an objective reality which does not change in tune with changing political, social and economic circumstances is vital. As an example, when Catholics and other Christians argue that same-sex marriage is against the natural law, they are accused of 'being out of touch with the times'. This completely misses the point. If something is against the natural law then it will *always* be against the natural law and in all circumstances. Although we may be accused of intolerance by adhering to absolute fundamental principles of natural law, they give us a clear point of reference when faced with tyranny and oppression, a point to which we shall return later.[17]

Natural Law Principles in Practice

We saw in Chapter 3 how natural law had influenced the development of English law and before we look at the idea of natural law in detail let us look at the case of *Hales v. Petit,* decided in 1585, when the idea of applying natural law had more currency than it does now.[18] The case involved the question of whether suicide was contrary to natural law, and this topic is very relevant today when it is suggested that euthanasia should be legalised.

The judges held that suicide was indeed against natural law for three reasons: First, it is against nature, as it is contrary to the rule of self-preservation. It is a fundamental instinct of every living thing to defend itself from destruction. Second, it is also against natural law, as it is against God since it breaches the fifth commandment, 'Thou shalt not kill'. Finally, it is against natural law 'as it is against the sovereign, who has lost a subject'. Clearly the final argument would not mean much to people today and the second argument would only appeal to Christians, but the first argument should command more general agreement.

Let us now turn to natural law and its application today.

The basic idea behind natural law was expressed by Aquinas as: 'Good is to be done and pursued, and evil is to be avoided'.[19] It is worth pausing here and noting that this principle is itself a moral one and thus the natural law above all provides a basis for morality in society.[20] Even so, as Finnis points out, this will only be if we apply our reason in the doing of good and avoidance of evil.[21] Going forward, there are, I think, three fundamental principles which flow from the idea of natural law: those of human dignity and the common good, linked by the upholding of relationships, which in a sense bind the other two principles together.[22] In his Introduction to the document issued by the Roman Catholic Bishops of England and Wales in 1996,[23] Cardinal Basil Hume, then Archbishop of Westminster, linked the two basic principles by pointing out, first, that the foundation of the social teaching of the Church is the dignity of the human person, but then emphasising that as our human dignity consists in our being made free by God: 'Society should respect this freedom by enabling men and women to assume responsibility for their own lives and encouraging them to co-operate with each other in the common good'.

Human Dignity

One principle which our reason tells us must be fundamental in any system of law is that of the innate dignity of each human being which flows from the fact that we are children of God (Jn 1:8).

The question is not the supposed value of that person's life or the contribution which they make to the community. Instead, we as Christians proclaim that all human life has an intrinsic value in itself. It is for this reason that legislation which legalises abortion and euthanasia is opposed by Christians. These are two absolutely fundamental points: if the law cannot guarantee the sanctity of life both at its beginning and at its end, then what value does life have? At the moment, as is well known, abortion is lawful subject to certain conditions as laid down in the Abortion Act 1967 as amended by the Human Fertilisation and Embryology Act 1990. One area which Christians find particularly objectionable is the provision that an abortion can lawfully take place where there is a substantial risk that if the child were born it would suffer from such physical or mental abnormalities as to be seriously handicapped. In this case the abortion can take place at any time even up to the term of the pregnancy, whereas in the case of some other grounds the term is fixed at 24 weeks. Not only is this provision objectionable in itself, as allowing the destruction of a human being, but the singling out of those with serious handicaps carries with it the sinister implication that their lives are of less worth than those who are not handicapped.

Euthanasia, in the sense of actively encouraging and promoting the death of a person, is not lawful. This means that Christians have the duty to resist attempts to make it lawful. The way in which the law has developed is an interesting example of how changes can slip through. Under the Suicide Act 1961, it is a crime to aid, abet, counsel or procure the suicide of another with a maximum penalty of fourteen years imprisonment. There is a good reason for this. Suppose that someone has been left a large sum of money in the will of an elderly aunt. There is, regrettably, an incentive for that relative to seek to persuade that aunt to, for instance, take such a large dose of sleeping tablets that she dies. This is one of the main reasons why we have a law against assisted suicide. However, there has been a continuous campaign to legalise suicide in cases where, for example, a person is incurably ill and has expressed a wish to die. Catholics and other Christians have been at the forefront of resistance to this. Not only would this offend the principle that 'We are stewards, not owners, of the life that God has entrusted to us' (*Catechism of the Catholic Church*, 2280) but, as we have seen above, legalisation of assisted suicide would bring grave practical dangers. What has happened is instructive, and an example of how we as Christians must be eternally vigilant. Assisted suicide is not actually legal and the words in the Suicide Act 1961 still stand. However, the Director of Public Prosecutions has issued Guidelines, which did not require Parliamentary debate, stating the criteria which would be applied in considering a prosecution. You can find these on the website[24] where you will see that the first two factors against a prosecution are: when 'the victim had reached a voluntary, clear, settled and informed decision to commit suicide' and 'the suspect was wholly motivated by compassion'. So, by stealth, the law is altered: it is easy to see how the application of these guidelines will mean that there will be very few cases of prosecutions for assisting a suicide. The message for Christians is that we must insist that important changes to the law are at least the subject of an Act of Parliament so that they can be properly debated.

However, the principle that law must uphold the dignity of life goes further than opposition to abortion, euthanasia and cloning. In his introduction to the Catholic Bishops Conference document '*Cherishing Life*'[25] Cardinal Cormac Murphy-O'Connor said: 'In our society, there are many signs of the ways in which human life is cherished: respect for those who live with disability, debate about adequate healthcare for the elderly and widespread concern for the protection of children from harm'. Thus any law which denies human dignity is to be opposed by Christians and correspondingly one which promotes it is to be supported. A clear example of a law which all Christians must oppose would be one which permitted slavery. An example of a law which could be said to have promoted human dignity was the Minimum Wage Act 1998 which, as its title indicates, set a minimum wage for all workers.

The Common Good

The fundamental natural law concept of the common good is not separate to that of human dignity but part of it for, as Thompson puts it: 'Human beings are innately social. Humans are born dependent on others and remain interdependent throughout their lives.'[26] Thus human dignity is realised in community. The idea of

the common good is set out in the *Catechism of the Catholic Church*:
'Law is a rule of conduct enacted by competent authority for the
sake of the common good'.[27] This was emphasised in fuller detail by
Pope John XXIII in his encyclical *Pacem in Terris* where he stated:

> The attainment of the common good is the sole reason for the
> existence of civil authorities. In working for the common good,
> therefore, the authorities must obviously respect its nature, and at
> the same time adjust their legislation to meet the requirements of
> the given situation.[28]

However, he went on to say:[29]

> The civil power must not be subservient to the advantage of any one
> individual, or of some few persons; inasmuch as it was established
> for the common good of all.[30] Nevertheless, considerations of
> justice and equity can at times demand that those in power pay
> more attention to the weaker members of society, since these are at
> a disadvantage when it comes to defending their own rights and
> asserting their legitimate interests.

In fact, as David McIlroy points out,[31] this is not so far distant from
the view of the secular philosopher John Rawls,[32] that government
has a duty to maximise the available resources to those worse off in
our society.[33]

Thus the encyclical *Evangelium Vitae* (at II, 71) states that: 'the
real purpose of civil law is to guarantee an ordered social existence
in true justice' (see 1 Tm 2:2). Although, as John Finnis points
out,[34] the common good is generally appropriately served by individuals performing their own obligations. Nevertheless, there is a
wider dimension where we must as Christians look more broadly at
how the law can remedy those injustices in society which injure the
common good.

One good example of legislation for the common good has been
the legislation to prohibit discrimination against those who have
what are called 'protected characteristics'. These are listed in the
Equality Act 2010 as age, disability, gender reassignment, marriage
and civil partnership, race, religion or belief, sex and sexual orientation. Discrimination means treating a person less favourably
because of any of these characteristics and all Christians must
surely applaud this as to discriminate against a person in these
cases would be to act against their dignity as humans.

The concept of the common good is vital at a time when it is felt by many that too much attention is paid to the satisfaction of individual needs and desires with personal autonomy regarded as the ultimate good. Mario Conti, Archbishop Emeritus of Glasgow, pointed to 'the increasing acceptance, wittingly or unwittingly, of a particular ideology which considers all structures and ethical systems as inimical to human freedom'.[35] Christians must point to the destructive effects which this ideology will have in relation to legislation of many kinds. A belief that the claims of the common good come before personal autonomy would lead Christians, on the one hand, to oppose legislation making it possible for employers to exercise their autonomy by dismissing employees without reason and, on the other, for individuals to exercise their autonomy by contracting a same-sex marriage.

In this we are at one with others, who may not be Christians. Jesse Norman, in his recent evaluation of the eighteenth-century politician and thinker Edmund Burke,[36] criticises the idea of what he calls 'liberal individualism' which, he says, considers the human individual as 'the basic unit of account in morals, in politics and in economics'. As he says, the result is that 'they have moral priority over society itself and their interests are to be generally preferred over the constraints imposed by society'. However, as Norman points out, society is what makes individuals into human beings, because growing up in society is a process by which we become human.[37] Christians have rightly tended to oppose the notion of personal autonomy based on liberal individualism when speaking of economics but have not always applied this critique to personal morality. In truth the whole concept is based on mere selfishness. Moreover, over-emphasising autonomy is dangerous as it has led, for instance, to the foolish notion that the use of certain drugs should be de-criminalised in spite of the fact that drug use is responsible for over 85% of all acquisitive crime, such as burglary and shoplifting, in the UK.

The Death Penalty

Clearly, preserving the common good includes rendering an aggressor unable to inflict harm,[38] and so the Church has always recognised that the civil authorities have the right and duty to punish wrongdoers 'commensurate with the gravity of the crime'. Paragraph 2266 then says that this does not exclude the death penalty 'in cases of extreme gravity'.

Pope John Paul II said that society 'should not go to the extreme of executing the offender except in cases of absolute necessity; in other words where it would not be possible otherwise to defend society'. He then went on to say that 'as a result of improvements in the organization of the penal system, such cases are very rare, if not practically non-existent'.[39] Pope Francis seems to have gone further, although it is not clear if his remarks are official Church teaching. In an address to delegates from the International Association of Penal Law on October 23, 2014, he said:

> All Christians and people of good will are called today to struggle not only for abolition of the death penalty, whether legal or illegal, and in all its forms, but also to improve prison conditions, out of respect for the human dignity of persons deprived of their liberty.

He then extended his remarks to the morality of life imprisonment by saying that: 'And this I connect with life imprisonment. Life imprisonment is a hidden death penalty.'

Relationships

I would also contend that natural law emphasises the upholding of relationships. In *The Catholic Faith*, Roderick Strange tells of a monk who had spent his life in meditation. You must, he said, meditate 'until your eyes bleed. And then perhaps you may be able to perceive some small truth'. And what was this? : 'That relations are real'.[40] The same point was made graphically by Martin Luther King: 'All life is interrelated. All men are caught in an inescapable network of mutuality, tied in a single garment of destiny'.[41]

The Christian life is founded on the relationship between Father, Son and Holy Spirit in the Trinity, and relationships are at the heart of the actual living out of that life in the command to love our neighbour. Human dignity is upheld in the context of the common good but what enhances both the dignity of all humans and the common good are particular relationships and especially, although this is by no means the only example, relationships founded on the family. The trend over the last century has been to emphasise the citizen's relationship with the State but the danger is that people see their relationship purely with the State. Natural law, I suggest, requires that the law protects and upholds that vast tissue of relationships essential in any healthy society. It is worth mentioning that this stress on relationships is also part of the Hindu tradition: Menski draws attention to 'the dynamising concept of *karma*, the principle of "action and reaction", signifying that whatever humans do, they are interlinked entities'.[42]

Amongst these are of course churches, which leads to a principle that religious freedom must be respected, together with that of the family, and it is ultimately on the principle that the institution of marriage between a man and a woman is part of the natural law that Christians base their opposition to same-sex marriage.[43] Another category of relationships is the vast network of voluntary organisations, most of which are registered as charities under the Charities Act 2011. The use of charities to provide public services to tackle what the Government calls 'our most deep-rooted social problems' is a cornerstone of the 'Big Society' idea of David Cameron, the present Prime Minister. This is fine in itself but we must be careful that charities do not become simply an arm of the State by being sucked into its grasp. Christians must see that legislation and government policy safeguard their independence.

This idea of the protection of relationships finds its echo in the principle of subsidiarity, rooted in the natural law, one of the consistent themes of Catholic Social Teaching. This principle was first fully enunciated by Pope Pius XI in his encyclical *Quadragesimo Anno*, in 1931. He stated that: 'Just as it is gravely wrong to take from individuals what they can accomplish by their own initiative and industry and give it to the community, so also it is an injustice and at the same time a grave evil and disturbance of right order to assign to a greater and higher association what lesser and subordinate organizations can do.'[44] Thus the principle is, on one level, aimed at ensuring that Governments do not take over the functions of local authorities and that, wherever possible, autonomy is granted by the State to bodies, often operating at a local level or within a specific area. It is sometimes loosely described as requiring decisions to be taken at as low a level as possible but in fact it goes deeper than that, as Pope Benedict XVI characteristically recognised in *Caritas in Veritate* when he said: 'the principle of subsidiarity is an expression of inalienable human freedom. Subsidiarity is first and foremost a form of assistance to the human person via the autonomy of intermediate bodies'.[45]

Subsidiarity operates alongside the principle of solidarity, which is the recognition by all of us that we do not live alone and for ourselves alone but, through our relationships with one another, we are interdependent. As Pope St John Paul II put it in his encyclical *Sollicitudo Rei Socialis* (1987): 'When interdependence becomes recognized in this way, the correlative response as a moral and social attitude, as a "virtue", is solidarity. This then is not a feeling of vague compassion or shallow distress at the misfortunes of so many people, both near and far. On the contrary, it is a firm and persevering determination to commit oneself to the common good'.[46]

Automony v. Communitarianism

It is important not to let discussion of natural law remain at the level of abstract theory but to evaluate how a belief in natural law, leading to a belief in human dignity, the importance of relationships and the common good, might work in actual practice. As has been well said: 'Natural law is not an abstraction, to be read as a text, or indeed to be picked apart by casuists. It is simply reason at work.'[47] A belief in the common good of necessity implies that we are not autonomous. We have already mentioned some instances, here is another one. 'Autonomy' refers to a person who lives according to his own law and it is, of course, a valuable principle in, for instance, medical law and ethics where it emphasises respect for the patient's own wishes. But it is dangerous when it is treated as a kind of 'Holy Grail' to which all other considerations must defer. An example of this is the editorial in the *British Medical Journal* which supported Lord Faulkner's Bill to legalise euthanasia under certain conditions on the basis that:

> In recent decades, respect for autonomy has emerged as the cardinal principle in medical ethics and underpins developments in informed consent, patient confidentiality, and advance directives. Recognition of an individual's right to determine his or her best interests lies at the heart of this journal's strategy to advance the patient revolution in health care.[48]

This is so often linked to the mantra of 'choice' but a moment's reflection will show that an argument based on autonomy as absolute is fallacious. If we were all completely autonomous there would be no need for any laws at all.

Moreover, an over-emphasis on autonomy can lead to selfishness. Let us take an example from an area not often used in these debates, that of entitlement to the home where the parties are not married.

In the case of *Burns v. Burns* in 1984, Patrick and Valerie Burns set up home together in 1961 in rented accommodation where their first child was born. She was known as Mrs Burns, although they did not marry.[49] In 1963, when Valerie was expecting their second child, Patrick decided to buy a house in London. The house was purchased in his name and he paid for it. Valerie remained at home to look after the children and to perform domestic duties, and was thus unable to earn a salary until 1975, when she started working as a driving instructor. She used her earnings to pay the rates and the telephone bills and to buy fixtures, fittings and certain domestic chattels for the house and redecorated the interior. Valerie left Patrick in 1980 and brought court proceedings claiming that she was entitled to an interest in the house. In effect she was claiming that she was entitled to a share of its value.

The court held that as she had not made any contribution to the cost of acquisition of the house she had no rights and, thus, after nineteen years together, living in a house as a family, she was left without any rights in the property. The fundamental reason was that the courts applied what is known as the 'common intention approach' to deciding these issues, which involves giving effect to what the parties had intended by any agreement or arrangement that gave effect to their common intention. The problem was that, in this case, there was no evidence of any such intention that Valerie should have an interest in the home and so she was awarded none. One could say that this is an example of the 'autonomy approach' in that it gives effect to what the parties wanted with the consequence that, if there is no evidence of this, then the party in whose name the house is will win.

The law has moved on since then as it recognises a wider range of factors in deciding what the common intention of the parties was. The main source of these today is in the judgement of Lady Hale in the case of *Stack v. Dowden* in 2007,[50] but even so, the basis of the approach is still to find what the parties have intended. In an article in 2012, the authors argue that:

> If the intentions of the parties are to be paramount then this shows respect for their autonomy as we are saying that what they say counts. If on the other hand we look at supporting the family relationship then this is really emphasising the family as a community at the expense of the autonomy of its individual members.[51]

Thus on the communitarian approach, which is giving effect to the common good, one might argue that what matters is the common good of the family and not what can be an artificial search for what the parties intended. Thus in the case of *Burns v. Burns* we saw that there was a family unit with a father, mother and two children. Would the promotion of the common good have meant that the mother should have been entitled to a share in the house to recognise her contribution to that common good?

Natural Law as the Product of Reason

It is vital to see this chapter as a continuation of the previous one for it is the contention not only of Christians but of others that law is the product of reason. Christians would then go on to say that this reason stems from our faith. Furthermore it is the Christian belief that, just as all human beings share in the divine Sonship of Christ and so have, whether knowingly or not, the stirrings of faith, so all human beings have that reason that comes from faith. What is the alternative? It can only be that law is the product of the will of the lawmaker. This derives from the principle of voluntarism, which, in this context, emphasised the absolute freedom of God as against his creatures and thus, as Pope Benedict XVI has pointed out, could give rise to a sundering of reason from faith so that 'our reason, our sense of the true and good, are no longer an authentic mirror of God'.[52]

If we deny the validity of natural law and make the will of the lawmaker the sole criterion of the validity of a law, then we must face up to what happened in Nazi Germany when all the actions of Hitler and the Nazi party were strictly within the law and indeed were valid law on the principle that Nazi laws were undoubtedly the product of Hitler's will.[53]

Legal Positivism

There is another viewpoint which is that of legal positivism, of which one of the main exponents was the English jurist John Austin (1790–1859). Legal positivism argues that the existence and content of law depends on social facts and not on its merits. Thus whilst legal positivists are interested in the merits of law, they say that the merits or otherwise of a particular law do not determine whether that law exists. There is much in this of course. For example many Christians would say that the provisions of the Abortion Act 1967 are profoundly wrong but there is no doubt that it is the law. It may be, though, that a law is passed which is so hideously immoral that Christians would say that it is not law at all and here we would part company with the legal positivists. In the end, though, we must ask whether there is any real difference between this approach and the one referred to above where law is seen purely as an expression of the sovereign will.

Natural Law, the Nazis and the Second World War

Take laws passed in Nazi Germany. It must be remembered that the processes by which the Nazis came to power in 1933 were entirely legal and so any laws passed in the Nazi era were, in the strict sense, law. Moreover, the Nazis acted in accordance with strict legal forms when they actually came to power. By the Empowering Act of March 23, 1933, Hitler was given power to alter or suspend certain articles of the German Constitution, and in a further law of 1934 he was given authority to make new constitutional law. Thus, according to strict legal positivism, all of the legislation, however abhorrent it was, passed by the Nazi regime, was law.

In a sermon preached in the heat of the Second World War in St Dunstan's Church, Fleet Street, London on May 9, 1943, before an audience of lawyers from the Temple, Rev. Nathaniel Micklem put it this way:

> The Germans used to boast that theirs was a Reichsstatt, that is, a political community resting on law ... you know that in Germany today the whole structure of law has been overthrown ... that the only principle of law recognised is the so called 'sound feeling of the people', which means the whim of the Nazi party. But wait! Nothing illegal has been done by Hitler. He has always kept scrupulously within the law.[54]

Micklem then drew an important distinction between the fact that for practical purposes law is indeed seen as the will of the lawgiver and is the view of Hitler but, in truth, law 'may never be severed from justice, nor justice from the eternal Reason' which is natural law.

The German jurist Gustav Radbach (1870–1949) was also perturbed by the fact that, in strict law, Hitler had acted perfectly legally, so that the situation was what he termed one of 'statutory lawlessness'. Thus he developed his theory of 'intolerability'. This means that where statute law stands in unbearable contradiction to the demands of justice, then that law must be set aside so that justice can be fulfilled. There is debate on whether this is natural law theory or not but whatever the label it performs the same function as natural law in opposing a higher principle to the strict letter of the law.

The operation of this principle[55] can be seen after the end of the Second World War when the West German courts had to deal with cases involving the treatment of Jews and others during the Nazi era, and later when, following reunification, the courts of unified Germany had to deal with cases involving East German border guards shooting those trying to escape. The West German Constitution adopted the principle that there should be no retrospective punishment and this meant that acts would be judged according to the laws in force at the time. This would have meant that those who participated in the killings of Jews, the disabled, homosexuals, gypsies and others could not have been found guilty of any crime. In addition, East German border guards who killed those attempting to flee East Germany would likewise have escaped punishment. However, the courts used the intolerability principle and in this way the laws which allowed these horrors were declared not to be law and so acts done under them were unlawful and could be punished. If we adopted the idea of legal positivism, then we would have to regard all laws passed by the Nazis as valid. Is this what we want? We could, I suggest, replace the phrase 'demands of justice' with 'fundamental Christian precepts'. How could we tell if a law stood in 'unbearable contradiction' to Christian principles? To some degree, this would be an instinctive reaction: would one, as a Christian, simply recoil from such a law and say: this just cannot stand!

Thus Christians, instead of the intolerability principle, would have said that, as we are made in the image of God and are thus endowed with an inalienable dignity, these laws under which the Nazis and the East German border guards acted were in direct affront to that dignity and so were not law at all. What is vital is that we uphold objective standards by which laws can be judged under the principle of justice.

It is worth mentioning that the International Military Tribunal, which conducted the war crimes trials in Nuremburg after World War Two, acted under general principles such as that there can be a crime against humanity, and war crimes, and crimes against peace. It has been argued that in one sense the jurisdiction of the Tribunal was founded on positive law, as it was said to rest on existing (i.e. positive) law but on the other hand the trials themselves were said to be a matter of justice and this surely indicates a natural law foundation.[56] This idea of trying war criminals has continued since with, for instance, trials involving war crimes arising out of the conflict in Bosnia. In addition, following the Rwandan genocide, in which some 800,000 Tutsis were killed by Hutu over a period of 90 days, the United Nations Security Council established an International Criminal Tribunal for Rwanda. This development of an international criminal law is one which all Christians should unreservedly support.

Natural Law and Human Rights

In a lecture at the University of Swansea, the lawyer and theologian David McIlroy argued that:

> Natural law theory, in its pagan Greek, Christian, Roman and Christian mediaeval forms turns out to be a sort of human rights theory: a theory that there is an objective moral order of right and wrong which determines how human beings ought to be treated and that governments should be held accountable when they violate that objective moral order.[57]

This last point is important as McIlroy argues, and I think that he is right, that the very idea of inalienable human rights is one that comes from natural law. In his lecture he argues that there is in effect a train of thought running from natural law theory to a theory of natural rights and then onto the modern doctrine of human rights. We shall have more to say on human rights in Chapter 10, but the point for us now is that, as McIlroy puts it: 'Christians are in large part responsible for the invention of human rights.' Thus, when some Christians are fearful of human rights and see them as a weapon to be used against Christians by aggressive secularists, we should say: 'No, human rights are a Christian concept! The language of human rights is our language!'

Notes

1 In *Natural Law and Natural Rights* (Oxford: Oxford University Press, 2011), pp. 398–403.
2 Ibid., p. 400.
3 In *Thomas Aquinas* (London: Penguin Books, 1955), p. 221. See also the discussion in B. Davies, *Thomas Aquinas' Summa Theologiae, A Guide and Commentary* (Oxford University Press, 2014), esp. pp. 212–229.
4 At 16. I have used the version by Austin Flannery *The Basic Sixteen Documents; Vatican Council II* (Dublin: Dominican Publications, 1995). A very valuable collection of Aquinas' writings on this topic is A. D'Entrèves, *Aquinas' Selected Political Writings* (Oxford: Blackwell), 1965).
5 *Catechism of the Catholic Church*, English translation for the United Kingdom (London: Geoffrey Chapman, 1994).
6 This is a quotation from *Dei Filius*, 2.
7 R. Waterfield, (trans.), Plato, *Theaetetus*, 172 a-b (London: Penguin, 1987).
8 International Theological Commission, *In Search of a Universal Ethic: A New Look at the Natural Law* (London: CTS, 2012), p. 13.
9 See further on this, W. Menski, 'Hindu Law' in *Law and Justice*, 164 (2013), pp. 45–62.
10 In *Search of a Universal Ethic*, p. 16. This pamphlet has a most valuable section on the extent to which the concept of natural law is recognised worldwide. See pp. 13–20.
11 J. Laing and R. Willcox, (eds), *The Natural Law Reader* (Oxford: Blackwell, 2013) is a good, representative anthology of natural law thinking from the ancient Greeks to the present.
12 In 'What's at Stake in Natural Law?' *New Blackfriars*, 89 (2008), pp. 508–521. See also the noble defence of reason and natural law from the Congregational point of view in N. Micklem, *Law and the Laws being the marginal comments of a theologian* (London: Sweet and Maxwell, 1952).
13 J. Macquarrie, *Principles of Christian Theology* (London: SCM Press, 1966).
14 In *Faith and Politics* (London: DLT, 2010), pp. 36–41. His whole discussion of this topic is worth reading.
15 In *Faith and Politics*, p. 39.
16 Civil law in this context means the law of the State rather than civil law as distinct from criminal law. Readers will find it helpful to refer to 'The Natural Law and Common Law' by Richard O'Sullivan in B. Wortley, (ed.), *The Spirit of the Common Law* (Tenbury Wells: Fowler Wright Books, 1965), and to N. Doe, *Fundamental Authority in Late Medieval English Law* (Cambridge: Cambridge University Press, 1990), especially Ch. 3: 'Natural Law: the Superior Moral Law'.
17 This section has inevitably only touched on natural law theory. Readers seeking a fuller account are recommended to read J. Laing and R. Wilcox, (eds), *A Natural Law Reader* (Oxford: Blackwell, 2013).
18 I am indebted to the analysis of this case in an essay by Richard O'Sullivan, QC, entitled 'The Philosophy of the Common Law', in B. Wortley, (ed.), *The Spirit of the Common Law*. See note 16, above. This is a collection of the papers of Richard O'Sullivan.
19 *Summa Theologiae* 1-2, q. 94, a. 2, c. Note that this is not quite the usually quoted formula: 'do good and avoid evil'.

20 See the discussion in A. D'Entrèves, *Natural Law*, 2 ed. (London: Hutchinson University Library, 1970), pp. 44–45.
21 J. Finnis, 'Natural Law' in Vol. I, *Reason in Action* of the *Collected Essays of John Finnis* (Oxford: Oxford University Press, 2011). The topic of reason and its relationship to faith was considered in Chapter 4.
22 It is of course both possible and right to seek to take these principles further and apply them to concrete situations but there is not the space to do this here. A fascinating example is provided by R. M. Helmholz 'Natural Law in the Trial of Thomas More' in *Thomas More's Trial by Jury* (Woodbridge, Suffolk: The Boydell Press, 2011).
23 'Common Good and the Catholic Church's Social Teaching' – available at togetherforthecommongood.co.uk/.../whats-the-common-good.html? (accessed February 20, 2014). This excellent document should be more widely studied than it is.
24 Policy for Prosecutors in Respect of Cases of Encouraging or Assisting Suicide: www.cps.gov.uk
25 London: CTS, 2004.
26 J. Thompson, *Catholic Social Thought* (New York: Orbis Books, 2010), p. 58.
27 At 1951.
28 At 54.
29 At 56.
30 This sentence is a quotation from Pope Leo XIII's encyclical letter *Immortale Dei*, (1885).
31 D. McIlroy, *A Biblical View of Law and Justice* (Milton Keynes: Paternoster Press, 2004), p. 36.
32 J. Rawls, *Theory of Justice*, rev. ed. (Oxford: Oxford University Press, 1999), p. 53.
33 The meaning of justice in a Christian context is discussed further in Chapter 7.
34 J. Finnis, *Natural Law and Natural Rights*, 2nd ed. (Oxford: Oxford University Press, 2011), p. 305.
35 Statement on Scottish Government proposals to legalise same-sex marriages – issued by the Scottish Catholic Media Office, October 2011.
36 J. Norman, *Edmund Burke* (London: William Collins, 2013), p. 241. The whole of Chapter 9 on 'Liberal Individualism', which Norman argues that Burke's thought is opposed to, is well worth reading.
37 Ibid., p. 246.
38 *Catechism of the Catholic Church*, 2266.
39 In *Evangelium Vitae*, 56.
40 R. Strange, *The Catholic Faith* (Oxford: Oxford University Press, 1996), p. 183.
41 'Beyond Vietnam' in J. M. Washington, (ed.), *A Testament of Hope: The Essential Writings of Martin Luther King, Jr.* (San Francisco: Harper and Row, 1986), p. 254.
42 W. Menski, 'Hindu Law' in *Law and Justice*, 164 (2013), p. 54.
43 This topic is considered further in Chapter 9.
44 At 79.
45 At 57.
46 At 38.
47 J. Bishop, 'Natural law and ethics: some second thoughts', in *New Blackfriars*, September 1996, pp. 381–389, at p. 384.

48 *British Medical Journal*, 5 July 2014, (vol. 349, issue 7965).
49 Had they been married, Valerie Burns would have been in a better position to claim a share in the house and this is still the case today.
50 A later decision is that of *Jones v. Kernott* in 2011.
51 S. Gardner and K. Davidson, 'The Supreme Court on family homes', *Law Quarterly Review*, 128 (2012), pp. 178–183.
52 Quoted in J. Schnall, *The Regensburg Lecture* (South Bend, Indiana: St. Augustine's Press, 2007), p. 137. See also the discussion of voluntarism in International Theological Commission, *In Search of a Universal Ethic: A New Look at the Natural Law*, pp. 26–27.
53 This point is discussed in more detail below.
54 Afterwards published by Oxford University Press under the title of *The Theology of Law* and reproduced in N. Micklem, 'The Theology of Law', in *Law and Justice*, 172 (2014), pp. 4–9. Much of Middle Temple lay in ruins at the time, through German bombing, which must have given added piquancy to this talk.
55 See, for a succinct account, B. Schlink, *Guilt About the Past* (London: Beautiful Books Ltd, 2010), pp. 58–62.
56 See A. D'Entrèves, *Natural Law*, 2nd.ed., p. 106.
57 D. McIlroy, 'A Christian Understanding of Human Rights', a lecture delivered at Swansea University on 20 March 2013 and available at https://lawcf.org/resources/.../Christian-understandings-of-human-rights. Human Rights is considered as a theory in Chapter 10, and in practice in Chapter 12.

Chapter 6

Christians, Conscience and the Law

'We will not be silent. We are your bad conscience.
The White Rose will not leave you in peace.'

(*Fourth leaflet of the White Rose*, Munich 1942)

Introduction

Mary Doogan and Concepta Wood were midwives who worked for many years in the labour ward at the Southern General Hospital, Glasgow, as Labour Ward Co-ordinators. As practising Roman Catholics, they were able to take advantage of one of the few concessions which the law in this country gives to conscientious objection and so they registered a conscientious objection to taking part in abortions as permitted by Section 4 of the Abortion Act 1967. This provides that 'no person shall be under any duty, whether by contract or by any statutory or other legal requirement, to participate in any treatment authorised by this Act to which he has a conscientious objection'.

As a result of registering their objection, they were not required actually to participate in the treatment of patients having an abortion. For many years medical terminations of pregnancy were carried out in the labour ward if the foetus was more advanced than eighteen weeks. Otherwise they took place in the gynaecological ward. However, from 2007, all abortions took place in the labour ward, where the two midwives worked, and so their position became more acute.

The two midwives sought confirmation that, having expressed a conscientious objection to the termination of pregnancy, they would not be required to delegate, supervise and/or support other staff in the participation and provision of care to patients undergoing medical termination of pregnancy at any stage in the process, but this was refused. They appealed but the decision of their employers, the Greater Glasgow and Clyde Health Board, was that: 'delegating to, supervising and/or supporting staff who are providing care to patients throughout the termination process does not constitute providing direct 1:1 care and having the ability to provide leadership within the department is crucial to the roles and responsibilities of a Band 7 midwife, therefore this part of your grievance is not upheld.'

The Supreme Court in *Greater Glasgow Health Board v. Doogan and Another* (2014) held that the nurses were not covered by s. 4 of the Abortion Act, as they were not actually 'participating' in an abortion. In some ways this decision was expected as, in an earlier case, *Janaway v. Salford Health Authority* (1988), the term 'participate' was narrowly defined and did not include a medical receptionist at a Health Centre who refused to type letters of referral from general practitioners to specialists with a view to termination of a woman's pregnancy. However, the case of the two midwives was inherently stronger as they were actually involved in the medical process. Nevertheless Lady Hale, who gave the only detailed judgment and with whom the other Supreme Court Justices agreed, held that Parliament, in passing the Abortion Act in 1967, must have intended that the word 'participate' should have a narrow meaning and not cover what she termed 'the host of ancillary, administrative and managerial tasks' that might be associated with an abortion service. In this she disagreed with the Inner House of the Court of Session in Scotland. Here the midwives had won their case[1] as this court had held that 'the right of conscientious objection extends not only to the actual medical or surgical termination but to the whole process of treatment given for that purpose.' Interestingly, the court also referred to the observations of the court in the South African case of *Christian Education SA v. Minister of Education* (2000) that legislation such as this should be interpreted in a way which allows the parties to be true to their beliefs while remaining respectful of the law.[2]

This last point is important as Lady Hale, in her Supreme Court judgement, mentioned that the midwives had other possible claims under the European Convention of Human Rights (ECHR) and the Equality Act 2010. The ECHR issue is considered further below and both are dealt with fully in Chapters 10 and 12. For now it is worth noting that clause 5 of the Assisted Dying Bill (2013), which seeks to legalise euthanasia in some cases, also uses the word 'participating' when it gives a right of conscientious objection to 'participating in anything authorised by this Act to which that person has a conscientious objection'. We can see from the cases of Mary Doogan and Concepta Wood just how limited a protection that would be.

I have discussed this case in detail because, in the end, issues involving conscience concern the individuals themselves: no one, for example, stood with the Lutheran pastor Dietrich Bonhoeffer in Flossenbürg Concentration Camp on the morning of 9 April 1945, nor with Thomas More on Tower Hill on 6 July 1535. However, although ultimately decisions based on conscience are for us to make personally, how should we make them and to what extent should the law respect decisions based on conscience?

What is Meant by Conscience?

Let us start with the word 'conscience'. It is derived from the Latin *conscientia* and means 'knowledge in oneself'. There is an echo of this, I think, in Hamlet where Polonius advises his son Laertes: 'To thine own self be true ...'[3] The word 'conscience' is often misunderstood. As Herbert McCabe puts it: 'Nowadays we speak of someone "consulting her conscience" rather as someone might consult a cookery book or a railway timetable'.[4] Conscience is, he says, seen 'as a private repository of answers to questions' which amount to a 'personal set of guidelines' and not in any deeper sense. So often people casually toss out the remark: 'Oh, it's against my conscience'.

It is this that Pope Benedict XVI refers to when he speaks of the identification of conscience 'with the superficial consciousness and the reduction of man to his subjectivity'[5] and which leads to us being 'completely dependent on the prevailing opinions of the day'. In simple terms, a claim to a conscientious belief cannot and should not be just an assertion of my individual beliefs but must be based on something deeper, and it is only when it is based on this 'something deeper' that it can truly be called a conscientious belief. John Finnis puts it this way:

> in forming one's conscience one is not so much seeking to form oneself, or to secure one's personal identity or authenticity, as to discern the truth about the meaning and worth which human existence is meant by its divine author to have, and does in each human life have, for good or ill, for heaven-haven or shipwreck.[6]

This does not mean that only religious people have consciences: what it does mean is that that inner spark, that something deeper, is present in us all.[7] If conscience is properly understood in this way, then, as Pope Benedict has emphasised, it is the antidote to moral relativism.

On this basis, Cardinal George Pell has written that he does not favour the phrase 'primacy of conscience' and that: 'It is truth, or the word of God, which has primacy, and we have to use our personal capacity to reason practically, that is, exercise our conscience, to try to recognise those particular truths'.[8] Thus conscience is indeed vital, but in the end it is conscience in the service of truth. The idea that we should abandon the notion of the primacy of conscience may startle some but, understood correctly, Cardinal Pell's view accords with many Christian thinkers.

For many Christians, and particularly, but by no means exclusively, Roman Catholics, the truth, in the sense of what is good, is to be found in what is called the 'natural law', a concept which was explored in Chapter 5 and which amounts to a fundamental insight into what is good. St Paul explains:

> For instance, pagans who never heard of the Law but are led by reason to do what the law commands, may not actually 'possess' the Law but can be said to 'be' the law. They can point to the substance of the Law engraved on their hearts – they can call a witness, that is, their own conscience – they have accusation and defence, that is, their own mental dialogue.[9]

It is in this sense that Thomas Aquinas views what he calls *synderesis* as being what Pope Benedict XVI refers to as a kind of 'primal remembrance of what is good and true'.[10] Conscience is then regarded by Aquinas in the sense of being able to formulate a judgement in the light of this basic understanding of the good[11] and thus we come back to what we said in Chapter 4 on the relationship between faith and reason.

Claims in Conscience not to be Bound by a Law

There are many biblical references to claims not to be bound by an unjust law, as in conscience it is not binding. In the Second Book of Maccabees,[12] Eleazar, a highly-respected Scribe, was at a banquet and was forced to open his mouth to swallow pig's flesh. He refused and resolved instead to die 'with honour rather than to live disgraced'. However, those in charge of the banquet took him aside and attempted to persuade him to adopt the stratagem of *appearing* to eat the meat as prescribed by the king but *in reality* to eat meat of a kind which he could eat. He roundly refused and declared that he would not bring 'defilement and disgrace on my old age'. Instead, he said, he would die because: 'Even though I may avoid execution by man, I can never, living or dead, elude the grasp of the Almighty'. With these words, we are told, he 'went straight to the block'. In modern times, the Second Vatican Council emphasised in *Dignitatis Humanae* that the individual must not be forced to act against conscience nor be prevented from acting according to conscience, especially in religious matters, and based this right on the dignity of the human person.[13]

Note the words of Eleazar: 'elude the grasp of the Almighty'. Here Eleazar is making a link between a secular law and the higher law of God. An easy answer would be to say that, for Christians, it is to be found in the precepts of Christianity and that a Christian would be justified in disobeying any law which conflicted with those precepts. This, however, takes us too far and too quickly, for it begs the question of what those precepts are, especially in the context of conscientious objection to a law.

For Pope Benedict and others 'it is faith that awakens conscience'.[14] However, it is the claim of many Christians that, just as the natural law applies to all of us, so all, believers or not, have a right of conscientious objection to an unjust law.[15] So in Sophocles' *Antigone,* Antigone defies the order of Creon to leave her brother Polynices unburied and says in answer to Creon:

> That order did not come from God. Justice,
> That dwells with the gods below, knows no such law,
> I did not think your edicts strong enough
> To overrule the unwritten unalterable laws
> Of God and heaven, you being only a man.
> They are not of today, but everlasting,
> Though where they came from, none of us can tell.[16]

When Can Claims Based on a Conscientious Belief Justify Disobedience to a Law?

The British Humanist Association (BHA) has said that: 'The concept of conscientious objection acquires its problematic character from the conflict between two powerful, but diametrically opposing, moral requirements. One is the requirement to obey the law; the other, the requirement to follow the dictates of one's own conscience'.[17] Whilst Christians will not be likely to agree with the conclusions of the BHA, this is a clear way of putting it. When, then, can the moral requirement to follow one's conscience be justified?

The claims of conscience can often be seen in terms of the individual's resistance to power. For Pope Benedict XVI, 'conscience is the recognition of claims that arise from our dignity as creatures of God answerable to him for ourselves and others.'[18] Further, power is limited by these claims because claims of conscience are 'claims capable of giving direction to those in authority about how they should use their power'. Moreover, as he says, power must be resisted by the person of conscience protesting against the exploitation of the powerless. As he concludes: 'This will inevitably entail suffering, which is the only way, ultimately, that injustice can be overcome'.

This idea that conscience resists the unjust exploitation of power is an important one but we now need to go further and try to identify situations where this will be so. For a claim by me that I should not be bound by a law on grounds of conscience is a very serious one to make. It amounts to saying that I, as an individual, claim that a law should not apply to me and so I should be exempt from it.

Moreover there is a consistent thread running through the writings of both St Peter and St Paul that wherever possible obedience should be given to the government. St Paul writes:[19] 'You must obey all the governing authorities. Since all government comes from God, the civil authorities were appointed by God and anyone who resists authority is rebelling against God's decision, and such an act is bound to be punished'. On the other hand, although St Paul does advocate obedience to the authorities, he points out very clearly that 'all government comes from God' and this is where the Christian's right to refuse obedience to a law comes in.

A Christian can, I suggest, make such a claim in two types of cases:

(a) The first will be where a Christian feels that the whole system of laws on which the State is based is so fundamentally anti-Christian that he/she cannot give any allegiance to its legal system at all. One example, from very many examples of heroic Christian witness in Nazi Germany, is that of Frank Rienisch, a priest who was beheaded for refusing to take the military oath of allegiance on the ground that, as he put it: 'The present government is not an authority willed by God, but a nihilistic government that has attained its power only through force, lies and deceit.'[20]

(b) The second will be where the Christian gives general assent to the laws of a State but refuses to do so in particular circumstances. One could say that, assuming that a government respects the principles of democracy and those of human rights,[21] then such claims will be rare, but we always need to come back to the theme of resistance on grounds of conscience to the unjust exploitation of power.

How Does UK Law Deal with Claims Based on Conscientious Objection?

English law has granted a right of conscientious objection for many years but in very narrowly defined cases. Quakers were exempted from military service in 1803, and a general right of conscientious objection was introduced by the Military Service Act 1916. Sikhs are exempt from the requirement, under the Road Traffic Act 1988, that motorcyclists must wear a helmet and are also exempt from the requirements of wearing safety helmets on construction sites (s.11, Employment Act 1989). There is also a general right of conscientious objection in s. 38 of the Human Fertilisation and Embryology Act 1990 to 'participating in any activity governed by this Act'.

One of the best known instances is probably s. 4 (1) of the Abortion Act 1967, which was considered in the introduction. Even this hard-won exemption is by no means secure. In October 2010, the Parliamentary Assembly of the Council of Europe (PACE) passed a resolution which said (in part): 'No person, hospital or institution shall be coerced, held liable or discriminated against in any manner because of a refusal to perform, accommodate, assist or submit to an abortion.' This has been roundly rejected by Swedish parliamentarians who voted 271 to 20 to instruct the Swedish delegation to the Council that, 'Sweden should support efforts which make abortions free, safe and legal for all women' and thus to reject this resolution.

Professional Guidance and Conscience Clauses in the Health Care Professions

The General Medical Council has issued Guidance stating that the conscience clause in s. 4 of the Abortion Act 1967 does not apply to situations where a patient who is awaiting or has undergone a termination of pregnancy needs medical care, as this will not be *participation* in an abortion and the lawfulness of this seems, unfortunately, to be confirmed by the recent Supreme Court decision in *Greater Glasgow Health Board v. Doogan and Another* (2014), considered above.

There is also a duty to tell patients of their right to see another doctor and Lady Hale, in her Supreme Court judgement in the above case, confirmed the lawfulness of this when she said that 'it is a feature of conscience clauses generally within the health care profession that the conscientious objector be under an obligation to refer the case to a professional who does not share that objection'. With respect, this dilutes conscientious objection to nothingness and morally puts the conscientious objector in an even worse position. For if doctor X, for example, believes that abortion is wrong but has to refer the patient to doctor Y who she knows will enable the abortion to happen then, in doctor X's view, she would not only be complicit in a morally repugnant act of an abortion but in doctor Y's moral guilt in facilitating it. The General Pharmaceutical Council has issued Guidance[22] to pharmacists stating that if their beliefs prevent them from providing a pharmacy service, such as the morning-after pill, then if they refer the patient to another pharmacy they must check that there is another pharmacist who can provide the pill and has the relevant stock. The pharmacist might as well provide the pill anyway! It is noteworthy that the two midwives in the Glasgow case were not supported by the Royal College of Midwives which instead argued that treatment to which the conscience clause could extend only encompassed treatment which actually causes the termination.

Moreover, the General Medical Council has now drafted new

guidelines (2013) ('Personal beliefs and medical practice') which state that doctors could be struck off for refusing to prescribe contraceptive pills to unmarried women. The guidelines state that it would be 'discriminatory' for a doctor to refuse to prescribe the pill or the morning-after pill on the grounds that they do not believe in sex outside marriage. Here is a clear case where a threat to conscientious beliefs is threatened and doctors are surely entitled to resist. A doctor who refuses to prescribe the morning-after pill can say that what is at stake is the dignity of a human being whose life would be terminated by this. What about discrimination against the unborn child? Thus we can say that professional bodies in the health care professions, far from upholding conscience clauses on behalf of their members in the area of abortion, seem determined to increase their scope.

Protection of Freedom of Conscience under the European Convention on Human Rights

The topic of human rights will be considered further in Chapters 10 and 12, but it is important at this juncture to note that the European Convention on Human Rights (ECHR) explicitly protects freedom of conscience, as Article 9 (1) provides that:

> Everyone has the right to freedom of thought, conscience and religion; this right includes freedom to change his religion or belief and freedom, either alone or in community with others and in public or private, to manifest his religion or belief, in worship, teaching, practice and observance.

Article 9 (2) then qualifies Article 9 (1) by these words:

> Freedom to manifest one's religion or beliefs shall be subject only to such limitations as are prescribed by law and are necessary in a democratic society in the interests of public safety, for the protection of public order, health or morals, or for the protection of the rights and freedoms of others.

It will be noted that the protection given to freedom of conscience is in the same Article of the Convention which protects religion. Thus most claims by Christians have been based on freedom of religion and this issue is considered in more detail in Chapter 12. However, as an example of how freedom of conscience is protected by the ECHR, we can take the case of Leading Medical Assistant Michael Lyons of Plymouth, who was told in May 2010 that he would be deployed to Afghanistan. However, he decided that it would be morally wrong to be part of British involvement there and applied for conscientious discharge. His application was refused and he began a written appeal to the Advisory Committee on Conscientious Objection. In September 2010 he attended obligatory operational deployment weapons training and refused to take part. After attempts to persuade him to change his mind he was charged with intentionally disobeying a lawful command and sentenced at court martial to seven months' military detention, reduction to the rank of Able Seaman and dismissal. He then appealed against his conviction and sentence on the grounds that the order was unlawful because it contravened his rights under Article 9 of the ECHR.

The Court of Appeal did not agree. It held that the procedure for dealing with claims of conscientious objection satisfied the requirements in Article 9 (2) above of being 'prescribed by law' and 'necessary in a democratic society'. Further, it felt that if a person who had voluntarily joined the military sought to be discharged on the grounds of conscientious objection, then it was right that there should be a proper process for deciding whether or not that claim was well-founded. Until that had been established, Michael Lyons and others should continue to be subject to the requirements of military service and discipline, otherwise a claim would simply be an escape-route, regardless of the consequent risk to others and whether or not the claim was well-founded.

A Way Forward?

Where does all of this leave us today? I suggest four guidelines in this area:

(a) That wherever possible, Christians give obedience to the law and work within it to secure the promotion of the common good and the dignity of each individual.
(b) That as a last resort Christians should claim a right not to be subject to a law which stands in 'unbearable contradiction' to these principles.
(c) That in many cases it will be possible for reasonable adjustments to be made to a law to accommodate the beliefs of

Christians, and Christians should be alert to recognise these situations and to press for these reasonable adjustments. We shall examine this in Chapter 10 when we discuss Christianity, Equality and Human Rights. As mentioned above, Lady Hale, in the Supreme Court case of *Greater Glasgow Health Board v. Doogan and Another* (2014), suggested that the midwives pursue their claim, which is still with an Employment Tribunal, on the basis of Article 9 or that of the Equality Act 2010, and it may be that the action brought on the basis of the conscience clause in the Abortion Act was misconceived. Certainly the result of that litigation has left the law in a less favourable state then ever.

   (d) Christians should not just regard the question of conscience and the law in a negative light in the sense of refusing to be bound by laws that go against conscience but should promote a conscience-based approach to law itself.

Finally Christians can and should promote the idea of the law being based on conscience. In fact, a conscience-based jurisdiction already exists in English law and is known as 'equity'. This system was originally applied by the medieval Chancellors, who were invariably ecclesiastics, and came to combine a concern for moderating the strict letter of the law[23] with a focus on personal conscience. An example of this can be seen in cases involving the family home.

Suppose that a house is bought in the name of one partner (Charles) but the other (Sue) has contributed half of the purchase price, with Charles contributing the other half. Although in strict law only the one in whose name the house is put, Charles here, has any rights, equity is likely to intervene and say that the house is held on trust for both Charles and Sue, as both have made contributions to the price. In doing so, equity is in effect saying that it would be against conscience that a person with whose money a house was bought, Sue in our example, should have no rights over it.

In fact equity does not operate over the whole of English law, being mainly, but not exclusively, confined to property matters, but this idea of a conscience-based jurisdiction repays further study by Christians.

Conclusion

But when all is said and done, there will be cases where there is a stark choice to be made for the Christian: to abide by a law which offends fundamental Christian principles or not. In this case there is no room for fudge or compromise and the consequences of Christian witness must be squarely faced. Thomas More famously did this when faced with denying Henry VIII's Act of Supremacy. What rings down the centuries and is an inspiration to all Christians who follow him are his words following his conviction for denying the royal supremacy when he declared: 'This indictment is grounded on an Act of Parliament directly contrary to the laws of God and his Holy Church' with the result that the indictment is 'in law, amongst Christian men insufficient to charge any Christian man'.

It is the example of those such as More and others who, when faced with a direct conflict between the law and deeply held conscientious beliefs, did not flinch but, in the last analysis, were prepared to die for their beliefs, that we must cherish and which can serve as an inspiration to us all. This was so with the Munich students too, quoted at the head of this chapter, who formed the 'White Rose' group and who called themselves the bad conscience of the Nazis as they were highlighting the evil of Nazism. We too may be called to a similar witness.

Notes

1 This was what resulted in the appeal to the Supreme Court.
2 In fact, in this case the court decided against Christian schools who wanted an exemption from the law banning corporal punishment in schools, but the general point made by the court is important.
3 Hamlet, 1.3.81.
4 In *God Still Matters* (London and New York: Continuum 2005), p. 152.
5 'If you want peace ... conscience and truth', printed as Chapter 5 of J. Ratzinger, *Values in a Time of Upheaval* (San Francisco: Ignatius Press, 2006), p. 83.
6 In 'Faith, Morals and Thomas More', included in Vol. V of J. Finnis, *Collected Essays: Religion and Public Reasons* (Oxford: Oxford University Press, 2011), p. 171.
7 See K. Brownlie, *Conscience and Conviction* (Oxford: Oxford University Press, 2012), which makes a case for disobedience to the law in some cases on grounds of conscientious moral conviction rather than a religiously-based conviction in conscience. It is instructive to contrast these two approaches.

 8 Quoted in T. Livingstone, *George Pell, Defender of the Faith Down Under* (San Francisco: Ignatius Press, 2002), p. 407.
 9 Rm 2:14–15.
10 'If you want peace ... conscience and truth', printed as Chapter 5 of J. Ratzinger, *Values in a Time of Upheaval*, p. 92.
11 My grateful thanks to Fr Robert Ombres, O.P., of Blackfriars, Oxford, for much illumination on Aquinas and conscience, although he must not be thought responsible for what I have written.
12 6:18–31.
13 *Dignitatis Humanae*, 2.
14 Quoted in V. Twomey, *Pope Benedict, the Conscience of our Age* (San Francisco: Ignatius Press, 2007), p. 109.
15 Other Christians would reject the notion of natural law but still uphold the right of conscientious objection to an unjust law on the basis that it is contrary to the Word of God.
16 I have used the translation in the edition in the Penguin Classics by E. F. Watling, (Harmondsworth: Penguin, 1974).
17 Introduction to '*Right to Object? Conscientious Objection and Religious Conviction*', BHA, 2011.
18 Quoted in Twomey, *Pope Benedict, the Conscience of our Age*, p. 110.
19 Rm 13:1–3.
20 See H. Gollwitzer, K. Kuhn and R.Schnieder, (eds), *Dying We Live: Letters written by prisoners in Germany on the verge of execution* (London: Fontana Books, 1958), pp. 47–48. This marvellously inspiring little book contains many such accounts.
21 By human rights I am not advocating any particular system or classification of human rights but simply a respect for human rights as based on the Christian principle of the dignity of each person.
22 *Catholic Herald*, 12 August 2011.
23 The concept of equity in the law is also discussed in Chapter 7 of this book. It exists in Scots law too but not as a separate branch of the law.

Chapter 7

Law and Justice

'Yahweh says this, "Let the sage not boast of wisdom, nor the valiant of valour, nor the wealthy of riches! But let anyone who wants to boast, boast of this: of understanding and knowing me. For I am Yahweh, who acts with faithful love, justice, and uprightness on earth; yes, these are what please me," Yahweh declares'.

(Jer. 9:22–23)

Introduction

One might ask why there needs to be a separate chapter on the theme of justice in a book concerned with Christians and the law. Surely justice and law are synonymous? Unfortunately this is not always so. Mrs. Bagnet, in Dickens' *Bleak House*, put it succinctly when she observed that her friend Sergeant George, wrongly accused of murder, needed a lawyer to defend him as: 'It won't do to have truth and justice on his side; he must have law and lawyers'.

This chapter explores the meaning of that elusive term 'justice' and then goes on to examine justice in the particular context of access to justice. There is a real problem here: increasing numbers of people are finding that, although they have a valid legal claim, they are unable to bring it to court as they cannot afford to do so. On the one hand Christians do not want to encourage unmeritorious claims but, on the other, a denial of justice, often to the most vulnerable members of society, is an affront to us all.

The theme of justice is strongly stressed throughout the Old Testament, both in the justice of God and in relation to God's justice on earth, as the quotation above shows. But how should Christians today see this in relation to their own lives, and how can Christians use the demands of justice as a practical tool to measure whether the State, in its activities, is living up to its demands? Although this chapter does not aim to give a complete answer to these questions, it does aim to give some signposts.

What is Justice?

Each of us has an instinctive feel for what is unjust. We cry out and say: 'That's unjust!' Pope Benedict XVI, in his encyclical *Deus Caritas Est*, puts it this way:

> Justice is both the aim and the intrinsic criterion of all politics. Politics is more than a mere mechanism for defining the rules of public life: its origin and its goal are found in justice, which by its very nature has to do with ethics. The State must inevitably face the question of how justice can be achieved here and now. But this presupposes an even more radical question: what is justice? The problem is one of practical reason; but if reason is to be exercised properly, it must undergo constant purification, since it can never be completely free of the danger of a certain ethical blindness caused by the dazzling effect of power and special interests.

So there are two issues: the first is to arrive at a criterion of justice by which we may judge if an act is just or not and by which we can arrive at a standpoint by which we may achieve justice in society, and, secondly, how to exercise what Pope Benedict calls our practical reason so that justice can be achieved in actual concrete situations.

A Search for a Workable Idea of Justice

The constant difficulty with concepts such as justice is to relate them to everyday situations so that the concept is made to have an effect on the everyday lives of people and does not remain within the narrow confines of academic discussion. How to begin our search? First we need to recognise that the term 'justice' is used in two different ways: in the sense of God's justice and in the sense of justice in society. However, I would argue that, although these are often spoken of separately, there is no distinction between these two applications of the term 'justice', nor is it right to make any. For what lies behind any attempt to distinguish between God's justice and ours is the notion that our justice is of a lesser standard than God's. I suggest two areas for initial discussion: the first is, obviously, the meaning which we attach to the term 'justice', and the second is the extent to which what may be a rigid rule should not be applied in particular cases in the interests of justice.

What Meaning Should We Attach to the Term 'Justice'?

The search for a workable meaning of justice is one which has occupied many philosophers down the ages. Although we need to say something about the different ways in which the term justice has been explored, my primary concern is not to add to this philosophical debate but, instead, to suggest some principles which can govern us in our search for justice from a Christian perspective.

I suggest that any Christian idea of justice must focus on two points: justice for each individual and justice for the common good. In particular, a Christian approach must resist the temptation to cast the debate about what justice means in terms of personal autonomy, a point which was made in previous chapters.[1]

We can start with Plato who, in *The Republic*, referred to justice as giving every man his due.[2] This may not seem to amount to saying much but it is useful to note the context in which this was said. This was a dialogue between Polemarchus and Socrates and, later, Polemarchus agrees that to give every man his due means to 'do good to one's friends and harm one's enemies', a statement with which Socrates agrees. Here the Christian immediately disagrees, but is this not, in fact, what often happens? Here we see the way in which the idea of justice is often clouded by that ethical blindness of which Pope Benedict spoke in the passage above. Not only this but, later in the dialogue, Thrasymachus arrives and gives another definition: that justice means that which is in the interests of the stronger party.[3] Although this is wrong, the advantage of this definition is that it makes clear what justice often becomes.

The basic idea of justice as giving to everyone what is their due has, as Sagovsky points out,[4] been enormously influential. It has influenced Roman Law and, most importantly for our purpose, it influenced Aquinas in his discussion of justice in the *Summa Theologiae*. As Sagovsky explains, the attraction of this idea is that we can know what is due to a person. I remain sceptical of this idea, as there lies behind it the notion that a person has done something or is something, and from this they have a right to what is their due. What of the seriously disabled person or the unborn child? They are totally dependent on us and a notion of what is their due implies that unless they have made some measureable contribution to society, there is nothing due to them. I prefer to link the idea of justice to that of human rights which is based on the principle that whoever we are we all have some basic inalienable rights. As the preamble to the Universal Declaration of Human

Rights puts it: 'Whereas recognition of the inherent dignity and of the equal and inalienable rights of all members of the human family is the foundation of freedom, justice and peace in the world.' As Sagovsky puts it: 'With our contemporary understanding of human rights, we have a whole framework of rights we consider to be due to any person, no matter who they may be'.[5]

This idea of the inalienable rights of each person, which I argue must be the foundation of every system of justice, is thus in conflict with utilitarianism which, of course, argues that the right thing to do is to maximise utility and this means that we must do everything that produces happiness and everything that avoids pain. It thus follows that the object of laws and legal systems should be the promotion of the greatest happiness of the greatest number of people.[6] As Michael Sandel argues,[7] 'the most glaring weakness of utilitarianism is that it fails to respect individual rights', and this criticism can be applied to other theories which stress the importance of individual autonomy as a foundation for a system of justice. We looked at the dangerous prevalence of this idea of autonomy in Chapter 5, but it is worth mentioning it here in connection with a Christian idea of justice.

The most influential recent thinker on justice was the American, John Rawls who, in his *Theory of Justice*,[8] put forward two fundamental principles of justice. The first is that: 'Each person is to have an equal right to the most extensive scheme of basic liberties compatible with a similar scheme of liberties for others'; and the second principle, which follows from the first and is subordinate to it is that: 'social and economic inequalities are to be arranged so that they both are (a) reasonably expected to be to everyone's advantage and (b) attached to positions and offices open to all.'

The stress on liberties in the first principle strikes many Christians as unfortunate. Of course we all desire liberty but, to those in desperate need of the basic means of subsistence, this talk of liberties means nothing and is redolent of affluent Western societies. To be fair, later on Rawls does introduce the 'difference principle' which is that, in relation to the second principle, only those social and economic inequalities are permitted that work to the benefit of the least advantaged members of society. This by itself sounds fine, and much in accordance with Christian thinking, but when Rawls' thinking is examined in more detail, it is not clear what he means by 'benefit'. As Sagovsky points out,[9] he speaks at one point of 'minimal advantage' and then of 'greatest expected benefit'. What I would find more compelling as a

Christian would be a commitment to removing social and economic inequalities. Moreover the notion of 'arranging' inequalities seems paternalistic. Who would choose how and when to apply the difference principle?[10]

Not only this, but Christians have argued that we need to set the demands of justice in the context of the doctrine of Original Sin. We live in a fallen world, and will do so until Christ comes again to gather all things to Himself. So any system of law must provide strong measures to deter wrong-doers while at the same time recognising that we are all capable of redemption. This is why many Christian lawyers are interested in the idea of Restorative Justice, which enables victims to meet or communicate with the offender to explain the real impact of the crime the offender has committed. This serves to help the offenders to recognise how their actions affect others, and to understand that they are responsible for their choices and must be held accountable for them.

In the end we have, as Christians, to rest our search for justice on the radical demands of the gospel. When I began to write this chapter, I toyed with the notion of drawing up a kind of checklist of what Christian justice demands of us in contemporary society, but I then realised that this would be fruitless. This chapter cannot tell us where our search for justice will end but it can tell us where it begins: with wisdom. As McIlroy says,[11] 'justice is a divine quality, to be discerned with wisdom' and it is clear that this quality is the essence of reaching right decisions. 'Evil men do not understand justice; but those who seek the Lord understand it fully'.[12]

Justice and Equity

One perennial problem in the search for justice is the fact that a general rule stated in law may well result in justice in most cases but when applied in particular circumstances in may result in injustice. A starting point can be found in the *Nicomachean Ethics* of Aristotle (Book 5)[13] where Aristotle observes that there is a need at times to have a kind of corrective to legal justice. This is because a law is obviously universal in that it applies to all in particular situations without being able to take account of individual circumstances. This is where equity comes in as it can take account of these circumstances and, as Aristotle puts it: 'say what the legislator would have said had he been present'. He uses the term *epieikeia to* describe this.

Aquinas, in the *Summa Theologiae,* takes up this idea of Aristotle and regards *epieikeia* as 'a higher rule for human actions'.[14] As Sagovsky says, 'the implications of this are enormous,'[15] for what Aquinas is suggesting is that it is possible to enter into the 'spirit' of justice so that one can discern clearly where the normal rules of justice do not apply.

This notion is still present in English law today.[16] Here is an example: the case of *Inwards v. Baker* in 1965. John Baker was the legitimate son of (another) John Baker and was planning to buy some land and build a bungalow on it when his father said: 'Why don't you build the bungalow on my land and make it a bit bigger.' The son did so, paying some £150 of the cost whilst his father paid £200, although later the son repaid the father most of this. When the bungalow was completed in 1931, the son lived in it and continued to do so after his father's death in 1951. However, his father left all his property by will to Ethel Inwards and her son and daughter who were the illegitimate children of Mr Baker. They allowed John Baker to live in the bungalow for some time but then, in 1962, they sought possession.

John Baker's problem was that in strict law he had no rights to the bungalow nor the land on which it stood as there had never been any formal deed which transferred it to him. Thus, in strict law, he was little more than a trespasser and could have been evicted. However, this would have ignored equity. Normally it is right for the law to insist on some formalities for the transfer of land, but this was not a usual case. John had built the bungalow himself, almost entirely by his own labour, and borne most of the cost of the materials.

The solution of Lord Denning in the Court of Appeal was to overlook, as it were, the lack of formalities and instead allow John to remain in the bungalow for the rest of his life after which it would revert to those entitled under his father's will.

Readers might like to consider if justice was done here: the son was allowed to stay, since, if he was forced to leave, he would lose the property that he built, but on his death it went to those legally entitled. I think that it was, and so we have an example of Aristotle's principle of *epieikeia* at work.

Justice and Mercy

Justice and mercy are often contrasted on the basis that whilst justice is a kind of regular standard of law, there is a need for mercy to be shown in particular cases to, as it were, temper the rigour of the law. Thus mercy stands above justice, purifying its application and modifying its rigours. Is this so?

Pope St John Paul II took this view in his encyclical *Dives et Misercordia* where he wrote, particularly in reference to the Old Testament:

> In this way, mercy is in a certain sense contrasted with God's justice, and in many cases is shown to be not only more powerful than that justice but also more profound. Even the Old Testament teaches that, although justice is an authentic virtue in man, and in God signifies transcendent perfection, nevertheless love is 'greater' than justice: greater in the sense that it is primary and fundamental. Love, so to speak, conditions justice and, in the final analysis, justice serves love. The primacy and superiority of love vis-a-vis justice – this is a mark of the whole of revelation – are *revealed precisely through mercy.*[17]

We can see this in the story of the repentant thief who admitted that he and his companion deserved their sentence: 'we are paying for what we did.' Nevertheless Jesus says to the thief: 'In truth I tell you, today you will be with me in paradise.'[18] Here we could say that justice, in the form of the operation of the law which had led to the conviction of the criminals, had been complied with but that Jesus had, in the words of St John Paul, 'conditioned justice' by this act of mercy through his all-embracing love.

In a secular sense we can see this in another well-known example, that of the speech of Portia in Shakespeare's *Merchant of Venice*. Here Portia, in her plea to Shylock not to insist on his lawful due of a pound of flesh, says:

> Though justice be thy plea, consider this:
> That in the course of justice, none of us,
> Should see salvation. We do pray for mercy,
> And that same prayer should teach us all to render
> The deeds of mercy ...

In a lecture, Fr Robert Llewelyn said, when referring to the thought of Julian of Norwich, that 'justice is swallowed up in

mercy'.[19] Julian herself says that 'the Lord beheld his servant with
pity and not with blame'.[20] This thought is continued by Lord
Hailsham, a former Lord Chancellor, who ends his book, *A
Sparrow's Flight*, with 'The Sparrow's Prayer' which says:

> Hear this, Thy weary sparrow, when he calls,
>   Mercy not justice is his contrite prayer.[21]

Yet despite all of this, I have an uneasy sense that it is wrong to see
justice as some kind of second-best that operates in this fallen
world; that it is mercy that is in the premier league, as it were, and
that justice languishes in the lower divisions. The lawyer and
theologian David McIlroy[22] links justice and mercy in a different
way and rejects the idea that they are contradictory. He argues that
justice and mercy are seen in the Bible 'as concepts linked through
deliverance'. Thus Isaiah wrote of justice: 'But Yahweh is waiting to
be gracious to you, the Exalted One, to take pity on you, for
Yahweh is a God of fair judgement; blessed are all who hope in
him.'[23] On the other hand, as McIlroy observes, God's mercy is
seen at work 'by the Old Testament writers in his acts of delivering
his people *even when they do not deserve it*'.[24] So both God's justice
and his mercy are demonstrations of his love.

McIlroy regards the contrast as between mercy and judgement
rather than mercy and justice. So St James puts it: 'Whoever acts
without mercy will be judged without mercy but mercy can afford
to laugh at judgement'.[25]

I said at the start of this chapter that it was vital to relate notions
of justice, and for that matter, of mercy and judgement also, to
concrete situations. How, then does this distinction between mercy
and judgement apply in actual life? Take the tragic case of
Wendolyn Marklow.[26] Her son, Patrick, was disabled and his
condition worsened significantly when he was in his 20s. He
developed a severe form of autism and started to hit himself so
violently in his right eye, sometimes punching it as hard as he
could twenty times in half an hour, that he became blind in that
eye. In addition he suffered chronic insomnia, often only sleeping
for two to three hours a night, waking up screaming and shouting.
His mother appealed for help to social services but, the day after
an emergency appointment with the GP, Mrs Marklow gave Patrick
fourteen sleeping pills and suffocated him with a sleeping bag.

She was tried for manslaughter. Had the charge been murder
then the court must impose a sentence of life imprisonment, but

for manslaughter there is a discretion. She pleaded guilty and was given a two-year suspended sentence.

In terms of actual judgement it was, I suggest, right that Mrs Marklow was convicted. The legal system must take action when one person ends the life of another, even in circumstances as unbearably tragic as this. Furthermore, bringing a person before the courts is often a means of enabling them to be given help and to put their lives back on the right track, although obviously this did not apply in this case. Yet clearly the legal system could not impose any actual punishment on Mrs Marklow who had already suffered unendurably. Mercy was not only right, it was the only possible course, and the suspended sentence meant that, in effect, there was no punishment, as it would only be activated if she committed a similar offence, which was out of the question.

So in the sense of actual judgement, the law was right: a conviction for manslaughter. But in terms of mercy it was also right: in effect, no punishment at all. This is how the law needs to work.

In other cases, the matter may be more difficult. Take the decision by the Scottish Government in 2009 to release the terminally ill Lockerbie bomber al-Megrahi. The noted human rights lawyer, Geoffrey Robertson, argued trenchantly that: 'Mercy should season justice but only when extended to persons who can rationally be pitied or forgiven', and that the decision of the Scottish Government was wrong, as: 'We show mercy to the merciless by abjuring torture and the death sentence'.[27] It follows that, in the case of an unrepentant terrorist bomber, mercy can extend no further. Many will agree.

Accessing Justice

If we return to our original contention that justice is giving to every person what is their due, then clearly that person must have the means to enforce their rights to what is due to them. What, however, if they cannot afford to pay for legal advice and, if need be, representation in court?

This is a real problem and one where Christians should be concerned. Take this example: I agree with Fred, a plumber, that he will do some plumbing work on my house. Let us say that the cost is £15,000. However, I am dissatisfied with the work when it is done and I am only willing to pay Fred £5,000. Fred therefore takes me to court. It is quite possible for the costs of such a case, with experts' reports, witness statements beforehand and then cross examination at the actual trial, to end up at £150,000.

In order to ensure that those without means to pay were not excluded from the legal system, Legal Aid in England and Wales was established in 1949. It has remained an integral part of the British justice system but, and here is where Christians have cause for concern, its scope has been eroded over the years. For instance, when I started in the law over forty years ago, it was common for a person with a civil claim for, say, compensation for personal injuries, to be able to claim legal aid. Legal aid in civil cases has now been replaced in most cases by the 'no win, no fee' system.

In 2013 the Government announced a further round of cuts to legal aid, following on the Legal Aid Sentencing and Punishment of Offenders Act 2012 (LASPO) which came into force on 1 April 2013. This Act had the aim of cutting the legal aid budget by a quarter (£320m) within a year. It removed legal aid for the majority of cases – with some specific exceptions – involving divorce, welfare benefits, clinical negligence and child contact. In addition many migrants and prisoners will no longer be eligible for legal aid, and there are plans to remove a further £220m each year until 2018. The government's argument is that, with an annual budget of £2bn per year, England and Wales' legal aid system is the most expensive in the world and it needs reform.

However, the current situation remains worrying. An article in the *New Statesman*[28] gave a particular example of how lack of legal aid can cause injustice: It told the story of Liz, aged 16, who had a daughter, Emily, who was just over a year old. She lived with her mother, who was an alcoholic. Liz realised that she could not carry on any longer by herself and so she asked Emily's father if he could look after the baby, at the same time voluntarily putting herself into foster care. However, this went wrong. Emily's paternal grandmother accused Liz of domestic abuse, and filed a legal claim for custody of Emily. Liz, by this time in foster care, did not contest the claim. She was frightened and could not understand the wording of the legal documents or the charges against her.

A court hearing was scheduled but Liz was told that she was not eligible for legal aid because the case was a private matter. Liz, a vulnerable young person in care, could not afford lawyer's fees. Although she did receive advice from social services and a charity, she had to represent herself at the hearing against a qualified barrister. We do not know the end of the story, whether Liz won or lost the case, but that is not the point anyway. But we do know that she was left traumatized by the system. The difficulty here is that many people are profoundly unsympathetic to many cases, such as that of, say, a teenage refugee who does not qualify for legal aid to apply for permission for her family to come to the UK, and is left traumatised and isolated. Yet we should be.

Yet it is not just a question of asking the Government for more money for the legal aid budget, as so many campaigners seem to think. There is a strong argument that the cost of litigation is too high and Christians involved in the practice of the law, as well as others, must ask some searching questions about how we conduct cases and whether the cost could be lowered. In Germany, for example, the cost of litigation is much lower and it is much easier to see at the outset what the total costs are likely to be.

Here is an issue on which Christians can and should be in the forefront of the argument, putting the case for adequate legal aid. 'Blessed are those who hunger and thirst for uprightness: they shall have their fill.'[29] Shall we be part of a system that denies this?

Notes

1   See especially Chapter 5, Natural Law.
2   Plato, *The Republic*, H.D.P. Lee, (trans.), (Harmondsworth: Penguin Classics, 1955), p. 56.
3   Ibid., p. 65. Note also the discussion of justice by Aristotle in the *Nicomachean Ethics*, Bk 5.
4   N. Sagovsky, *Christian Tradition and the Practice of Justice* (London: SPCK, 2008), p. 19.
5   Ibid., p. 18. See Chapters 10 and 11 for a more detailed discussion of human rights.
6   See the illuminating account of the influence of this theory on nineteenth-century England in A. Dicey, *Law and Public Opinion in England*, 2nd ed. (London: Macmillan, 1963), pp. 126–210.
7   In *Justice: What's the Right Thing to Do?* (London: Penguin, 2010), p. 37.
8   *Theory of Justice*, rev. ed. (Oxford: Oxford University Press, 1999).
9   *Christian Tradition and the Practice of Justice*, p. 129. The whole discussion of Rawls' theories in Ch. 6 of this book is recommended.
10 A point made by Sandel in *Justice: What's the Right Thing to Do?*, p. 152.
11 In *A Biblical View of Law and Justice* (Carlisle: Paternoster Press, 2004), p. 81. Readers wishing to find a concrete application of basic principles of justice should turn to T. Bingham, *The Rule of Law* (London: Penguin Books, 2011). There is much to be said for his first principle: that the law must be accessible and, as far as possible, intelligible, clear and predictable.
12   Prov. 28:5.
13 Aristotle, *Nicomachean Ethics*, D. Ross, (trans.), (Oxford: Oxford University Press, 1925).

14 ST, 2a.2ae.120.2.
15 *Christian Tradition and the Practice of Justice*, pp. 114–115.
16 Scottish lawyers would look at the notion of equity differently. See S. Allison, 'Stair and Natural Law', *Law and Justice*, 169 (2012), pp. 189–209.
17 Pope John Paul II, *Dives et Misercordia*, 4.
18 Lk 23:39–43.
19 This was the Annual Julian Lecture, *Julian Then and Now* (Norwich: The Julian Centre, 1997).
20 *The Revelations of Divine Love of Julian of Norwich,* J. Walsh, (trans.) (Wheathampstead: Antony Clarke Books, 1980). This quotation is from Ch. 82.
21 London: Fontana, 1990.
22 In *A Biblical View of Law and Justice,* pp. 12–13.
23 Is 30:18.
24 Author's italics.
25 James 2:13.
26 This case made national headlines at the time. My source here is *The Guardian*, November 8, 2005.
27 'We should be ashamed that this has happened', *The Guardian,* 22 August 2009. This piece contained other contributions for and against the decision to release al-Megrahi.
28 *New Statesman,* January 13, 2014.
29 Mt 5:6. See the Theos pamphlet by A. Capland and D. McIlroy, *Speaking Up – Defending and Delivering Access to Justice* (London: Theos, 2015) for a powerful Christian critique of the present system of access to justice.

Chapter 8

The State and Morality

'Law needs a moral basis but this does not mean simply equating
law with morality. What it does mean is that we need to start a
public debate about not just what is right but also about the
common good for our society'.

(David McIlroy, essay on 'Does the law need a moral basis?'
in *Religion and Law*)

Introduction

In his lecture to the Law Society's Family Law Annual Conference
on 29 October 2013,[1] Sir James Munby, a senior judge who is
President of the Family Division, recalled the decision of the High
Court in *Upfill v. Wright* in 1911. The question was whether a
landlord could recover the unpaid rent, amounting to £72.50, on
a flat in South London which had been let to a woman who was the
mistress of the man who actually paid the rent. The court decided
that the rent was not recoverable as there was evidence that the
woman was in fact a prostitute and using the flat for purposes of
prostitution. But that was not the basis of the decision. Mr Justice
Darling described her as 'an immoral woman, being the kept
mistress of a certain man' and the rent paid by him was therefore
'the price of her immorality'. He continued:

> I do not think that it makes any difference whether the defendant is
> a common prostitute or whether she is merely the mistress of one
> man, if the house is let to her for the purpose of committing the sin
> of fornication there. That fornication is sinful and immoral is clear.
> The Litany speaks of 'fornication and all other deadly sin,' and the
> Litany is contained in the Book of Common Prayer which is in use
> in the Church of England under the authority of an Act of
> Parliament.

Here, then, we have an example of the courts basing a decision squarely on moral grounds: the judge took the view that the conduct of the woman was immoral, and Mr Justice Darling based his decision on this ground.[2] The question for this chapter is whether it is appropriate for the courts to take questions of morality into account.

There are in fact two important issues here which need to be separated: the first is that morality is a wide term and when people speak of morality in this context they usually do so in the sense of what may be called a High Victorian Morality with censorious overtones. If we adopt this line of thought, we are in danger of conceding the argument that moral issues should play no part in the law as this type of morality is often found quite unacceptable today. The second point is that morality is usually thought of as Christian principles of morality but in a pluralistic society this may not be so.

The Courts and Morality

It is certainly true that at one time the courts did indeed take moral reasons as the grounds of their decisions in a way that would not be the case today. The case of *Upfill v. Wright* is an example of a clause commonly found in leases providing that the property leased must not be used for an immoral purpose. But what does this mean? For example, in a case in 1977 which followed *Upfill v. Wright, Heglibiston Establishment v. Heyman and Others,* the question was whether an unmarried couple living in a flat together were living there for an immoral purpose. The Court of Appeal dismissed this argument peremptorily: the object of the covenant in clause 10 of the lease not to use the flat for any immoral purpose was to prevent it from being used for an immoral *purpose,* e.g. being systematically used as a brothel or used for prostitution and did not apply where two people who, though not married, lived together as man and wife in a flat for the purpose of their home for a substantial period. The issue in this case was whether the landlord was entitled to claim possession for breaches of this covenant and others but it was held that he could not.

Thus there is no doubt that the attitude of the courts has moved on from the days of *Upfill v. Wright.* But how far? What has certainly changed are the overt statements of judges that they have a kind of residual jurisdiction, founded on what is called 'public policy' to enforce certain principles of public morality. The last echo of this was probably the speech of the then Lord Simonds, a former Lord Chancellor, in the case of *Shaw v. Director of Public Prosecutions,* in 1962. The defendant published a booklet which contained the names, addresses and telephone numbers of prostitutes, photographs of nude female figures and, in some cases, details of willingness to indulge in what were described as various perverse practices. He was convicted of various offences, including conspiracy to corrupt public morals.

Lord Simonds upheld the convictions and said this:

> In the sphere of criminal law I entertain no doubt that there remains in the courts of law a residual power to enforce the supreme and fundamental purpose of the law, to conserve not only the safety and order but also the moral welfare of the State, and that it is their duty to guard it against attacks which may be the more insidious because they are novel and unprepared for ... there is in [the] court a residual power, where no statute has yet intervened to supersede the common law, to superintend those offences which are prejudicial to the public welfare. Such occasions will be rare, for Parliament has not been slow to legislate when attention has been sufficiently aroused. But gaps remain and will always remain since no one can foresee every way in which the wickedness of man may disrupt the order of society ... Let it be supposed that at some future, perhaps, early, date homosexual practices between adult consenting males are no longer a crime. Would it not be an offence if even without obscenity, such practices were publicly advocated and encouraged by pamphlet and advertisement? Or must we wait until Parliament finds time to deal with such conduct?

The date of this case, 1962, and the reference by Lord Simonds to homosexual practices, is significant. For it was at that time that there did indeed occur a marked change in social attitudes with the case of *R v. Penguin Books,* where it was held that *Lady Chatterley's Lover* by D.H. Lawrence and published by Penguin Books, was not an obscene publication despite the fact that it contained many sex scenes and repeated use of four-letter words. Then, in 1967, Parliament passed the National Health Service (Family Planning) Act 1967, removing the restrictions on providing contraception for social rather than purely medical reasons, the Sexual Offences Act 1967, decriminalising homosexuality, and the Abortion Act 1967, legalising abortion.

The Hart-Devlin Debate: Is There a Distinction Between Private and Public Acts?

It was against this background that what became known as the Hart-Devlin debate took place, which was largely concerned with the criminal law. The issue was whether the law should be concerned with morality as such or only with acts which harmed others.

The impetus for the debate was a proposed relaxation of the criminal law in the area of sexual conduct. There had long been a feeling that, in principle, it is not the business of the criminal law to concern itself with matters of private morality. For instance, in 1927, The Street Offences Committee 1927, under the Chairmanship of Mr Hugh Macmillan, K.C., had stated:

> As a general proposition it will be universally accepted that the law is not concerned with private morals or with ethical sanctions. On the other hand, the law is plainly concerned with the outward conduct of citizens in so far as the conduct injuriously affects the rights of other citizens.

What brought the matter to the fore was the Report of the Committee on Homosexual Offence and Prostitution (the Wolfenden Committee) in 1957 which recommended that homosexual acts between consenting adults in private should be legalised. More than this, it set out a vision of the criminal law as one which attempted to:

> preserve public order and decency, to protect the citizen from what is offensive or injurious, and to provide sufficient safeguards against exploitation and corruption of others ... It is not, in our view, the function of the law to intervene in the private lives of citizens, or to seek to enforce any particular pattern of behaviour, further than is necessary to carry out the purposes we have outlined.[3]

It is arguable, however, that it is not in fact possible to make such a sharp dividing line between public and private morality, and this was the argument of Lord Devlin, a distinguished judge. He argued that: 'Societies disintegrate from within more frequently than they are broken up by external pressures. There is disintegration when no common morality is observed and history shows that the loosening of moral bonds is often the first stage in disintegration, so that society is justified in taking the same steps to

preserve its moral code as it does to preserve its government and
other essential institutions'.[4]

What Lord Devlin did not argue was that in all cases the law
should be used to punish acts done in private, such as homosexual
acts between consenting adults, and in fact he supported a change
in the law here. But his argument that society needed a shared
morality was challenged by Prof. Hart in *Law, Liberty and Morality*,[5]
who argued that Lord Devlin had moved from the 'acceptable
proposition that some *shared*[6] morality is essential to the existence
of any society to the unacceptable proposition that a society is
identical with its morality'.

I myself would say that Lord Devlin did not say that, and what he
did say, and what I contend Christians should agree with, is that
some shared morality is essential to any society and that it is in fact
impossible to draw a sharp distinction between private acts which
may or may not harm me but with which the rest of society has
nothing to do, and acts which do harm others and with which the
rest of society does have something to do.

What is unfortunate is that this debate still seems to be
conducted about issues of sexual conduct, and indeed Lord Justice
Munby's speech, quoted at the beginning of this chapter, was
mainly concerned about this. For Christian morality has much
more to say about a wide range of other issues. Take, for example,
the recent controversy over 'payday loans'. These are short term
very high interest loans given by credit agencies when the borrower
cannot get a loan from the bank and are called 'payday' as the idea
is that, when payday arrives, the loan can be repaid. But what if it
cannot? A search of the internet reveals that if, for example, the
loan is not repaid for a year then the rate of interest can be as
much as 500%. Thus for every pound borrowed £5 will be
repayable.

It was concern that desperate people could be tempted into
taking on commitments of this kind that they were unable to meet
that led the Archbishop of Canterbury, Justin Welby, to criticise
the payday loan company 'Wonga', and said that the church would
drive it out of business by helping its own credit unions.[7] Following
the debate, the Chancellor of the Exchequer, George Osborne,
announced on 25 November 2013 that the Government would
amend the Banking Act going through Parliament to introduce a
cap on the cost of payday loans and said: 'This is all about having
a banking system that works for hardworking people and making
sure some of the absolutely outrageous fees and unacceptable

practices are dealt with. It's all about the government being on the side of hardworking people.'

It could be said that this is but one instance among very many of where the law does intervene to control unacceptable practices but that is not my point. What was clear here was that the Government was responding to a sense of moral outrage and thus on this basis, making law.

If the law is solely concerned with public acts then why did the authorities intervene here at all? If I am silly enough to take out a payday loan, then surely that is my fault and no one is harmed except me. In fact however, society took a view on this matter just as in the 1960s it took a view on consenting acts in private between homosexuals. In one it took action, in the other it decided that the law should change so that these matters were outside the law's remit. What this does not give us is a general principle that there is a sharp dividing line between law and morality.

It may be objected that offering payday loans was not a private act but a public one but, even if we return to what I contend is a false distinction, the case for confining the law to these is still not made out. Take the case of *R v. Brown,* decided by the House of Lords in 1993. Here five men were charged with offences arising out of consensual homosexual sadomasochist activities. The question was whether their consent to these activities amounted to a defence. The House of Lords held that it did not and one of the judges, Lord Templeman, said: 'Society is entitled and bound to protect itself against a cult of violence. Pleasure derived from the infliction of pain is an evil thing. Cruelty is uncivilised' Similarly Lord Lowry said that what the accused:

> are obliged to propose is that the deliberate and painful infliction of physical injury should be exempted from the operation of statutory provisions, the object of which is to prevent or punish that very thing, the reason for the proposed exemption being that both those who will inflict and those who will suffer the injury wish to satisfy a perverted and depraved sexual desire. Sadomasochistic homosexual activity cannot be regarded as conducive to the enhancement or enjoyment of family life or conducive to the welfare of society.

Thus it is clear that both judges regarded wider moral considerations as relevant and did not accept any rigid private/public distinction. By contrast, Lord Mustill, who was in the minority, advanced the classic so-called libertarian view that:

> What I do say is that these are questions of private morality; that the standards by which they fall to be judged are not those of the criminal law; and that if these standards are to be upheld the individual must enforce them upon himself according to his own moral standards, or have them enforced against him by moral pressures exerted by whatever religious or other community to whose ethical ideals he responds. The point from which I invite your Lordships to depart is simply this, that the state should interfere with the rights of an individual to live his or her life as he or she may choose no more than is necessary to ensure a proper balance between the special interests of the individual and the general interests of the individuals who together comprise the populace at large. Thus, whilst acknowledging that very many people, if asked whether the appellants' conduct was wrong, would reply 'Yes, repulsively wrong', I would at the same time assert that this does not in itself mean that the prosecution ... is well founded.

Euthanasia

For the Christian there can be no sharp divide such as Lord Mustill contends. Instead the issue in each case should be the appropriateness of using the law to punish any kind of conduct that is deemed wrong. What those who adhere to Lord Mustill's view are contending for is a kind of individual autonomy which, for the Christian, opens the door to mere selfishness. Here is another example taken from a topical area, that of the possible legalisation of euthanasia. We touched on this in Chapter 5, but the subject needs a fuller treatment in the context of law and morality.

It is vital at the start to be clear about terminology. What is argued for is voluntary euthanasia, where a person freely and voluntarily decides to end their life. What is not argued for is involuntary euthanasia, where a person's life is ended against their will.

As mentioned in Chapter 5, under the Suicide Act 1961, it is a crime to aid, abet, counsel or procure the suicide of another with a maximum penalty of fourteen years imprisonment. This is, of course, known as 'assisted suicide' and the issue is the extent, if any, to which this law should be relaxed to permit a person to assist another to end their life by, for example, the administration of a lethal drug. However, all UK law must now be compatible with the European Convention on Human Rights, and in this case supporters of euthanasia argue that it is incompatible with Article 8 which provides that everyone has the right to respect for his private and family life.[8] The argument is that a ban on what is termed 'assisted suicide' infringes that right on the basis that a person should have the right to kill themselves in an appropriately dignified manner.

From time to time cases are brought before the courts by those seeking a declaration that a person seeking to assist them to commit suicide will not be prosecuted and the latest of these involves Tony Nicklinson, who has since died, and another person whose identity has not been revealed and who is referred to as AM.

Both of them suffered 'locked-in syndrome': both were totally dependent on their carers, both could communicate only by eye-movements detected by their computers. Neither were terminally ill and they both faced the prospect of living for many years. Mr Nicklinson, from Melksham in Wiltshire, had described his life as a 'living nightmare'.

As mentioned in Chapter 5, the Director of Public Prosecutions (DPP) issued Policy Guidelines in 2010, which did not require Parliamentary debate, stating the criteria which would be applied in considering a prosecution. In this particular case AM sought an order that the DPP should clarify his published policy so that other people who may, on compassionate grounds, be willing to assist either of the parties to commit suicide at Dignitas in Switzerland, would know 'whether they would be more likely than not to face prosecution in England'. He also sought declarations from the court that, if the order requiring the DPP to clarify his policy was granted, then a doctor or solicitor who played a part in helping him commit suicide via Dignitas should not face disciplinary proceedings from the General Medical Council and the Solicitors Regulation Authority. Finally, he sought a declaration that s. 2 of the Suicide Act 1961 violated Article 8 of the European Convention on Human Rights. Mr Nicklinson also sought a declaration that Article 8 was violated and another declaration that, on grounds of necessity, it would not be unlawful for his GP or another doctor to terminate or to assist the termination of his life.

I have set out the grounds on which the court was asked to rule in some detail as they show the complex way in which different areas of the law interrelate in this, and indeed other areas. When the matter came before the Supreme Court in June 2014, Lord Neuberger, for the majority of the justices, held that the court could (and this was the crucial point) make a declaration that s. 2 of the Suicide Act was incompatible with Article 8 of the European Convention on Human Rights, which would have the effect that the prohibition of assisted suicide in s. 2 would end, thus making it legal. He gave various reasons for this, for example that: 'the arguments in favour of the current law are by no means overwhelming' and that: 'the present official attitude to assisted suicide seems in practice to come close to tolerating it in certain situations'.[9] However, he held that it would not be appropriate at this stage to make an order which would require the DPP to amend the 2010 Policy Guidelines. Rather, Lord Neuberger said, 'I think, it is appropriate to leave it to her to review the terms of the 2010 Policy, after consultation if she thinks fit, with a view to amending it so as to reflect the concerns expressed in the judgments of this Court, and any other concerns which she considers it appropriate to accommodate.' The message seems to be clear: the Supreme Court expects the guidelines set out by the DPP to be changed so as to make it much less likely that any prosecutions can be successfully brought for assisting in a suicide. This looks very much like the legalisation of euthanasia by the back door. At the same time a bill introduced by the former Labour Lord Chancellor, Lord Faulkner, to legalise euthanasia in certain circumstances received its second reading in the House of Lords on 18 July 2014 but failed to complete all its Parliamentary stages before the May 2015 General Election.

Where do Christians stand on this? In *Evangelium Vitae*, Pope John Paul II said:

> Suicide is always as morally objectionable as murder. The Church's tradition has always rejected it as a gravely evil choice. Even though a certain psychological, cultural and social conditioning may induce a person to carry out an action which so radically contradicts the innate inclination to life, thus lessening or removing subjective responsibility, suicide, when viewed objectively, is a gravely immoral act. In fact, it involves the rejection of love of self and the renunciation of the obligation of justice and charity towards one's neighbour, towards the communities to which one belongs, and towards society as a whole.[10]

In effect a person who wishes to commit euthanasia is asserting that they have complete and absolute autonomy and that this extends even to a decision to take their own life. However, in their insistence on what they see as autonomy they are involving others, as we saw in the case above. Whatever natural human sympathy we may have with someone such as Tony Nicklinson, voluntary euthanasia is a step too far.

It may be objected that the words of Pope John Paul are specifically based on religious grounds and as Christians we must not seek to impose our views on others. However, we must remember the relationship between faith and reason considered in Chapter 4 and our belief in natural law which we looked at in Chapter 5. Through this we reject the idea of autonomy and instead propose the richer concept of the common good. For there can be no doubt that once voluntary euthanasia is legalised then there will be cases of involuntary euthanasia where someone's life is ended because it is felt that they do not have a life worth living. Indeed, it is arguable that this has already happened in the case of Tony Bland, who deteriorated to a persistent vegetative state as a result of injuries sustained in the Hillsborough disaster in 1989. In 1992, the House of Lords granted an order that the hospital where he was could lawfully discontinue life-sustaining treatment and medical supportive measures designed to keep Tony Bland alive, including the termination of ventilation, nutrition and hydration by artificial means.

In crossing this Rubicon, the judges were much influenced by the American philosopher, Ronald Dworkin, who has argued that the life of those in a persistent vegetative state: 'is not valuable to anyone.' Indeed, he goes further: 'There is no way in which continued life can be good for such people' and to care for them shows 'pointless and degrading solicitude'.[11]

I personally find this language offensive, in the same way that I find the words of Prof. Glanville Williams offensive where, in the context of abortion, he speaks of abortion up to term, where there is a substantial risk of the child being born seriously handicapped, as being justified because the lives of the parents 'may well be blighted by having to rear a grossly defective child'.[12] How it contrasts with the Christian insistence of the innate worth of each human being and our rejection of the notion, implicit in Dworkin's words, that a person is only of worth when they can be of worth to others.

A Moral Nihilism?

What those who advocate euthanasia want is actually a moral nihilism where the only morality that counts is what I want. As Pope John Paul II put it in *Evangelium Vitae*:

> Finally, the more radical views go so far as to maintain that in a modern and pluralistic society people should be allowed complete freedom to dispose of their own lives as well as of the lives of the unborn: it is asserted that it is not the task of the law to choose between different moral opinions, and still less can the law claim to impose one particular opinion to the detriment of others.[13]

Thus those who insist on the absolute autonomy of each person will say that in fact they are not advocating any moral position at all and therefore it is wrong that others, such as Christians, should put forward a view explicitly based on morality. In fact, just as with the secularists as we saw in Chapter 2, so here also those insisting on autonomy are themselves taking a moral position. In this sense it makes no sense to speak of a divide between law and morals: each position on each law is itself based on a view of what is morally right.

Christians can take some heart from the judgement of Lord Sumption in the Tony Nicklinson case (see above) when he remarked that although the principle of autonomy is a fundamental value: 'There is, however, another fundamental moral value, namely the sanctity of life. A reverence for human life for its own sake is probably the most fundamental of all human social values.' One can only agree and say that once we lose sight of this principle then we lose all right to be considered a civilised society.

Conclusion

At the head of this chapter, I quoted the words of David McIlroy[14] on the need for a public debate on what is for the common good of our society. This chapter has attempted to contribute to that debate by maintaining that there can be no rigid divide between law and morality, nor can there be one between what are called private acts and public acts. This does not mean, of course, that the law should seek to intervene in each case where there may be immoral conduct. For instance, one may well term adultery immoral but there is no suggestion that it should be punishable by law.[15]

As Thomas Aquinas argues: 'Human law is established for the collectivity of human beings, most of whom have imperfect virtue ... so human law does not prohibit every kind of vice from which the virtuous abstain'.[16] Here we have the essence of the matter: we need to look, not at whether an act is private or public but at the great principles of human dignity and the common good, and take into account these common sense words of Aquinas.

A final thought: in Belgium where euthanasia for adults has been legalised since 2002, the Belgian Parliament, in 2014, passed a law where a child of any age may request euthanasia. There are indeed conditions: the child must be terminally ill, face 'unbearable physical suffering' and make repeated requests to die. In addition parents, doctors and psychiatrists would have to agree before a decision is made. Yet the fact remains, as pointed out by the Archbishop of Brussels, Andre-Joseph Leonard: 'The law says adolescents cannot make important decisions on economic or emotional issues, but suddenly they've become able to decide that someone should make them die.' Is this what we really want? Is not the Christian vision of human life infinitely preferable?

Notes

1   His address was entitled 'The sacred and the secular: religion, culture and the courts' and can be found at www.judiciary.gov.uk/.../JCO/.../law-morality-religion-munby-2013.pd. See also Chapter 3.
2   The effect was, of course, that the woman benefitted as she did not have to pay the rent!
3   Cmnd. 247. HMSO, London.
4   *The Enforcement of Morals* (Oxford: Oxford University Press, 1965), p. 13.
5   Oxford University Press, 1963. The quotation is from p. 51.
6   Author's italics.
7   It then emerged that the Church of England itself indirectly invested in Wonga through a 'pooled investment vehicle'. The archbishop said that: 'it shouldn't happen, it's very embarrassing' but at least he had made his point.
8   Note that Article 8 does not give a right to private and family life but only respect for this. This is an important distinction and one frequently missed.
9   The case is reported as *R (on the application of Nicklinson and another) v. Ministry of Justice* (2014) UKSC 38.
10 At para. 66.
11 These quotations are from various works of Dworkin and are cited in J. Finnis, *Human Rights and the Common Good*, Vol. III of the *Collected Essays of John Finnis* (Oxford: Oxford University Press, 2011).
12 Textbook of Criminal Law (London: Stevens and Sons, 1983).
13 At 68.
14 The essay from which this quotation is taken is in an excellent collection of

essays on the whole area of law and religion and is warmly recommended: N. Spencer, (ed.), *Religion and Law* (London: Theos, 2012).

15   Although this was not so even in fairly recent times: in 1948 there were 248 arrests for adultery in Boston, Massachusetts: Hart, *Law, Liberty and Morality*, p. 27.

16   ST I-II, 96.2.

Chapter 9

Religion and Public Debate

'Who would claim to lock up in a church and silence the message
of Saint Francis of Assisi or Blessed Teresa of Calcutta?'

(Pope Francis in *Evangelii Gaudium*, 183)

Introduction

Writing in the *New Statesman* on 10 January 2014, Christina Odone,
once Editor of the *Catholic Herald*, gave an example of how
Christians are becoming marginalised in public debate in an
article headed: 'The new intolerance'. In 2013 she was booked to
speak at a conference organised by Christian Concern as part of
the Government Consultation on its proposals to legalise same-sex
marriage. The title was 'One Man. One Woman. Making the Case
for Marriage for the Good of Society'. The speakers included a
retired professor of philosophy and a representative of the Roman
Catholic Archdiocese of Westminster. It was due to take place at
the premises of the Law Society in London, but a few days before
the event, the Law Society cancelled the booking on the ground
that the theme was 'contrary to our diversity policy' as it espoused
'an ethos which is opposed to same-sex marriage'. Another venue
was booked, the Queen Elizabeth II Conference Centre, but
twenty-four hours before the conference was to begin, it too was
cancelled, the manager saying that the subject was 'inappropriate'
and, when challenged, he too cited the organisation's diversity
policy. In the end, the conference had to be held in the basement
of a hotel.[1]

Nor is this something new. *The Guardian* columnist Jackie Ashley
wrote: 'If any MP really thinks their personal religious views take
precedence over everything else then they should leave the House
of Commons. Their place is in church, mosque, synagogue or
temple. Parliament is the place for compromises, for negotiations
in a secular sphere under the general overhead light of the liberal
tradition.'[2] The term 'liberal tradition' should be noted, as the

implication is that religion is contrary to that 'liberal tradition' and as such has no right to be heard in public debate. What caused her outburst was the statement by Roman Catholic cardinals on the fortieth anniversary of the passage of the Abortion Act 1967, which endeavoured to remind legislators of their moral responsibilities in the area of abortion.

There is a real problem here: note that the reason for the cancellation of the conference was the same in both cases: the organisation's 'diversity policy'. There was no suggestion that the conference was in any way illegal. There is undoubtedly a creeping move to deny Christians a voice in what is often called 'the public square'. This chapter aims to counter this trend by setting out why and how Christians can and should insist on their right to contribute to public debate.

How Christians Should Contribute to Public Debate

There is a view that Christians as Christians should be wary of involvement in public debate at all. There is an echo of this in Edward Norman's *Christianity and World Order,*[3] based on the Reith Lectures which he gave in 1978. Norman feared that some Christians were adopting wholesale the values of the secular world and failing to bring an authentic Christian voice to public debate. In his second lecture, 'Ministers of Change', he referred to the statement issued after the Medellin Conference of Roman Catholic bishops in 1968, which condemned neo-colonialism and endorsed the need for new and reformed political and economic structures.[4] He also referred in this lecture to the document *Uppsala Speaks* issued after the Fourth Assembly of the World Council of Churches held there in 1968 and which urged the peoples of the world 'to realise the need for revolutionary change'.[5] This tendency to, as he thought, see the world through the prism of secular and not Christian values, led Norman in his concluding lecture 'The Indwelling Christ' to argue for 'the separation of individual Christian action from the corporate witness of the Church'. He agreed that this would be seen as the 'privatisation of religion' but said: 'I think that is exactly what it is'.

This view may seem extreme to some but there is a real danger, when Christians engage in public debate, in simply becoming sucked into the prevailing mores of the world. Norman's criticisms were mainly directed at engagement in what amounted to left-wing views but there is the same danger when the Church is too closely identified with the right wing as this example shows.

In 1938, after visiting Hitler, following the invasion of Austria by Germany, Cardinal Theodor Innitzer, the Archbishop of Vienna, issued some directives to urge Austrians to vote in the forthcoming plebiscite for union with Germany and, having said that 'the exclusive mission of priests is to care for souls ... they must remain at a distance from politics', then seemed to contradict this by eulogising the idea of the 'nation' and saying that 'a truly religious life presupposes the practice of national virtues'. The Austrian episcopacy followed this by issuing explicit advice to their flocks to vote for union with Germany. It is important, though, to note that a swift rebuke followed from the Vatican.[6]

Thus in one way Edward Norman is right: Christians corporately must beware of too great an entanglement with the political world, but of course this by no means precludes involvement by Christians as individuals in politics. Indeed, I would go so far as to say that it is the duty of Christians to do so and clearly as individual Christians we will bring our own insights to bear. However, where I think that Norman is wrong is in drawing too sharp a line between corporate Christian involvement in the political world and individual Christian witness, and seeming to deny altogether any corporate Christian involvement at all. For if we place too great an emphasis on individual witness only, then we risk placing too great an emphasis on what in Catholic theology was termed the *societas perfecta*.[7]

This notion was used in scholastic theology to describe autonomous self-sufficient organisations such as the State and also the Church and, in the nineteenth century, it was used to define the Church over and against an increasingly secular society. If, however, we as Christians retreat into this model and thus retreat into ourselves, then we concede the field to secularists who are bent on our doing precisely this. At a time when the Christian point of view so desperately needs to be heard it would be a tragedy if the Church as a whole failed to give guidance on matters of Christian concern.

Political Theology or a Theology of Politics?

There is still a question of how the line between too great an involvement in political life and too great a detachment from it is to be drawn and I suggest that a helpful way forward is through the distinction between political theology and a theology of politics. This may seem semantic but it is not.

Fr Vincent Twomey in *Pope Benedict XVI, the Conscience of Our Age*[8] points out that Pope Benedict, as Joseph Ratzinger, rejected any theology which involves the 'instrumentalization of either the Church or the faith for political purposes or the attribution of sacral or salvific significance to politics'. Thus the term 'political theology' could do just that. However, we must not, on the other hand, disengage ourselves from political life and so we need a theology of politics. It is the theology which comes first, not the politics. How then does this idea of a theology of politics work?

In his address at Westminster Hall in September 2010, Pope Benedict said that 'the role of religion in political debate is not … to propose concrete political solutions, which would lie altogether outside the competence of religion – but rather to help purify and shed light upon the application of reason to the discovery of objective moral principles'.[9] In this way the Pope neatly gets past the familiar and often sterile point that somehow religious arguments in the public sphere must divest themselves of their religious nature before they are used in public debate. Instead, he is saying that as the source of all legal norms is reason and nature, so Christians, when making their arguments, do so on the basis of what they share with all humanity. In this way the argument from secularists is met that Christians only intervene in debate on the basis of religious dogmas. No again: Pope Benedict sees instead Christians taking part by using arguments accessible to all: reason and nature interconnected.

In his address to the Bundestag in Berlin on 22 September 2011,[10] the Pope took this further. He began by taking the passage in the First Book of Kings[11] where God invited the young King Solomon, on his accession to the throne, to make a request. Pope Benedict continued:

What will the young ruler ask for at this important moment? Success – wealth – long life – destruction of his enemies? He chooses none of these things. Instead, he asks for a listening heart so that he may govern God's people, and discern between good and evil. Through this story, the Bible wants to tell us what should ultimately matter for a politician. His fundamental criterion and the motivation for his work as a politician must not be success, and certainly not material gain. Politics must be a striving for justice, and hence it has to establish the fundamental preconditions for peace. Naturally a politician will seek success, as this is what opens up for him the possibility of effective political action. Yet success is subordinated to the criterion of justice, to the will to do what is right, and to the understanding of what is right.

This striving for justice must be seen in the context of promoting the requirements of the natural law in society[12] and this was given greater shape by Pope Francis in his Apostolic Exhortation *Evangelii Gaudium*[13] where he said (at para. 125) that:

> The Church's teachings concerning contingent situations are subject to new and further developments and can be open to discussion, yet we cannot help but be concrete – without presuming to enter into details – lest the great social principles remain mere generalities which challenge no one. There is a need to draw practical conclusions, so that they 'will have greater impact on the complexities of current situations'.[14]

He goes on to say in the same paragraph that: 'It is no longer possible to claim that religion should be restricted to the private sphere and that it exists only to prepare souls for heaven. We know that God wants his children to be happy in this world too, even though they are called to fulfilment in eternity, for he has created all things "for our enjoyment" (1 Tim 6:17), the enjoyment of everyone.' As the Pope tellingly observes (at para. 183): 'Consequently, no one can demand that religion should be relegated to the inner sanctum of personal life, without influence on societal and national life, without concern for the soundness of civil institutions, without a right to offer an opinion on events affecting society.' He then moves on with the telling observation with which this chapter began: 'Who would claim to lock up in a church and silence the message of Saint Francis of Assisi or Blessed Teresa of Calcutta?'

In Chapter Two of *Evangelii Gaudium*, the Pope gives more detail on some issues which should concern Christians and it is worth noting here in brief what they are: an economy of exclusion, an idolatry of money, a financial system which rules rather than serves, and an inequality that spawns violence. Another way of articulating fundamental Christian values is to base them on the Ten Commandments as suggested in *Good News for the Public Square*[15] so that we derive protection of freedom of religion from the first commandment, protection of the family from the commandments to honour your father and mother and against adultery, and the promotion of justice from the commandment not to bear false witness. The problem of course is that virtually everyone would agree that these are fundamental values which society should uphold: it is when we turn to the particular working out of these principles that we, as Christians, meet opposition.

The same applies to the fundamental principle of the innate dignity of human beings: put like this, no one is likely to disagree, but when Christians say that this means an end to abortion and absolute opposition to euthanasia, then they are met with objections from secularists of the kind that we saw at the start of this chapter. Given that as Christians we assert our right to contribute to public debate, on what basis should that contribution be?

Christians in Public Debate

The fundamental insight that Christians bring to public debate is that in any society there is a need for an agreed set of fundamental values within which that society can operate. This was well expressed by the Scottish theologian Lesslie Newbigin who said that: 'if there is no publicly accepted truth about the ends for which human beings exist, but only a multitude of private opinions on the matter; then it follows, first, that there is no way of adjudicating between needs and wants, and second, that there is no way of logically grounding needs and wants'.[16]

Furthermore, we believe, as Christians, that Christians provide that set of values. There is no need to be timid in asserting this: some Christians will say tentatively that: 'these are our views and we are just throwing them into public debate so that they can be considered along with others'. No: a bolder approach is needed. Our approach must be that society flourishes best when fundamental Christian values are applied. We cannot and must not seek to impose that view in any spirit of bigotry and intolerance, but there is no reason why we cannot argue for it strongly.

In fact, the right of Christians to engage in public debate as Christians only arises when the views of Christians conflict, or seem to conflict, with the prevailing mores of society. In *Talking God, the Legitimacy of Religious Public Reasoning*,[17] Jonathan Chaplin looks at the reaction to a march through central London, in 2008, by 600 Anglican bishops carrying placards past Downing Street and the Houses of Parliament to make their demands on behalf of the Millennium Development Goals. The Prime Minister, Gordon Brown, was among the audience and told them that he was 'humbled' to be among men and women for whom he had 'the utmost respect, the greatest admiration, and the highest affection.' Press reaction was favourable and Chaplin asks: 'Where was the familiar chorus telling us that this was a shameful attempt by a self-appointed, religious minority to impose its view on a (supposedly) secular majority?'

Chaplin then looks at a hypothetical situation where 600 Catholic bishops from around the world converge on Westminster.

> They march round Parliament Square and down Victoria Street carrying pro-life banners, ending up outside Westminster Cathedral where they listen to speeches calling for an end to abortion. Suppose that, again, the Prime Minister joins them and tells them that he has 'the utmost respect, greatest admiration and highest affection for them.'

As Chaplin points out:

> Imagine, if you can, the public reaction. Imagine the outrage, the accusations of undemocratic bullying, the calls for French-style secularism. The comment pages would be log-jammed with sermons informing us that religion is a private affair, and that we shouldn't mix up the things of God and Caesar.

Having said this, how should we as Christians operate in public debate?

There are two mistakes that Christians can make. One is to simply shout, for instance, that 'abortion is wrong. We know this because we are Catholics and that is what our Church teaches.' The statement is indeed true, but the way in which it is expressed will drive its hearers in the opposite direction. Instead, a more nuanced approach is needed which, without ever denying our faith, expresses it in such a way that non-believers will listen. At the same time there is the danger that Christians, out of a no doubt laudable desire to influence public debate on Christian principles, hitch themselves too closely to the ideology of one political party, whether of the right or left. We do well to heed the closing words of Herbert Butterfield: 'Hold to Christ, and for the rest be totally uncommitted'.[18]

Should the Christian Voice be Heard at All?

There is an argument, articulated, for example, by the American philosopher John Rawls,[19] that it is fundamentally wrong for Christians to put forward their views in public debate. This view is not specifically anti-Christian; instead it flows from his conviction that as there is what he calls 'the fact of reasonable pluralism' in the modern world, and thus disagreement about questions of religion and morality, so it is wrong for one group to seek to impose its view on others who do not share it. Thus if, for example, Christians put forward their view that euthanasia should be not be legalised, and they do this as Christians, then they are seeking to impose that view on others who might quite legitimately hold the opposite view.

For Rawls, then, the touchstone of any view is: 'how would our argument strike if presented in the form of a Supreme Court opinion?'[20] This would, says Rawls, mean that our arguments are neutral in the sense that no one view of public reason prevails and as such there is neutrality between different views of what is good for the human race.

In fact, as Michael Sandel points out,[21] if one looks closely at reasons given by the courts for their decisions, although they may be couched in the language of neutrality, in fact they are not neutral at all. He instances the opinion of the Chief Justice of the Massachusetts Supreme Court in *Goodridge v. Dept. of Public Health*, a case where the court held that a ban on same-sex marriage violated the constitution of that State. The Chief Justice held that the exclusion of same-sex couples from marriage was incompatible with: 'respect for individual autonomy and equality under laws'. Thus the Chief Justice argued that the issue was not the moral worth of the choice to enter into a same-sex marriage but the right of the individual to make that choice and so to marry their partner.

Sandel observes that, 'autonomy and freedom of choice are insufficient to justify a right to same-sex marriage.'[22] If we take this argument to its logical extent and the government is totally neutral on the 'moral worth of all voluntary intimate relationships' then the state would have no grounds for limiting marriage to two persons and polygamy would be legalised. As Sandel says: 'the real issue is whether same-sex marriages are worthy of honour and recognition by the community'. This is, by definition, a moral choice and is one, I contend, on which Christians are entitled to have a view.

Nevertheless, many Christians will see some force in the argument put forward by Rawls; we do live in a pluralist society and so we do need to think clearly about why we as Christians have the right to put forward a view in the hope that the rest of society will adopt it. How is this to be achieved?

An Alternative View

The argument that Christians should have the right to make their arguments heard in public debate has been lucidly articulated by Jonathan Chaplin[23] who distinguishes between what he calls 'candour in representation' and 'restraint in decision'. Chaplin starts from the proposition that legitimate political reasoning is *reasoning oriented to the moral purpose of the state*.[24] This then leads him to look at the purpose of the state such as the view of Oliver O'Donovan who speaks[25] of 'public judgment' as the state's moral purpose. Chaplin uses the term 'public good'. In this book we have defined the purpose of the state in natural law terms to promote the common good in the light of faith through reason. [26]

From that starting point, Chaplin advances the idea that 'The proposal is that in the *representative sphere*[27] of politics, free rein should be allowed for citizens to bring their rival faith perspectives to bear on the task of discerning the public good'. Thus, in contrast to the arguments of John Rawls, Chaplin sees no reason why, when a matter is the subject of public debate, Christians should not bring forward arguments explicitly based on their faith. This representative sphere includes, for instance, local council decisions, parliamentary votes on bills, Cabinet decisions and rulings of public agencies.

I would agree and say that Christians must insist on this, otherwise we are not accepting Christ as the Lord of all Creation.[28] Thus we have the right to put forward faith-based arguments and we ought to have enough confidence to say that we hope they will prevail. We are not, to use the language of John Rawls, seeking to impose our arguments on the rest of society but we are seeking to convince others, by the way in which we advance our arguments, that it is in the common good that they should be accepted.

However, Chaplin has some valuable ideas about exactly how, when Christians are being candid in representation, they should do this. He points out that: 'Placards and loud hailers, for example, are usually poor transmitters of confessional truth. Statements that simply assert the truth of a faith-based viewpoint without going on to unpack the public-good reasons flowing from them, or without acknowledging the presence of other sincerely-held perspectives, will generally not be persuasive.' This is clearly good sense and is in line with the argument made in Chapter 4 of this book that Christians must argue from faith through reason. It remains true, unfortunately, that too often Christians have not engaged in public debate in any nuanced way and that this has given ammunition to those who would deny Christians a voice in public debate. The more we contribute in the way that Jonathan Chaplin suggests and use our reason from our faith, the more we will be heard.

At this point we are simply at the level of public debate on a proposal. Let us take an example: a newly-elected government says that as it is so concerned about the level of immigration it intends to introduce an absolute moratorium on all immigration from every single country for a period of a year. Christians have put forward arguments for and against this based on their faith, one obvious argument against being the clear duty, emphasised in the Bible, of offering hospitality to a stranger.

The Government says that, having consulted on the proposal, it sees no reason to change its mind. We now come to the next stage of the actual debates in Parliament and once again there is no reason why Christians should not bring faith-based arguments to bear. As Chaplin says: 'Faith perspectives, then, may quite legitimately be brought explicitly into play in political debates, even in venues like Parliament, *insofar as they bear upon public policies which are thought to promote the public good.*'[29] He gives the instance of how Archbishop Tutu's confession that black South Africans were 'created in the image of God' advanced the public good because it spoke immediately and forcefully to a very specific public-good question: the injustice of the legislation maintaining apartheid.

Finally, suppose that this legislation is passed. Can the State say that it is justified on faith grounds? Here Chaplin says, and I think rightly, that this cannot be so. As he points out: The representative sphere can and must accommodate a plurality of voices, but when the State speaks *qua state* it must speak with one voice: the voice of the political community itself. And that community lacks the competence to endorse a particular faith perspective. This is what he calls 'restraint in decision' and here he is, I think, clearly right as the State's neutrality on matters of religion was emphasised by the European Court of Human Rights in *Refah Partisi (The Welfare Party) and Others v. Turkey* (2003): 'the State's duty of neutrality and impartiality [among beliefs] is incompatible with any power on the State's part to assess the legitimacy of religious beliefs ... and ... requires the State to ensure mutual tolerance between opposing groups.'

The Wish of Christians to be Popular

Despite what has been said above, I detect a reluctance among some Christians to swim against the popular tide. As Lord Mackay, the former Lord Chancellor has said, Christians must beware

> ... the wish to be popular or acceptable to public opinion ... We all must be conscious of this whatever church we support, established or disestablished, or if in our lives we are guided by moral principles which may have no religious base. Are we to go along with the tide or stick to our principles? It is usually easier to go along with the tide. Swimming against it involves strength of commitment.[30]

This is evident in the desire of some Christians apparently to swim with the tide and approve of the Same-Sex Marriage Act 2013. The fact that persons of the same sex wish to marry is not by itself a reason for allowing them to do so. If we argue that the churches should allow same-sex marriage then we must say that the Church has been wrong on this throughout the ages and should have allowed it from the very start of Christianity, otherwise we are upholding what Pope Francis has called a culture 'where each person wants to be the bearer of his or her own subjective truth'.[31] What we as Christians must do instead is to hold in balance the principle that marriage is between a man and a woman only whilst upholding as strongly as possible the equally valid principle of the innate dignity of each person which means that we condemn and more, we resist, the persecution of homosexuals which is happening in so many places across the world. By contrary, a striking instance of Christians being counter-cultural was the issue of the encyclical *Humanae Vitae* by Pope Paul VI in 1968, right in the heat of the 'swinging '60s', which proclaimed that the practice of artificial contraception was against the natural law and that openness of marriage to procreation was 'in harmony with human reason'.[32] At the time, I recall, many Christians, even Catholics, saying that they were in favour of artificial contraception because it was right 'in this day and age.' Although many have of course disagreed with *Humanae Vitae* on perfectly respectable grounds, that is not my point. Instead, what is noteworthy, is that the Pope rested his case, not on the mores of a passing age, but on what he saw as the dictates of natural law seen through reason.

In the case of Catholics, there is an often unconscious fear: that of being outcasts from the mainstream of society and current progressive thought. There is a dim echo from Recusant days of us being outcasts from English society, encouraging a desire to come in from the cold and no longer swim against the tide. It was, I believe, this thought that underlay some thoughts in a lecture given by the writer Paul Vallely in 2008 where he argued that: 'The task of good religion, therefore, is to seek mutual understanding rather than adding to the tensions of a polarising situation'.[33] No it isn't. The task of good religion is to proclaim the Truth. If that puts us at variance with the contemporary world and its mores then that is not a bad thing.

Christians must be constantly on the alert for the siren voices urging collaboration with the secular agenda. Another recent example is the formation of a group called: 'Accord Together'[34] which has as one of its aims: 'All state-funded schools should operate inclusive admissions policies that take no account of pupils' – or their parents' – religion or beliefs, and operate recruitment and employment policies that do not discriminate on the grounds of religion or belief.' The admissions policies of faith schools is, of course, in itself a matter for debate but what is startling is the support given to the group by Christians[35] on the grounds that, to quote two examples, they accord a privilege to church-goers and they damage community cohesion. What is entirely lacking is any mention, by the Christian supporters of this organization, of the fundamental value of Christian schools in actually teaching the Christian faith.

When Christ was presented in the Temple, it was Simeon who foretold to Mary that he was '*destined to be a sign that is rejected – and a sword will pierce your own soul too so that the secret thoughts of many will be laid bare*'.[36] Christ is not a sign of cosy engagement with the secular world but a sign of contradiction to it.

A Dilemma for Christians

Suppose that Christians are faced with a law that seems to them to be fundamentally unjust. What should be their attitude to it? Take the law on abortion, contained in the Abortion Act 1967 as amended by the Human Fertilisation and Embryology Act 1990.

The view of most Christians is that abortion is objectively wrong. Do we then simply campaign for the law to be repealed? However, the reality is that, as we know, this will not happen for a long time although, as Christians, we are confident that one day it will happen. If campaigning for an outright repeal of the law is not practical politics at the moment, do we then do nothing?

The answer lies, I think, in a twofold approach. We must never lose sight of the ultimate end of a repeal of the Abortion Act but we must also be alert to point out particular dangers in the details of the law. However, here we run into another danger: by remedying objectionable parts of the law we may simply make the law on abortion more acceptable and so make our aim of ultimate repeal less likely to be achieved. Here is an example:

Under the Abortion Act, virtually all abortions are carried out under s. 1 (1) (a) which provides that an abortion is lawful on the grounds that the pregnancy has not exceeded its twenty-fourth week and the continuance of the pregnancy would involve risk, greater than if the pregnancy were terminated, of injury to the physical or mental health of the pregnant woman. This reason accounts for the vast majority of all abortions (180,117 out of a total of 190,972)[37] in 2012. Of these, 99.94% were on mental health grounds – only 108 on physical health. However, although the statistics give a breakdown of when an abortion has been performed on physical health grounds (e.g. almost half [51 cases] relate to complications of pregnancy), there is no indication at all of the reasons for performing an abortion on mental health grounds, and it is believed that in most cases it is simply because the pregnant woman says that she is suffering from stress.

Is it then wrong to campaign for a change in the law to require a certificate to state clearly what mental health condition led to its being granted? The objection to this is that if the campaign succeeds it will simply tidy up what is in principle a bad law and we should have nothing to do with it. However, the fact that abortions are granted on the grounds of stress may well be felt wrong by others who may not share our absolute objection to abortion and so the number of abortions might be reduced and a specific wrong will have been redressed. Moreover we could say that there is a Christian duty to at least reveal the truth so that any public debate can take place in a more informed way.

Another example is the recent attempt in the House of Lords in the debates on the Assisted Dying Bill (2013) to insert the word 'suicide' into the bill. Lord Winston, the doctor and television presenter, spoke in favour of this on the basis that 'fragile, deranged, angry and distressed' patients would feel pressure to end their lives if the bill was passed with the title of 'assisted dying' and so, in effect, the word 'suicide' would make it clear to them and others exactly what they were doing. Whilst this may be true, one could argue that in this case the whole purpose of the Bill is so fundamentally opposed to Christian principles that any attempt to change its wording, however, well-motivated, is in itself morally compromised.

Christians and Political Philosophies

Many Christians as individuals are active in political parties but here I would suggest that the distinction between individual Christian witness and the corporate witness of the Christian Church is vital. For what is disastrous is when Christian churches, as such, endorse particular parties. What of political philosophies as distinct from parties? What of the Christian who says that support of a particular political philosophy is incompatible with Christian beliefs? The Scottish theologian Lesslie Newbigin thought that Christian belief had problems with the philosophies of both Left and Right. As he pointed out, they both shared an assumption derived from the Enlightenment as both speak in terms of individual rights: 'the Right asserts each individual's right to define and pursue a specific good on the grounds of a higher common good; the Left asserts that every person has the right to have their basic needs met by the community'.[38] Having said this, there is no doubt that many members of particular political parties of both Left and Right would rightly repudiate such a view that their set of beliefs necessarily led to such selfish ideas.

However, what we are concerned with here are political philosophies and, in fact, the prevailing political philosophy today is that of liberalism. But what exactly is liberalism? In *Religious Freedom and the Liberal State*[39] Rex Ahdar and Ian Leigh set out what they consider to be the defining characteristics of liberalism. They argue that for liberals the individual human being is the central focus with an emphasis on reason. Thus as they say: 'Religion is commonly seen by liberals as the province of subjectivism, emotion, even superstition'.[40] Moreover, a defining feature of liberalism is, Ahdar and Leigh argue, its commitment to neutrality or impartiality between competing conceptions of what constitutes a good and worthwhile life'.[41] Thus liberals would say that religion is just one of a range of conceptions of what constitutes the good for a person, whereas Christians would argue for the uniqueness of the Christian revelation. Thus whilst individual Christians may call themselves 'liberals' I suggest that a belief in a full-blown liberal philosophy, as I have outlined, is incompatible with Christian values and commitment. At the same time Christians will find much to admire in some aspects of liberalism, for example, its commitment to free speech and its emphasis on universalism, with liberalism's belief that 'generalisations about human dignity and freedom are taken to hold for all times and all places'.[42] This, I suggest, comes close to the insistence of many Christians on natural law principles of universal validity. Moreover, it is note-worthy that liberals who are strongly secularist in outlook have nevertheless been in the forefront of defending the right of Christians to free expression, as we shall see in Chapter 11.[43]

Conclusion

What is absolutely crucial for Christians when engaged in public debate is always to keep in mind that they are, in a sense, outsiders. As Michael Nazir-Ali points out, although as Christians we are often called to be the salt of the earth it is in fact as a light to the earth that we are called to be 'working against the grain in a prophetic and not merely a pastoral mode'.[44] We will pay no heed to the 'easy speeches that comfort cruel men', in Chesterton's phrase, but we find ourselves ever alert to point out and remedy the injustices of the kind which I mentioned earlier and so build up the Kingdom of God. For it is when Christians have been insiders in society that they have been weak: when they have been outsiders they have been strong. Tony Blair's 'Big Tent' was no place for us.[45]

Notes

1   Eventually, Christian Concern received an apology for the 'inconvenience' caused by the cancellation together with an insistence that there had been 'no intention' to discriminate against Christians (*Daily Telegraph*, 22 January 2015). To which one might reasonably ask: if their actions not did amount to discrimination, what would an act of discrimination be?

2   Jackie Ashley, 'Cardinals, back off from this war with women and state', *The Guardian*, June 4, 2007.

3   Oxford University Press, 1979.

4   The documents of this conference can be found, together with other documents relating to Catholic social teaching, including papal encyclicals, at www.shc.edu/theolibrary/cstdocs.htm? (accessed 12.1.14).

5   *Uppsala Speaks, Section Reports of the World Council of Churches* (Geneva: World Council of Churches, 1968).

6   The story is told in G. Passelecq and B. Suchecky, *The Hidden Encyclical of Pius XI* (New York: Harcourt Brace, 1997). Another example of crossing the borderline between the sacred and the secular is that of the Bavarian priest who, in post-war Bavaria, told his congregation that he would not instruct them how to vote but 'Make it Christian, make it Social, make it Union!'

7   The most helpful account I have come across of this, in relation to politics, is in R. Krieg, *Catholic Theologians in Nazi Germany* (New York: Continuum Publishing, 2004). See especially Chapter 1 which traces how it influenced and, most importantly, did not influence the German bishops in their dealings with the Nazis.

8   San Francisco: Ignatius Press, 2007. The discussion of a theology of politics is at p. 72.

9   This address was quoted in more detail in the Introduction. The whole of it can be found in *Benedict XVI and Blessed John Henry Newman, The State Visit, September 2010, The Official Record*, P. Jennings, (ed.) (London: CTS, 2010), pp. 102–106. The ideas in this paragraph are developed more fully in the essay by M. Cartabia and A. Simoncini, 'A Journey with Benedict XVI' in M. Cartabia and A. Simoncini (eds), *Pope Benedict's Legal Thought* (Cambridge: Cambridge University Press, 2015).

10 The full text can be found at www.catholicherald.co.uk.

11 1 Kg 3:9.

12 See chapter 4.

13 London: CTS, 2013.

14 This is a quotation from the *Compendium of the Social Doctrine of the Church* (Vatican: Pontifical Council for Justice and Peace, 2004), at para. 9.

15 T. Lawrence, (ed.), *Good News for the Public Square* (London: Lawyers Christian Fellowship, 2014), pp. 81–88. The whole of this little book is warmly recommended.

16 In 'The Welfare State: a Christian Perspective', *Theology*, 87, May 1995.

17 London: Theos Report, 2008.

18 In H. Butterfield, *Christianity and History* (London: Collins, 1949).

19 See his *Political Liberalism* (New York: Columbia University Press, 1993). Rawls died in 2002.

20 Ibid., p. 254.

21 In *Justice: What's the Right Thing to Do?* (London: Penguin, 2010). The discussion referred to in the text is at pp. 256–260.
22 At p. 257.
23 See *Talking God, the Legitimacy of Religious Public Reasoning*, (Chapter 5).
24 Author's italics.
25 In *The Ways of Judgment* (Grand Rapids: Eerdmans, 2005).
26 In Chapters 4 and 5.
27 Author's italics.
28 See Chapter 1.
29 Author's italics.
30 These words were in a lecture, 'Does Establishment have a Future?', which he delivered in Middle Temple on May 9, 2013, and which is reprinted in *Law and Justice*, 170 (2013), pp. 7–18.
31 In *Evangelii Gaudium* (London: CTS, 2014), 61.
32 *Humanae Vitae* (London: CTS, 1970), 13.
33 This was 'The London Newman Lecture' and was printed in *The Newman*, issue no. 74, May 2008, pp. 2–11.
34 'Bar entry by faith to religious schools', *Daily Telegraph*, 1 September 2014.
35 See its website: accordcoalition.org.uk
36 Lk 2:35.
37 Department of Health, Abortion Statistics, England and Wales, 2012.
38 These views of Newbigin are set out by Duncan B. Forrester in his essay on Newbigin in Nansie Blanche, (ed.), *A Time for Triumphs, Scottish Movers and Shakers of the Twentieth Century* (Edinburgh: Saint Andrew Press, 2005). See especially pp. 85–88.
39 2nd edition. (Oxford: Oxford University Press, 2013).
40 At p. 55.
41 At p. 56.
42 L. Woodhead, 'Liberal Religion and Illiberal Secularism', in G. D'Costa, M. Evans, T. Modood and J. Rivers, (eds.), *Religion in a Liberal State* (Cambridge: Cambridge University Press, 2013), p. 94. Readers will find her categories of what is meant by liberalism interesting.
43 Note also the discussion of 'liberal individualism' in the context of autonomy and natural law in Chapter 5.
44 In *Triple Jeopardy for the West* (London: Bloomsbury Publishing, 2012), p. 36.
45 As a footnote to the discussion in this chapter, readers may find it interesting to follow the work of the Commission on Religion and Belief in British Public Life, which was convened in 2013 by the Woolf Institute, Cambridge, to look at the issues discussed in this chapter and indeed in this book.

Chapter 10

Christianity, Equality and Human Rights

'But first We must speak of man's rights.'

(Encyclical of Pope John XXIII, *Pacem in Terris*, 11)

Introduction

In recent times the UK Government has adopted the twin goals of the promotion of equality and human rights, but Christians have often felt challenged by the language of equality and, perhaps to a lesser extent, that of human rights. This is because these concepts have been used by secularists to challenge Christian beliefs and they foster a lingering doubt among Christians as to whether the promotion of equality and the advancement of human rights are, in fact, desirable goals for Christians. As Vanessa Klug, for instance, puts it: 'Human rights are seen as a possible alternative common morality for the UK'.[1] The implication is clear: now that society no longer speaks a religious language common to most of us, human rights can supply this. Similarly government ministers and other politicians use the term 'equality' to justify actions of which some Christians disapprove. Here is a typical example from the former Deputy Prime Minister, Nick Clegg, who was reported as saying that the vote to legalise same-sex marriage was a *'landmark for equality in Britain'*. However, we are entitled to ask: in what sense *was* this a victory for equality and is, in fact, the pursuit of equality a desirable goal for any government and system of law? The same applies to human rights: is the pursuit of human rights a desirable goal for Christians? This chapter looks at the Christian response to both of these concepts and suggests a way forward. The next chapter looks at some actual court cases involving equality and human rights legislation involving Christians.

Equality in Secular Discourse

The term 'equality' is often bandied about in public discourse but with little or no thought as to what exactly it means. Thus, before we consider the Christian response, we ought to be clear about precisely what a commitment to equality involves. Equality, like all abstract concepts, is extremely difficult to pin down. A simple definition would be that it consists in treating everyone in the same way, often known as the 'equality as consistency' principle, but we know that this is not possible in reality. For example, minors are denied certain legal rights, not in order to discriminate against them but to ensure that they are not taken advantage of. Nor can we say that opportunities are always equal because there will always be cases where some individuals have greater access to particular rights through factors such as birth, wealth and position. This may not be desirable but it is the case.

In fact, the extent to which equality is actually promoted by the State in the UK is limited. Despite its title, 'The Equality Act 2010', this Act is not about promoting equality as such but protecting persons who possess certain characteristics, known as 'protected characteristics'[2] from discrimination, which means less favourable treatment on the ground of one of more of those characteristics.

Given even this caveat, there are various employment situations where there cannot be equality as consistency. In specific cases different treatment is required, such as that of pregnant women, and of disabled persons, to enable them to gain access to work and other opportunities. Under UK Employment Law pregnant women have much greater rights to take leave on the grounds of pregnancy than applies to other workers, and in the case of disabled persons, s. 20 of the Equality Act 2010 places an employer under a duty to make reasonable adjustments where disabled persons are put at a substantial disadvantage. This will be explored again in the following chapters, but a simple example would be special provision made for employees with a hearing loss, to enable them to hear a fire alarm.

In addition, in certain situations preferential treatment for certain groups in particular circumstances (generally known as positive discrimination) may be justified. For example, in Northern Ireland there has historically been discrimination against Roman Catholics.[3] The Fair Employment and Treatment (Northern Ireland) Order 1998, Art. 4, provides for the lawfulness of action (called affirmative action) designed to secure fair participation in employment matters by members of the Protestant and Roman Catholic community by the adoption of practices which encourage participation and the modification or abandonment of practices which restrict or discourage it.

A wider provision is found in s. 158 of the Equality Act 2010, which allows, but does not require, any action to be taken to support those with a protected characteristic,[4] as long as it is a 'proportionate means'. Such actions might include training to enable individuals to gain employment, or health services to address their needs. For instance, where the number of women in managerial positions in a particular firm is small by comparison with men, that firm may run training courses for women to enable them to apply for future managerial positions. Moreover by s. 159 an employer may take a protected characteristic into consideration when deciding whom to recruit or promote, where people having the protected characteristic are at a disadvantage or are under-represented – this positive action can be taken only where the candidates are similarly qualified. Thus where, for example, there are two applicants for the same managerial post, both equally qualified, one a man and one a woman, then the employer may decide to offer the position to the woman because there are fewer women in that type of post.

In all the above cases most people would argue that any unequal treatment was in fact justified. However, if we move to another field then we can find examples of deep inequality which are tolerated by the State. Take, for example, the 'personalisation' agenda which affects the lives of many involved with the care and support of persons with a disability as well as the disabled persons themselves. In 2007 the Government published *Putting People First: a shared vision and commitment to the transformation of adult social care.* This took the form of a concordat between central and local government departments, the third and private sectors, which officially introduced the idea of a personalised adult social care system, where people have maximum choice and control over their support, and services are tailored to meet the individual needs and preferences of users. What it has actually meant in many cases is the wholesale privatisation of social care.

Suppose that you are a disabled adult who needs to attend a day centre. You will no longer find very many of these run by local authorities. Instead they are increasingly run by private organisations. Suppose that you, as a service user or carer, have cause for complaint about the service you receive. You ask for the complaints policy: there is none. You ask social services to intervene: they cannot as the centre is not run by them. You contact the Care Quality Commission (CQC): they tell you that they can do nothing. If the centre had provided care for the elderly or residential care then the CQC could have taken action. Thus we have a large number of institutions caring for the most vulnerable in our society which are entirely unregulated. Anyone can set one up and, once it is set up, there is no inspection regime at all. Do politicians care? No. I asked one MP (of a type likely to be sympathetic) about this scandal and was told that it was 'not a political issue'. Yet here is blatant inequality: those in certain types of centres and homes have the benefit of a complaints and inspection system. Others do not.

The message of this discussion is this: it is a sham for politicians and others to say that the UK promotes equality. In some cases, as we have seen, equality is not desirable; in others it is desirable. But where the issue is not perceived to be a fashionable one, there is, in fact, no equality. The term 'equality' is simply a convenient shorthand to enable politicians to achieve what they want to achieve, such as same-sex marriage, for other reasons, whatever these may be.

Equality for the Christian

For the Christian, I suggest a much richer discourse than one based on the term 'equality'. We can start from St Athanasius who, in a bold phrase in reference to the Incarnation, said: 'God became man so that man might become God'. From this, we should speak of the uniqueness of each human being, deriving from their dignity a sharing in the life of Christ, which gives to their lives a sacred quality. Of course not everyone will agree with this, but that is not the point: this insight is the specific one that Christians bring to public debate. We are not speaking the language of the secular world but of our faith.

It is here that, as Christians, we need to set forth our vision of equality: not a flat and unattainable notion of equality but about something that goes to the heart of the Christian message. As Michael Nazir-Ali, a former Anglican Bishop of Rochester, puts it: 'the radical equality of all, no matter what appearances may suggest. This is about who people are and not necessarily about what they do or how they choose to live their lives'.[5] It is, I think, above all about *caring* for others. This notion of equality is, I suggest, best expressed by the idea of the innate dignity of each human being. The question is not the supposed value of that person's life or the contribution which they make to the community. Instead we as Christians proclaim that all human life has an intrinsic value in itself: as Nazir-Ali says: 'who people are'. Not only this, but Christians proclaim that the human dignity of us all is to be realised in community and in the search for the common good.

The Second Vatican Council links these two concepts in *Gaudium et Spes*. The common good:

> is the sum total of social conditions which allow people, either as groups or as individuals, to reach their fulfilment more fully and more easily ... At the same time, however, there is a growing awareness of the sublime dignity of human persons, who stand above all things and whose rights and duties are universal and inviolable.[6]

Thus, as Thompson points out: 'The common good is neither simply an aggregate as in utilitarianism ... which can be blind to the well-being of individuals and minority groups, nor a disaggregate as in individualism, which de-links personal flourishing from the health of the community or from a good society'.[7]

How much richer all of this sounds than the mantra of 'equality' uttered so ceaselessly! For the truth is that the current obsession with equality is in fact linked to a naked individualism of a kind that all Christians must reject. Not only this, but the emphasis on individualism is essentially nihilist as it rejects all moral authority and thus takes refuge in what turns out to be a cul-de-sac of worshipping at the secular god of equality. For the secular emphasis on equality turns out to be nothing more than the kind of relativism that Pope Benedict XVI so rightly condemned: All are equal. All life-style choices are of equal value. Nothing is good. Nothing is bad. We are all autonomous human beings.

Equality and Diversity

The terms 'equality and diversity' are often linked together, often without very much thought as to what they entail. Thus many organisations have 'equality and diversity' policies. In fact, diversity is at the heart of the Christian message, as Christ knows no boundaries. The most vivid example of this is after the first Pentecost, when the apostles 'were all filled with the Holy Spirit and began to speak different languages as the Spirit gave them power to express themselves'.[8] The list of tongues in which they spoke is surely diversity in action. Yet in the modern secular culture I detect a subtle use of the term 'diversity' to mean something else. Take this example from the report of the Care Quality Commission (CQC) into a residential home run by an order of Catholic nuns: 'Although an Order of Catholic Nuns are attached to the service and some are involved in delivering the service, people's diverse needs are recognised and respected. Two people we spoke to told us they were Catholic and attended Mass daily with the Sisters of the Order. Two were not Catholic and told us that this made no difference in how they were viewed or treated.' This is fine on the surface but is there an underlying message that *because* the home is run by a religious order there is *ipso facto* a danger that the diverse needs of service users might not be respected?

At the same time, it is important for Christians not to get caught up in scaremongering about perceived threats to religious rights when, in fact, none exist. In September 2014, the Government announced new school standards (contained in the Education [Independent School Standards] [England] [Amendment] Regulations 2014), requiring all academies, free schools and independent schools to actively promote British values which 'encourage respect for other people' such as tolerance, mutual respect and the rule of law.[9] There is no problem with this, but it is then often stated, quite inaccurately, that there is also a requirement to 'actively promote' the rights defined in the Equality Act 2010, including sexual orientation and transsexual rights. This is untrue: Government guidance states that schools and individuals are not obliged to 'promote' teachings, beliefs or opinions that conflict with their own, but nor is it acceptable for schools to promote discrimination against people or groups on the basis of their belief, opinion or background. Thus, schools should encourage tolerant attitudes to others' beliefs but this is not the same as promoting those beliefs.

Human Rights

Christians also tend to be ambivalent about the concept of human rights and this is, I think, because they feel pulled in different directions. There is an ongoing debate, a good deal of it unfortunately misinformed, about whether the European Convention on Human Rights, which we shall consider in the next chapter, should continue to be incorporated into UK law by the Human Rights Act 1998. This makes it vital that we bring a Christian perspective to bear on any discussion of human rights.

On the one hand there is the natural Christian impulse to promote basic human rights, particularly of those who are the victims of oppression, victimisation and torture. Pope John Paul II was a powerful advocate of human rights, especially in this context. For example, when he visited Khartoum in 1993, he ended his homily by voicing his 'solidarity with the weak and defenceless who cry out to God for help, for justice, for respect for their given dignity as human beings, for their basic human rights, for the freedom to believe and practice their faith without fear or discrimination'. These are powerful words and it is noteworthy that the Pope linked human rights with human dignity, a theme to which we shall return.[10]

However, this is countered by the realisation that to talk the language of human rights, when they are not grounded in a common religious ethic, leaves the way open to human rights being used to push a secularist agenda with elements in it of which Christians disapprove. It is this which the former Archbishop of Canterbury, Rowan Williams, was referring to when he remarked that: 'What makes the gap between religion and the discourse of human rights worrying is that the language of the Universal Declaration[11] is unthinkable without the kind of moral universalism that religious ethics safeguards.'[12] Moreover, there is a practical concern, as David McIlroy points out: 'The problem with the idea of rights as a human invention is that if rights are just a human invention, although we need rights to protect ourselves against the state, we also only have rights if they are created or enforced by the state'.[13]

Finally, and reinforcing this concern, Christians feel ambivalent about using the language of rights with its connotations of individuals asserting what they want at the expense of a Christian concern for others. To put it bluntly, a concern for human rights is seen as selfish.

Too often, Christians have been ready to concede the human rights argument to secularists. Here is an example: Peter Vardy and Paul Grosch in their book *The Puzzle of Ethics*[14] contrast the principles of natural law with those of human rights and remark, in the context of natural law, that: 'a human life is self-evidently sacred because that life is granted by God and, therefore should be interfered with by no one excepting God'. This is fine, but the authors then go on to say that: 'Human rights, on the other hand, are the actual products of moral, social and political agreements made between human beings'. This line of thought, with respect, plays right into the hands of the secularists as it locates human rights within agreements rather than in fundamental principles which I would argue were Christian ones.

Given this ambivalence we ought to consider what part Christians have played in the development of the concept of universal human rights and secondly whether this is a concept which Christians can and should support.

Christians and Human Rights

As the Catholic Bishops of England and Wales have pointed out, one theme 'inherent in the Church's understanding of human rights reflects the characteristically Catholic understanding that divine revelation and human reason ultimately confirm one another, since both of these express truth or are oriented to it.'[15] Thus we see how the twin ideas of faith and reason, considered in Chapter 4, find their practical expression in a commitment by the Catholic Church to human rights. However, it would be quite wrong to ascribe a commitment to human rights exclusively to the Catholic Church, as we shall see.

In fact, the part played by Christians over the centuries in establishing the idea that there are fundamental rights which attain to all humans is a notable one and it is a great pity that Christians have been so slow to point this out.[16] There is a strong argument that the very idea of human rights derives from natural law and is thus a specifically Christian concept.[17] Part of the problem is that Christians have always had a concern for others, which is of course an expression of Christ's command to love one another, but this has not been put in the language of human rights when perhaps it would be today. As Newlands points out: 'the Bible talks of release of captives, and Jesus speaks of visiting prisoners'.[18] In a more modern context St Wulfstan, Bishop of Worcester, visited Bristol, then part of his diocese in the late eleventh century, to preach against the slave trade.

However, as Ruston points out, the modern Christian concern with human rights can be traced to a great sermon preached by the Dominican friar Anton Montesimo, in 1511, in what is now the Dominican Republic.[19] The day was the second Sunday of Advent and the place was not a great cathedral or a university seminar, but a makeshift wooden church on the island of Hispaniola. The text of Montesimo's sermon was: 'a voice cries in the wilderness' and his audience, as Ruston puts it: 'were Spanish who had crossed the ocean to get rich in the Indies as quickly as possible'. The context was oppression by the Spaniards of the native Indians. Montesimo's central words were these:

> I am the voice of Christ in the wilderness of this island...such a voice you have never yet heard, more harsh, more terrifying and dangerous than you ever thought you would hear. This voice says that you are all in mortal sin and that you will live and die in it for the cruelty and tyranny with which you use these innocent people. Tell me, with what right, with what justice, do you hold these Indians in such cruel and horrible slavery? ... Are they not men? Do they not have rational souls? Are you not obliged to love them as yourselves? Don't you understand this? Can't you grasp this?

The sermon, Ruston relates, caused uproar, and complaints went to the Dominican Provincial and King Ferdinand of Spain. The King ordered the friars back to Spain to be punished and, regrettably, the Provincial took his side. Nevertheless, as Ruston puts it, 'there was sufficient moral unease at Court to prompt the King to call a meeting and laws were passed aiming to curb the brutalities of the colonists.' Following this, Pope Paul III in his encyclical *Sublimis Deus* of 1537, stated of the Indians that: 'They are to have, to hold, to enjoy both liberty and dominion, freely, lawfully. They must not be enslaved.[20] Should anything different be done, it is void, invalid, of no force'. Although the Catholic Church later placed less emphasis on a notion of universal human rights, this document of a Renaissance Pope stands forever as a ringing endorsement of the concept. Later indeed the Catholic Church did look with suspicion on claims founded on rights, due I think to its stress in the Enlightenment[21] and the connection between rights and a gospel of individualism. This last concern is still relevant today but we have anticipated and must first turn to the extent to which human rights were received in Protestant Christianity.

In addition to freedom from slavery, human rights were then, and still are, seen as vital in the area of freedom of religion. So with the break-up of a universal Christendom founded on the Catholic Church, and its replacement by many churches under the loose umbrella of 'Protestantism', believers claimed liberty of conscience and freedom of religion.

Furthermore it has been argued that the very advent of Protestantism virtually gave birth to the doctrine of human rights. Thus the German Reformed theologian Professor Jürgen Moltmann argues that human rights have a Christian origin because: 'Human rights and personal liberties, freedom of religion, freedom of belief and of conscience, democratic forms of government and liberal views of life: all these things grew up together with Protestantism'. I would not agree with this and would argue that human rights are such a fundamental principle of Christianity that no one denomination can claim them as their own. However, as we shall see later, there is no doubt that the Protestant ethic did contribute very greatly to the development of human rights as a concept.

As David McIlroy points out: 'A key turning point in the development from natural law to human rights comes with John Locke.'[22] Why was this so? It is because Locke (1632–1704) took the existing concept of natural law and natural justice and turned this into one of natural rights, one of which was the right of freedom of religion.[23] However, he went further and built his idea of natural rights around that of property. Private property was not seen as theft from the common good but was instead 'compatible with the natural common ownership which existed in the beginning of things'.[24] Few would disagree with the principle of this but the emphasis on rights of property as natural rights rather than, for instance, the right to freedom from poverty, made this, in McIlroy's phrase: 'a theory of human rights for rich men.'[25] Nevertheless, as he continues: 'But it is a theory which seeks to use rights to limit the power of government. Locke's ideas undoubtedly inspired the American Revolution and influenced the framers of the U.S. Declaration of Independence.' At the same time the French Declaration, *Des Droits de l'Homme,* had the anti-clerical slogan: '*ni Dieu, ni maitre.*' Note the stress on 'the rights of man'. Here we see the concept of human rights breaking away from its Christian origins and becoming what McIlroy calls: 'some kind of free-standing, self-supporting system of beliefs and values'[26] and this idea that human rights not only operate free from any Christian anchor but are to an extent the antithesis of Christianity and all religions is prevalent today as seen in Vanessa Klug's book *Values for a Godless Age,* referred to in the introduction to this chapter. So human rights act as a substitute for religion.

How is Christianity to Meet This Challenge?

In fact we could say that Christianity is already meeting this challenge by seeking to reclaim the language of human rights for its own but there is much work to be done. Our starting point must be to remind others of the noble part played by Protestant Christians in ensuring that human rights were included in the United Nations system after the Second World War.[27] This initiative eventually bore fruit in the 'Universal Declaration of Human Rights' issued in 1948. The moving spirit was Otto Frederick Nolde, an American, and the body which promoted the project was the World Council of Churches – in formation, established in 1938.[28] The impetus came from a desire, as one of its members, the Scottish theologian John Mackay put it: 'to write the peace'.[29]

It was recognised that, after the Second World War, there would need to be a reordering of international institutions, bodies such as the League of Nations having failed, and these new institutions should have a Christian underpinning. So, in 1941, the Federal Council of Churches, a USA body, began this process with a meeting at which a paper was circulated which stated that: 'We must bring into existence the common spirit without which such institutions (i.e. proposed international institutions) will be ineffective. Toward this common spirit Christianity has a vital contribution, for, through Christian witness, men in every land are led to believe in a purposeful God who governs the world in a brotherhood of man under their Father God'.[30] At the same time others were thinking in this direction, for example the subsequent Archbishop of Canterbury, William Temple, who convened a conference at Malvern in 1941 entitled: 'The Life of the Church and the Order of Society' which aimed to consider how Christian thought could shape society in its reconstruction after the War.[31] Although the moving spirit in all this came mainly from Protestants together with Catholics such as Jacques Maritain, it is worth recalling that they received inspiration from the Christmas war time radio broadcasts of Pope Pius XII,[32] and when the United Nations General Assembly gathered in Paris in 1948, the future Pope John XXIII, then Nuncio in Paris, was active in promoting what became the 'Universal Declaration on Human Rights'.[33]

Although the Declaration certainly puts forward Christian principles, there is no mention in it of Christianity. The Vatican had, according to Nurser, pressed strongly for this and Eleanor Roosevelt, who had chaired the Commission on Human Rights, which did much of the preparatory work, would have liked it also, but evidently Nolde was not too concerned, observing that: 'The Declaration is intended to affirm that man has the right to believe as he sees fit; it is not intended to declare what man should believe'.

What is also significant, especially in the light of later debates, is that the Universal Declaration covers both civil and political rights and also social and economic ones. So, starting from Article I, with its ringing statement that: 'All human beings are born free and equal in dignity and rights. They are endowed with reason and conscience and should act towards one another in a spirit of brotherhood', the Declaration moves on to look at civil and political rights such as the right to life, liberty and security of person (Art. 3), the principle that: 'No one shall be subjected to arbitrary arrest, detention or exile' (Art 9) and the right to freedom of thought, conscience and religion (Art. 18). It then moves on to social and economic ones such as the 'right to work, to free choice of employment, to just and favourable conditions of work and to protection against unemployment' (Art. 23) and 'the right to rest and leisure, including reasonable limitation of working hours and periodic holidays with pay' (Art. 24). This comprehensive statement of human rights is one, I suggest, that is very much in the spirit of Christian thought and can be contrasted with the emphasis in the European Convention on Human Rights (ECHR) of 1950, which covers only social and political rights. We shall have more to say on this below but the vital point is that whereas the ECHR is incorporated into UK law by the Human Rights Act 1998, the Universal Declaration is not and remains simply a touchstone of what human rights are, and a very powerful one at that.

The Universal Declaration is inevitably couched in general terms and thus liable to be treated as a justification for particular agendas. For example, in a letter to the *Daily Telegraph*,[34] Stephen Bowen, Director of the British Institute of Human Rights, and Dr Mark Porter, Chair of Council, British Medical Association, in marking the 66th anniversary of the Declaration, wrote that 'from ensuring equality for those receiving care services to equality for same- sex couples, our Human Rights Act is helping to deliver the promise of the UDHR in Britain ...' Clearly one agenda here is the promotion of same-sex marriage but the letter writers ignore both the fact that this would have been unheard of in 1948 and is controversial to the extent that it is disingenuous to claim it as a universal human right. So Christians, when engaged in the human rights debate, must ensure that they are promoting a specifically Christian version of universal human rights.

The Teaching of Recent Popes on Human Rights

As Nurser observes:[35] 'From the time of Pope John XXIII, the popes have been the most coherent and assertive speakers of the language of human rights'. This is certainly true, and the starting point is Pope John XXIII's encyclical *Pacem in Terris*. This speaks of human rights in the widest sense:

> Man has the right to live. He has the right to bodily integrity and to the means necessary for the proper development of life, particularly food, clothing, shelter, medical care, rest, and, finally, the necessary social services. In consequence, he has the right to be looked after in the event of ill health; disability stemming from his work; widowhood; old age; enforced unemployment; or whenever through no fault of his own he is deprived of the means of livelihood.

It is noteworthy that this list is introduced by the words: 'But first We must speak of man's rights'. Later on indeed duties are linked with rights: 'The natural rights of which We have so far been speaking are inextricably bound up with as many duties, all applying to one and the same person'. However, rights come first and are then linked with duties.

Ruston argues[36] that *Pacem in Terris* represented a *volte face* by the Catholic Church in its acceptance of universal human rights after 'two centuries of bitter opposition to the Rights of Man'. There is much truth in this but in fact the break was not so sudden. Before then popes had spoken of rights, albeit only in particular cases, such as Pope Leo XIII in *Rerum Novarum* who drew attention to the right to private property, the rights of the family and all in the context of the rights of workers. Pope Pius XII, in his Christmas broadcasts, so much derided by anti-Catholics and, sadly by some Catholics, had not only given inspiration to the nascent universal human rights movement, as we noted above, but provided a starting point for later developments in this area. For example, in his broadcast message at Christmas 1944, the Pope spoke of: 'The absolute order of living beings, and the very purpose of man – an autonomous being, the subject of duties and inviolable rights, and the origin and purpose of human society – have a direct bearing upon the State as a necessary community endowed with authority.'[37] Not only this but, in 1938, Pope Pius XI gave instructions for work to begin on what has become known as the 'hidden encyclical' (*Humani Generis Unitas*) which was never in fact issued but which, in its denunciation of racism in particular and concern for human dignity in general, showed a marked concern for human rights, although this exact term is never used.[38]

Following *Pacem in Terris,* the Second Vatican Council, although not speaking of human rights in general, did speak of the principle of religious freedom in *Dignitatis Humanae,*[39] and Pope Paul VI continued the Church's engagement with human rights in his encyclical *Populorum Progressio* issued in 1967. Here he was concerned in particular with the equitable distribution of the resources of the earth and he quoted the Second Vatican Council as teaching that 'God intended the earth and everything in it for the use of all human beings and peoples. Thus, under the leadership of justice and in the company of charity, created goods should flow fairly to all.'[40] As Pope Paul then taught: 'All other rights, whatever they may be, including the rights of property and free trade, are to be subordinated to this principle.'[41] This emphasis on human rights was continued by Pope John Paul II in his first encyclical, *Redemptor Hominis,* in 1979. Here he praises 'the magnificent effort made to give life to the United Nations Organization, an effort conducive to the definition and establishment of man's objective and inviolable rights' but at the same time remarks on the violation of human rights by concentration camps, violence, torture, terrorism, and discrimination in many forms.

Ruston detects a darker note in the later encyclical *Evangelium Vitae* of 1987 which he feels 'marks a serious falling out with the majority of world opinion on the subject of rights'.[42] The reason why Ruston feels this is because the encyclical attacks what Pope John Paul calls 'the culture of death'. Thus the pope praises what he calls 'the various declarations of human rights and the many initiatives inspired by these declarations'[43] as he says that they 'show that at the global level there is a growing moral sensitivity, more alert to acknowledging the value and dignity of every individual as a human being, without any distinction of race, nationality, religion, political opinion or social class.' However, he then goes on to point out that

> these noble proclamations are unfortunately contradicted by a tragic repudiation of them in practice. This denial is still more

distressing, indeed more scandalous, precisely because it is occurring in a society which makes the affirmation and protection of human rights its primary objective and its boast. How can these repeated affirmations of principle be reconciled with the continual increase and widespread justification of attacks on human life? How can we reconcile these declarations with the refusal to accept those who are weak and needy, or elderly, or those who have just been conceived? These attacks go directly against respect for life and they represent a direct threat to the entire culture of human rights.

I do not agree with Ruston here as, although the Pope does indeed refer to abortion in his reference to 'those who have just been conceived', he also refers to the weak, the needy and the elderly. Far from being open to attack from some as being too concerned with specifically pro-life issues it is clear that the Pope views attacks on the dignity of human life in the very widest sense.

This concern for human rights was a theme of Pope Benedict XVI also who linked the concept of human rights to natural law. On 15 April 2008, he gave an address to the U.N. General Assembly on the 60th anniversary of the 'Universal Declaration of Human Rights'. His address: *'Human Rights ... Must Be Respected as an Expression of Justice'*[44] made human dignity the bedrock moral foundation of the Universal Declaration and emphasised that human rights rested on the foundation of 'the natural law inscribed on human hearts and present in different cultures and civilization.' What is also interesting is his use, when Cardinal Ratzinger, of human rights language in the formulation of canon law so that this language of human rights can serve the Church in its own mission as expressed in the revised Code of Canon Law.[45]

Thus both the Christian inspiration behind the 'Universal Declaration of Human Rights' and the constant teaching of the Popes are evidence that human rights are by no means the product of a secular culture and Christians may rightly claim that the modern concern for universal human rights is largely indebted to the Christian churches.

Should Christians Use the Language of Rights at All?

Although, as we have just seen, Christians have been at the forefront of the modern campaign for universal human rights this does beg a deeper question: should Christians be concerned with rights as such? In principle, Christians emphasise not individual rights but, instead, the common humanity of us all. Furthermore, is talk of human rights another way of selfishly saying 'my rights', and rooted in the current obsession with the autonomy of the individual which in itself is profoundly anti-Christian? Pope Benedict XVI reflected this concern when he suggested that: 'Perhaps the doctrine of human rights ought today to be complemented by a doctrine of human obligations and human limits'.[46] There is no doubt that Christians and others should be having this debate, although we noted above that in *Pacem in Terris* Pope John XXIII began with the words: 'But first We must speak of man's rights', although later, duties were linked with rights.

The problem is this: in one way talk of rights can seem to be individualistic and not in accord with Christian thinking. Yet if Christians say that human rights do not exist for them, then is this denying humans redress against forms of injustice that offend the basic Christian principle of the innate dignity of each of us?

The philosopher Alistair McIntyre forcefully criticised the modern notion of human rights on the basis that, as Ruston puts it: 'a right, like a number of other key moral concepts, only makes sense when enacted within an identifiable tradition, and within the dissolution of the tradition to which it belonged it has ceased to be an instrument of the common good'.[47] There is no doubt that he is right that an insistence on *human* rights can all too often become an insistence on *my* rights but this does not, I contend, become a reason for abandoning a Christian commitment to human rights; instead it becomes a reason for setting them in a Christian context.

One point that needs to be made here is that any Christian understanding of human rights is precisely that: Christian, and so, as the Catholic Bishops of England and Wales have pointed out: 'Christians learn from the Gospel that life itself is not only a human right, but is also, and in fact firstly and ultimately, a divine gift. In the words of Jesus in Jn 10:10, "I have come that they may have life and have it to the full." This unique gift is something that only God can take back, and therefore the right to life does not entail the right to suicide or euthanasia.'[48] Moreover any discussion of rights in the Christian context needs to be conducted against the background that ultimately 'rights' are not my rights but rights in relation to God. Accordingly we need to set the exercise of human rights in the context of the common good and make clear that these rights are not to be asserted simply to satisfy my desires or wants but in order to promote the dignity of each

person in that context. David McIlroy, in considering the relationship between rights and responsibilities says: 'It is not that we have
rights and the correlative of our rights is that others have responsibilities towards us. It is that we have responsibilities towards
others and those responsibilities ... entail rights'.[49] The Catholic
Bishops of England and Wales put it neatly when they say that: 'To
claim a right for myself means my claiming it for others too'.[50]
Moreover there is also an obligation on us all to ensure that
everyone in our society is able to claim those rights and this means
that we must look very closely at how litigation is funded and at any
proposed government cuts in state funding of human rights
claims.

Yet there still remains a sense of uneasiness in Christians and
others about a culture of rights. I think that Jean Beth Elstain in
her article 'Thinking about Women, Christianity and Rights'
points a way forward: 'Rights are immunities from the depreda-
tions of the more powerful, which would violate human dignity,
rather than entitlements'.[51] If we see human rights through this
prism and in the context of the common good and with our
responsibilities towards others at the forefront, then Christians
should not only have nothing to fear from a culture of rights but
can positively enhance that culture.

It is all too easy for any discussion of human rights to become
too esoteric and to fail to grapple with actual lived situations. Here,
then, to conclude this section, is an example of how human rights,
in this case the provisions of the ECHR as given statutory force by
the Human Rights Act 1998, can make a difference to the lives of
vulnerable people in our society from a (sadly) true story.

Suppose that I have an elderly relative in a private care home.
Let us say that it is my father. His care is privately funded from his
savings. I visit him and see that he is not being cared for: he is not
being washed regularly and food is simply thrust at him. He cannot
feed himself properly and so remains of food cover his clothing.
Nor are his continence needs attended to. I complain to the
management of the care home who utter some meaningless words
such as: 'we regret that the standard of care in my father's case has fallen
below their usual high standards'. I then receive a letter from the
home saying that they are giving me four weeks' notice that they
can no longer care for my father. Clearly I do not want him to stay
there for much longer but I need longer to find alternative accommodation. Under Article 8 of the European Convention on
Human Rights (ECHR) there is a duty on the home to respect his

private and family rights which means that both their treatment of him and their peremptory notice when I complained are in breach of this. But does the ECHR apply? Under the Care Act 2014 this is now so as a result of a late amendment in the House of Lords.

Surely for the Christian the answer is clear: of course the ECHR should apply, and those who campaign for the UK's withdrawal from the Convention on the basis of misleading statements in the popular press should honestly answer this question: do they feel that people in my father's position should be left without the protection of the law or not?

Slavery and Torture

Before we leave the topic of human rights we should, albeit briefly, look at two areas where it has been alleged that the record of the Christian Church has been found wanting: slavery and torture, as, unless we confront the past record of the Church, our witness to human rights in the present will be compromised.

Take slavery first.[52] During the Old Testament period, the institution of slavery was in full possession of the social and economic systems of the Middle East, North Africa and indeed all ancient civilisations. At various times the Israelites were enslaved but among the Israelites themselves the Mosaic Law led to a more humane treatment of slaves. For example they had to be set free if seriously injured by their master (Ex 31:26–27), they retained their right to a day of rest so that their masters did not have absolute control of their lives (Ex 30:10; 33:12; Dt 5:14) and they could even marry their master's daughter (1 Ch 2:35). There was thus a striking difference between the humane slavery for the people of God and the cruel slavery practised under Roman law. Here a slave was a mere nullity at civil and praetorian law. He was denied the juridical attributes of personality and was reduced to mere property to be used and disposed of at will.

In the New Testament, St Paul presented two distinct doctrines on slavery: One was what might be called the dogmatic theory of slavery under which all who are baptized as Christians are equally and without distinction sons and daughters of the One Father, and so in Christ there is neither slave nor free (Gal 3:26–28; Col 3:2; 1 Cor 13:13). This theology was applied to the moral directives of St Paul on masters and slaves in what might be called a moral theology of slavery. (See Col 3:22–23; Eph 6:5–9; 1 Tim 6:1–2; Titus

2:9–10) These show that St Paul was forced to tolerate slavery under Roman law but only as a necessary evil and he recommended slaves to choose emancipation if offered (1 Cor 7:20–24). The logical conclusion, although not explicitly stated, is manumission according to Roman law. It is now considered that Sts Peter and Paul were referring to the 'household code' when speaking of slavery. Thus just as slaves should be obedient to their masters so also should wives obey their husbands (1 Pet 3:1) and in effect the Apostles were providing the legal relationship of slavery with a theological superstructure so that Christian slaves and wives could more easily learn the virtues of following Christ, and masters and husbands learn the virtue of care for their legal subjects. This household code of slavery remained a theme of Christian teaching throughout the first millennium of Christianity but the 'dogmatic theory of slavery' also insisted on the emancipation of slaves by their masters.

We have already seen above how Pope Paul III, in his encyclical *Sublimis Deus* of 1537, stated that native Indians must not be enslaved. There were various Papal Briefs forbidding the enslavement of American Indians but what is noteworthy is that there was no general condemnation of slavery as such. Thus it was not until the nineteenth century that Papal Briefs make reference to the enslavement of the native population in Africa and the transatlantic trade in slaves. It was left to Pope Gregory XVI in 1839, by the Constitution *In Supremo Apostalatus*, to condemn the slave trade, some thirty-two years after the UK parliament had abolished it.

Meanwhile it should be noted that the Catholic Church had been involved with the institution of slavery in other areas. For example, there was a very ancient privilege of the Roman magistrates to emancipate slaves who fled to the Capitol and appealed for their liberty. This had lapsed and in 1535 Pope Paul III decided to renew it. However, it was found that the reduced number of slaves in Rome and the surrounding areas caused problems and so the Pope was petitioned to change his mind. He acceded to this by a *Motu Proprio* of 1548 which declared the lawfulness of slavery and slave trading, including the holding of Christian slaves, in Rome. There are also records showing that from the fifteenth to the eighteenth centuries the Popes were involved in the purchase and use of galley slaves for the pontifical squadron in the war with the Turks.[53]

The process by which the Catholic Church moved to outright

condemnation of slavery in all cases was very gradual and the greater impetus to the abolition of slavery came from non-Catholic sources such as the Society of Friends, who campaigned for many years against slavery, particularly in America. It was indeed George Fox of the Society of Friends who denounced the slave trade as early as the 1670s and the Society who, in 1783, petitioned both the UK Parliament and the American Continental Congress to abolish it.[54]

As Shirley Williams points out, 'over the years the Popes consistently denounced slavery ... The difficulty was that local officials, ecclesiastical and secular alike, their careers dependent on pleasing monarchs and sometimes local bishops, were extremely reluctant to do anything about it'.[55] The eventual change of tone is shown by Pope Leo XIII who, in his encyclical *In Plurimus* (1888) condemned slavery outright: 'In the presence of so much suffering, the condition of slavery, in which a considerable part of the great human family has been sunk in squalor and affliction now for many centuries, is deeply to be deplored; for the system is one which is wholly opposed to that which was originally ordained by God and by nature.'[56]

Although much of the above may seem to be only of historical interest, it is not. Slavery still exists in many parts of the world and the remarks by Pope Leo XIII in his encyclical *Rerum Novarum* (1891) on the nature of the employment contract can be read in an anti-slavery sense and also in the sense of modern employment law. He remarks that human labour is personal as the active force inherent in the person cannot be the property of anyone other than the person who exerts it.[57] This thought was picked up and developed by the Catholic Bishops of Columbia in 1956 who argued that 'the wage contract is not a contract of sale, nor are the relationships between workers and employers simple commercial relationships, unless, in contravention of natural justice, an attempt is made to separate the work from the person.' In more recent times the tone has naturally changed and Christian churches are now in the forefront of attempts to tackle evils such as trafficking for cheap labour or prostitution. In 2014 there was an international conference at the Vatican on this and, in preparation for the conference, Cardinal Nichols of Westminster and the Home Secretary, Theresa May, in a joint article condemned modern slavery which 'damages not only the lives which are crushed by it. It violates human dignity and diminishes us all'.[58] As I write, the Modern Slavery Act 2015 has passed through

Parliament. This creates two new civil orders to prevent modern slavery, establishes an Anti-Slavery Commissioner and provides for the protection of modern slavery victims. Here is an area where Christians should be actively engaged in looking at the details of this Act and how it is implemented.

When we turn to torture,[59] we find that in 866 AD – in the midst of the 'dark ages' – Pope Nicholas I condemned the practice of torture in no uncertain terms.[60] He observed that: 'A confession must be spontaneous, not extracted by force. Will you not be ashamed if no proof emerges from the torture? Do you not recognise how iniquitous your procedure is?' But when the practice received the sanction of rediscovered texts of Roman Law in the twelfth century, it became, by the beginning of the thirteenth century, the accepted practice in Western Europe, and the Church did not protest against this. In particular, heresy was regarded as treason against God and thus the severest measures were needed to extirpate it. The same applied to sorcery and witchcraft, and Ross[61] estimates that witchcraft trials would claim the lives of between 200,000 and one million lives in the period roughly between 1500–1700. Not all of this directly involved the churches, but it has to be said that they should have been active in seeking to prevent this practice and they were not. The one plea that can be entered in mitigation is that in the judicial torture of the Middle Ages and early modern times, there were rules, and limits imposed, as for example in Pope Innocent IV's authorisation of torture by the Inquisition in Northern Italy in 1252: '*Citra disminutione membri*' – no bones were to be broken.[62]

So Christians must admit that in these two cases of slavery and torture there has been a falling in the standards expected of us but it is better to admit this than to compromise our witness to human rights today by indulging in sophistic reasoning to explain what went on. Human Rights remains a challenge for us all, not least for the churches.

Notes

1 In *Values for a Godless Age* (Penguin: London, 2000), p. 192.
2 These are set out in the Equality Act 2010 and will be examined in the next chapter in more detail. They are: age; disability; gender reassignment; marriage and civil partnership; pregnancy and maternity; race; religion or belief; sex; sexual orientation.
3 Thus Catholics with the same educational qualifications were twice as likely

to be unemployed as Protestants (Fair Employment Commission 1995). It is fair to say that in recent years the position has improved: see for example the Fair Employment Monitoring Report (Belfast: Equality Commission for Northern Ireland, 2004).

4   See footnote 1 above.
5   In *Triple Jeopardy for the West* (London: Bloomsbury Publishing, 2012), pp. 140–41.
6   At 26.
7   J. Thompson, *Introducing Catholic Social Thought* (New York: Orbis Books, 2010), p. 59.
8   Acts 2:4–5.
9   But why 'British' values? Are these not basic human values?
10 This link between dignity and human rights has not escaped criticism: see M. Glendon, 'Foundations of Human Rights: The Unfinished Business', *American Journal of Jurisprudence*, 44 (1999), pp. 7–14, in Laing, J. and Wilcox, R., (eds), *A Natural Law Reader* (Oxford: Blackwells, 2013), pp. 431–436.
11 'The Universal Declaration of Human Rights'. This is considered below.
12 In 'Reconnecting human rights and religious faith', in *Faith in the Public Square* (London: Bloomsbury Publishing, 2012), p. 161.
13 D. McIlroy, 'Human Rights Theory: Fit For Purpose, Fundamentally Flawed or Reformable?,' *Law and Justice*, 173 (2014), pp. 129–144, at p. 132.
14 London: Harper Collins, 1999, p. 199.
15 *Human Rights and the Catholic Church*, Reflections on the Jubilee of the 'Universal Declaration of Human Rights'.
16 The best account of the development of a Christian tradition of human rights is that by Ruston in *Human Rights and the Image of God* (London: SCM Press, 2004).
17 See, for an exposition of the Christian viewpoint, D. McIlroy, 'A Christian Understanding of Human Rights', a lecture delivered at Swansea University on 20 March 2013 and available at https://lawcf.org/resources/.../Christian-understandings-of-human-rights
18 In G. Newlands, *Christ and Human Rights* (Aldershot: Ashgate, 2006), p.13. This book presents a thorough discussion of a Christian engagement with human rights and is enormously stimulating. See also J. Mahoney, *The Challenge of Human Rights* (Oxford: Blackwell Publishing, 2007), which looks at the struggle for human rights from a wider perspective.
19 I owe this account to Ruston, *Human Rights and the Image of God*, pp. 66–68.
20 The question of slavery is dealt with below.
21 See also Chapter 4.
22 In 'A Christian Understanding of Human Rights'. See note 18 above.
23 See in particular Locke's *Two Treatises on Government*, ed. M. Goldie (London: Dent, 1993).
24 Ruston, *Human Rights and the Image of God*, p. 208.
25 D. McIlroy 'Human Rights Theory: Fit For Purpose, Fundamentally Flawed or Reformable?', *Law and Justice*, 173 (2014), pp. 129–144, at p. 134.
26 Ibid., p. 133.
27 The story is well told in John S. Nurser, *For All Peoples and All Nations* (Geneva:, WCC Publications, 2005).
28 The World Council of Churches was formally established in 1948.
29 Nurser, *For All Peoples and All Nations*, p. 49.

30   Quoted in Nurser, *For All Peoples and All Nations*, p. 58.
31   Nurser, *For All Peoples and All Nations*, p. 59.
32   Ibid., p. 165.
33   Ibid., p. 171, n. 27.
34   December 10, 2014.
35   Nurser, at p. 168.
36   Ruston, *Human Rights and the Image of God*, p. 18.
37   Pope John XXIII quoted this passage in *Pacem in Terris* at 47.
38   The fascinating story of this projected encyclical is told in G. Passalecq and
     B. Suchecky, *The Hidden Encyclical of Pius XI* (New York: Harcourt Brace and
     Co., 1997).
39   At 2.
40   *Gaudium et spes*, 69.
41   *Populorum Progressio*, 22.
42   At p. 22.
43   The parts quoted are all in 18.
44   Pope Benedict XVl, *Address of 18 April 2008 before the General Assembly of the
     United Nations Organisation in New York* (AAS 100, 2008), p. 335.
45   See V. Twomey, *Pope Benedict XVI, The Conscience of Our Age* (San Francisco:
     Ignatius Press, 2007), pp. 87–88.
46   In 'Was die welt zusammenhalt' (What keeps the World Together') an
     address given on January 19, 2004, at the Catholic University of Bavaria
     anniversary and published as Chapter 2, 'Searching for Peace, Tensions and
     Dangers' in *Values in a Time of Upheaval* (San Francisco: Ignatius Press, 2006),
     p. 40.
47   Ruston, *Human Rights and the Image of God*, p. 12.
48   In *Reflections of the Catholic Bishops of England and Wales on the Jubilee of the
     Universal Declaration of Human Rights, proclaimed by the United Nations General
     Assembly, 10 December 1948* (1998), see para. 7. This whole document is a most
     valuable attempt to put the Christian, and specifically, Catholic case for
     human rights and should be studied most carefully.
49   D. McIlroy 'Human Rights Theory: Fit For Purpose, Fundamentally Flawed
     or Reformable?,' *Law and Justice*, 173 (2014), pp. 129–144, at p. 142.
50   *Reflections of the Catholic Bishops of England and Wales on the Jubilee of the
     Universal Declaration of Human Rights*, para. 5.
51   In Witter and Van der Vyver, *Religious Human Rights in Global Perspective* (The
     Hague: Martinus Nijhoff, 1996), quoted in Newlands, *Christ and Human
     Rights*, p. 116.
52   The most comprehensive treatment of this topic from a Catholic viewpoint is
     in J. F. Maxwell, *Slavery and the Catholic Church* (Chichester: Barry Rose, 1975).
     My account is greatly indebted to this really excellent book which confronts
     frankly the mixed record of the Church in this area.
53   See, for example, a letter from Pope Urban VIII to his treasurer dated 31
     January 1629. R. Chirografi, 1628–1630, folio 126.
54   See J. Walvin, *A Short History of Slavery* (London: Penguin, 2007), especially
     Ch. 10.
55   S. Williams, *God and Caesar: Personal Reflections on Politics and Religion*
     (London: Continuum, 2003), p. 79. This thoughtful book is recommended
     for many other insights into the relationship between religion and politics.
56   At 3

57 Para. 34.

58 *Daily Telegraph*, April 9, 2014.

59 This section draws heavily on J. Bishop, 'A Question of Torture', *Law and Justice*, 159 (2007), pp. 103–113.

60 *Response to the questions of the Bulgars* (866), chapter LXXXVI.

61 J. Ross, 'A History of Torture', in *Torture*, K. Roth and M. Worden, eds (New York: New Press, 2005), p. 11.

62 Bull, *Ad extirpanda*, 26, in *Bullarium Privilegiorum ac Diplomatum Romanorum Pontificum amplissima collectio* (Romae, 1740), vol. III, p. 326. See also *Torture, A Human Rights Perspective* edited by K. Roth and others (New York: Human Rights Watch, 2005).

Chapter 11

Christians and Religious Liberty

'Freedom only to speak inoffensively is not worth having'.
(Lord Justice Sedley in *Redmond Bate v. DPP* [2000])

Introduction

This chapter looks at two areas where Christians and, indeed, members of other religions, have argued that their freedom of expression has been infringed by either laws passed by the State or by the too-zealous following of those laws by other bodies, usually in the public sector.[1] It is worth reminding ourselves that this is not a new situation. Take the disturbance which occurred at Ephesus which is recorded in Acts 19:23–41.

St Paul had preached that 'gods made by human hands are not gods at all'. This threatened the lucrative trade of silversmiths who made silver shrines of the goddess Diana of the Ephesians and thus, under the leadership of one Artemis, they began a disturbance shouting: 'Great is Diana of the Ephesians!' with the result that the town was in an uproar. In the end the matter was settled by the good sense of the town clerk who pointed out that St Paul and his companions had done nothing illegal and that if there was any justified cause of complaint, it could be dealt with in legal proceedings. Eventually St Paul left the city and set out for Macedonia.

This passage illustrates a vital point that arises constantly. Who was to blame for the disturbance? Was it the person who uttered the words, in this case St Paul, or was it his hearers? What of the situation where a person deliberately inflames a crowd with violent and incendiary language? Are they then to blame for the resulting disturbance? Possibly so. What of the opposite situation where the speaker does not say anything inflammatory at all but there are those in the crowd determined to cause trouble and they do so. Are they then to blame?

These issues arise in many contexts but it is with cases involving the expression of religious opinions that we are concerned.

Expression of Opinions Held by Christians

Let us start with the events that occurred in Weston-super-Mare in 1882. The Salvation Army held parades through the town headed by, as the judge in the case put it: 'musical band and flags and banners'.[2] There is nothing unusual in that, of course, and the Salvation Army still parade today through our streets. But on that occasion another group, known as the Skeleton Army, opposed the Salvation Army, due to the vigorous opposition of the Salvation Army to the sale and consumption of alcohol. In the words of the judge: the Skeleton Army 'assemble to dispute the passage of the Salvation Army through the streets and places, some to discourage such passage with shouting, uproar, and noise, to the great terror, disturbance, annoyance, and inconvenience of the peaceable inhabitants of the town, and to the endangering of the public peace' and therefore 'free fight, great uproar, blows, tumult, stone throwing, and disorder has ensued.' This happened on a number of occasions and culminated on 26 March 1882, when the Salvation Army once again marched but were as usual accompanied by a 'tumultuous and shouting mob of some hundred persons'. The police had obtained an order from the magistrates that prohibited anyone from assembling to the disturbance of the public peace in the town and told the leaders of the Salvation Army procession that they were in breach of this notice and their procession must disperse. However, they refused to do so and were arrested.

The magistrates convicted the local leaders of the Salvation Army of unlawful assembly but the High Court disagreed. The Salvation Army had indeed come together for a lawful purpose and had no intention of carrying it out unlawfully. However, they did know that their procession would be opposed and they had good reason to suppose that a breach of the peace would be committed by those who opposed it. Nevertheless, as the judge put it: 'everyone must be taken to intend the natural consequences of his own acts.' What were the natural consequences of the acts of Salvation Army in marching? Put this way, it was clear that they were not guilty because the disturbance was caused by their antagonists.

This strong and robust line of thought, if applied consistently by the courts, would have saved many Christians from conviction for expressing their views but, unfortunately, it has not.

Let us go forward to Bournemouth in 2001 and the case of Harry

Hammond, who was an Evangelical Christian and had been a preacher for twenty years. He was elderly and mildly autistic. On Saturday, 13 October 2001, Mr Hammond positioned himself in the town centre and began preaching, holding up a sign saying: 'Stop Immorality', 'Stop Homosexuality', and 'Stop Lesbianism'. It also said, in each of the four corners of the sign, 'Jesus is Lord'. A group of thirty to forty people gathered around him, arguing and shouting. Some threw soil at Mr Hammond, and a bucket of water was poured over his head. He was arrested by the police and charged under s. 5 of the Public Order Act 1986, which made it a criminal offence to use threatening, abusive or insulting words or behaviour, or disorderly behaviour, or display any writing, sign or other visible representation which is threatening, abusive or insulting, within the hearing or sight of a person likely to be caused harassment, alarm or distress thereby.

As we shall see below, this section has recently been amended but, at that time, there were three alternative offences: the use of words or behaviour that is insulting or abusive or threatening. Mr Hammond was charged with insulting behaviour. The High Court, on appeal from the Magistrates Court, found him guilty.[3] It is vital to appreciate how the legal system works in this context. Where there is an appeal from the Magistrates Court, the High Court is reluctant to interfere with any findings made by the magistrates on the actual facts of the case, as it is the magistrates who will have heard the oral evidence of the witnesses. Instead, the High Court concentrates on whether the magistrates applied the correct law. So in this case the High Court held that it was open to the magistrates to conclude as a matter of fact that the words on the sign were insulting within the meaning of the Act. The words appeared to relate homosexuality and lesbianism to immorality. Although it was accepted that Mr Hammond was, according to his understanding, exercising his right to free expression of his religious views, the court held that the magistrates could conclude that his conduct was not reasonable for various reasons, including the pressing need to show tolerance to all sections of society and the fact that his conduct was provoking violence and disorder.

This was widely felt to be a most unfortunate decision.[4] One cause for concern was the way in which the word: 'insulting' had been interpreted to deny Mr Hammond the right to express perfectly lawful views simply because some in his audience found them unacceptable. Moreover the reference by the High Court to the need to show tolerance, although by itself laudable, could be seen as an extra restriction on freedom of speech of Christians at a time when their views are increasingly at variance with some sectors of society.

Problems with the Word: 'Insulting'

In fact, s. 5 of the Public Order Act was used to criminalise behaviour on the grounds that it was insulting in a number of cases including the arrest and prosecution of an Oxford student for asking a police officer, 'Do you realise your horse is gay?', which Thames Valley police described as homophobic and 'offensive to people passing by', and the arrest of a 16-year-old for holding up a placard that said: 'Scientology is a dangerous cult'. As a result, there was a campaign to remove the word 'insulting' which united both Christian and secular groups, and which was led by the comedian Rowan Atkinson, the human rights campaigner Peter Tatchell and the former shadow home secretary David Davis. Finally the Home Secretary, Theresa May, announced that Section 57 of the Crime and Courts Act 2013 would remove the word 'insulting' from the Act with the result that it will now be an offence to use threatening or abusive behaviour but not insulting behaviour. This came into force in February 2014. Interestingly, Keith Porteous Wood, Executive Director of the National Secular Society, said:

> We congratulate the home secretary for removing a much-abused catch-all provision where the police could charge anyone for using trivial words that irritated them. The police did not even need to identify the victim that allegedly had been insulted. The change is likely to prevent street evangelists preaching against homosexuality being charged.[5]

The campaign to remove the word 'insulting' was of course motivated by other groups as well as Christians but still there is a wider message here for Christians in their relations with the State: where there is a valid cause, as here, and Christians argue it reasonably, and enlist the support of others, then there is a fair chance of success.

However, the maxim that the price of liberty is eternal vigilance is vividly illustrated by another current battle being fought in the interests of free speech on the part of Christians and others. Under the Anti-social Behaviour, Crime and Policing Bill 2013, an order known as Injunctions to Prevent Nuisance and Annoyance (IPNAs) was proposed to replace Anti-social Behaviour Orders (ASBOs). In the past, where a court injunction has been sought in noisy neighbour cases in social and private housing, the test has been whether the person was engaging in 'conduct capable of causing nuisance or annoyance to any person'. Under this bill, the government had proposed to extend this test to all cases of alleged anti-social behaviour so that it would apply to preachers such as Mr Hammond and, in the opinion of a former Director of Public Prosecutions, Lord Macdonald of River Glaven, even a lone individual standing outside the entrance to a bank holding a sign objecting to its role in the financial crisis, could meet the criteria and threshold for such an order. The Government, following a heavy defeat in the House of Lords, gave in and announced that the bill would be amended so that, except in social and private housing, the much higher threshold of 'conduct that has caused, or is likely to cause, harassment, alarm or distress to any person, will be required for the issue of an injunction.'[6]

The European Convention on Human Rights and Free Expression

In the case of Mr Hammond there was a further argument that his conviction violated his rights under Articles 9 and 10 of the European Convention on Human Rights. We have met these in the previous chapter and will meet Article 9 in more detail in the next one but, briefly, Article 9 provides that: 'Everyone has the right to freedom of thought, conscience and religion', and Article 10 provides that: 'Everyone has the right to freedom of expression. This right shall include freedom to hold opinions and to receive and impart information and ideas without interference by public authority and regardless of frontiers.' Moreover, Article 11 can be relevant: this protects the right to free assembly. Would these have availed Mr Hammond? The High Court thought not and, unfortunately, Mr Hammond died before the matter could be taken to the European Court of Human Rights.

A possible pointer to how someone in the position of Mr Hammond would have fared is the case of *Alekseyev v. Russia*, decided by the European Court in 2010. The Mayor of Moscow had banned various gay rights marches on grounds of public order and the protection of health and morals, and the rights and freedoms of others. In May 2006 he had been quoted as saying that 'the Church, the Mosque and the Synagogue' were against gay pride marches and had described an attempt to lay flowers at the Tomb of the Unknown Soldier in the Aleksandrovsk as 'a desecration of a holy place'.

The Court rejected the Government's contention that propaganda promoting homosexuality was incompatible with religious doctrines and the majority's moral values and might harm children or vulnerable adults. Moreover the fact that there had been vociferous opposition from both Orthodox and Muslim groups to the march was not a legitimate reason for prohibiting the march. Some will say that the distinction between these two cases is that here the march was by homosexuals and the opposition came from religious groups whilst in the case of Mr Hammond he represented a religious point of view and was opposed by homosexuals. I hope that this is not so. I would prefer to rest the difference on this simple point: the opposition of others prevented Mr Hammond from expressing a lawful view; by contrast, the Mayor of Moscow was told by the courts that the opposition of others could not stop lawful views from being expressed. The latter decision was as right as the decision in Hammond was wrong.

There was a different approach in the UK case of *Redmond-Bate v. DPP* in 2000, although there was a different offence charged: that of obstructing a police officer in the execution of his duty. Here there were three women belonging to a small organisation called Faith Ministries who, among other things, preach to passers-by in the street. They had agreed with the police that they would on this occasion do this from the steps of Wakefield Cathedral. However a crowd of more than a hundred had gathered, some of whom were showing hostility towards the women. Fearing a breach of the peace, a police officer asked the women to stop preaching and, when they refused to do so, arrested them all for breach of the peace.

The High Court held that they were not guilty. Lord Justice Sedley observed first that: 'If the public promotion of one faith or opinion is conducted in such a way as to insult or provoke others in breach of statute or common law, then the fact that it is done in the name of religious manifestation or freedom of speech will not necessarily save it'. This is of course right, but then he added these words:

Free speech includes not only the inoffensive but the irritating, the contentious, the eccentric, the heretical, the unwelcome and the provocative, provided it does not tend to provoke violence. Freedom only to speak inoffensively is not worth having. What Speakers' Corner (where the law applies as fully as anywhere else) demonstrates is the tolerance which is both extended by the law to opinion of every kind and expected by the law in the conduct of those who disagree, even strongly, with what they hear. From the condemnation of Socrates to the persecution of modern writers and journalists, our world has seen too many examples of state control of unofficial ideas.

One often feels that there is too much timidity in this area today, often in the name of political correctness, where the one thing that must be avoided at all costs is causing offence to others. Lord Justice Sedley reminds us that this is not the point: the one border-line drawn by the law is where words are intended to provoke violence, or at the very least, harassment, alarm or distress. As some Christian views become steadily outside the mainstream, we must not be afraid to proclaim them, reasonably indeed, but also firmly and we must insist that in doing so we have the support of the law.

Criminal Offences Protecting the Expression of Religious Belief

From looking at freedom of expression by Christians we now turn to areas of the law which can be used to protect the expression of opinions that may be offensive to Christians. The best known of these was the offence of blasphemy.

Blasphemy may well have arisen out of the medieval laws against heresy and was originally an offence that protected society in the sense that everyone was assumed to be a Christian, and so an attack on Christianity weakened the bonds that held society together. This is brought out in the judgement of Chief Justice Hale in the case of *R v. Taylor* in 1676 where he is reported as observing: 'to say, religion is a cheat, is to dissolve all those obligations whereby the civil societies are preserved'.[7] Moreover, he continued: 'Christianity is parcel [i.e. part] of the laws of England; and therefore to reproach the Christian religion, is to speak in subversion of the law'. Thus in *Whitehouse v. Lemon* in 1979 (the well-known *Gay News* case), Lord Diplock explained that: 'In the post-Restoration politics of seventeenth- and eighteenth-century England, Church and State were thought to stand or fall together. To cast doubt on the doctrines of the established church or to deny the truth of the Christian faith upon which it was founded was to attack the fabric of society itself'.[8]

In fact, prosecutions for blasphemy were rare and, in time, the offence came to be seen as part of public order law so that in *R v. Hetherington* in 1841, it was established that simply denying the tenets of the national religion 'in a sober and temperate manner' was not blasphemous.

The last case where there was any serious attempt to bring a prosecution for blasphemy was *Green v. City of Westminster Magistrates Court* (2007) where Mr Green, the Director of an organisation called 'Christian Voice', tried to bring a prosecution for blasphemy resulting from the theatrical production and TV screening of a play called 'Jerry Springer: the Opera'. This was a parody of Mr Springer's chat show and in it he imagined his descent into hell. Characters appeared as Satan, Christ, God, Mary, and Adam and Eve, and Mr Springer treated them as chat show guests. As one of the judges put it: 'in their behaviour and language they exhibit considerable excesses, as his terrestrial guests habitually do.'

Nevertheless the attempt to bring a prosecution failed. The court emphasised that the law had moved on and that it had long been the case that a successful prosecution for blasphemy required not only 'contemptuous, reviling, scurrilous and/or ludicrous material relating to God, Christ, the bible or the formularies of the Church of England' but also 'the publication must be such as tends to endanger society as a whole, by endangering the peace, depraving public morality, shaking the fabric of society or tending to cause civil strife'. In this case, there was no evidence that the play would lead to any of these consequences.

It might have been thought that the offence could have survived given that it was in effect confined to cases where the opinions expressed could lead to civil disorder but, in fact, it was abolished by section 79 (1) of the Criminal Justice and Immigration Act 2008, which simply states that: 'The offences of blasphemy and blasphemous libel under the common law of England and Wales are abolished'.

One reason for abolition was, according to the Government, that there was now new legislation to protect religious believers. The Racial and Religious Hatred Act 2006 amended the Public Order Act 1986 to create Part 3A entitled 'Hatred against persons on religious grounds'. Part 3A includes numerous criminal offences protecting groups of believers from threatening words or behaviour[9] that might stir up hatred against them, believers being defined by reference to religious belief or lack of religious belief. However, a prosecution can only be brought if the defendant *intended* to stir up religious hatred and this means that the chance of a successful prosecution is very small.[10]

In any event there is a subtle but important difference between the new offence and that of blasphemy which it replaced. The new law is part of public order law and protects religious *believers* whilst the old offence of blasphemy protected religious *belief* as such.[11] The abolition of blasphemy was advocated by secularist MPs such as Evan Harris and, although the Government denied that abolition of the crime of blasphemy does not 'represent further evidence of a drift towards secularisation', there was the feeling among many Christians that that was precisely what it was.

Religious Liberty and Managerial Practices

One of the main threats to religious liberty comes, not from the law, but from over-zealous managerial practices which insist on observance of codes of conduct and other documents which go far beyond the requirements of the law. The result is that those who, in particular, express the orthodox teaching on marriage are discriminated against. The case of Adrian Smith, a housing manager employed by Trafford Housing Trust, may serve as an example.

Mr Smith saw an article on the BBC News website headlined 'Gay church marriages get go ahead' and linked the article on his personal Facebook page, adding the comment: 'an equality too far'. His Facebook page could only be viewed by friends, and friends of friends. A colleague, having read the remark, posted a response asking Mr Smith to explain what he meant. He replied with a post that said: 'I don't understand why people who have no faith and don't believe in Christ would want to get hitched in church. The Bible is quite specific that marriage is for men and women.'

Despite the fact that this appeared only on his personal Facebook page, he was demoted to a non-managerial position with a 40% reduction in salary. His employer argued that posting such comments on Facebook had the potential to prejudice the reputation of the Trust and breached the staff Code of Conduct (by promoting religious views to colleagues and customers), and that this amounted to gross misconduct. It is vital to emphasise that Mr

Smith's words were no more than an expression of opinion and were perfectly lawful. There is nothing in the Equality Act which prevents individuals from expressing their own personal opinion nor were his words a criminal offence. What his employer was doing was using his position as an employer to prevent an employee expressing his own personal views.

Many Christians, and others too, are inclined to give in when matters reach this stage and have 'no stomach for the fight'. To his great credit, Adrian Smith was not one of these and took the matter to court, arguing that his dismissal was wrongful. The High Court agreed,[12] in what was a significant victory, not only for Christians but for all who cherish the importance of free speech. The court said that although Mr Smith had listed his occupation as a manager at the Trafford Housing Trust on his Facebook page, no reasonable reader would thereby conclude that his postings were made on the Trust's behalf. It decided that Adrian Smith had a right to promote his religious views in his own time; this included his Facebook page, as colleagues and customers had the option of whether or not to subscribe to it. To suggest that a Code of Conduct could be interpreted to extend so far into an employee's private life as to fetter his religious expression outside of work would amount to an infringement of rights of freedom of expression and belief and was unsustainable.

Sadly, many employers, especially those in the public sector, are all too likely to take the same line as did the Trafford Housing Trust. It is up to Christians to resist them and for the churches to give their support.

Another example is that of Dr Hans-Christian Raabe, who is a leading member of the Manchester-based Maranatha Community, dedicated to 're-establishing Christian values in society'. He co-wrote a paper in 2005 called 'Gay Marriage' and Homosexuality – Some Medical Comments.' The other six co-authors were a radiologist, a cardiologist, a paediatric neurologist, a family physician, a neurologist and a dermatologist. The Paper had seven headings: Background, Health risks of the Homosexual lifestyle, Homosexuality and paedophilia, 'Gay marriage', Biological evidence regarding gender development, Benefits of traditional marriage and Adverse effects of family breakdown. The format was the making of a number of statements under each heading followed in each case by a series of bullet points apparently designed to support the statements. Some of them quoted sources, others made further statements and others expressed opinions.

Dr. Raabe was subsequently appointed to the Advisory Council on the Misuse of Drugs (ACMD) as the GP member but then a number of other ACMD members questioned the suitability of Dr Raabe for this appointment in view of what he had said in this paper, especially as ACMD frequently considered the misuse of substances which appeared to be used largely within nightclubs favoured by the LGBT (lesbian, gay, bisexual, and transgender) community.

The Home Office then put out a statement saying his appointment to the ACMD had been revoked and they would be starting a recruitment campaign for a replacement GP shortly. What is disturbing about this case is that there was no suggestion at any time that Dr Raabe had allowed his professional judgement as a member of the ACMD to be influenced by the views he had expressed. Had he done so, then that would have been a different matter. The only point was that he had been asked at the interview if there was anything in his personal or professional history that may cause embarrassment, and he had not mentioned this article. His answer was that he did not think it would cause embarrassment as everything they referred to had been in the public domain for many years and was nothing new.

Dr Raabe challenged his removal by a High Court action in which one of his claims that was that his removal was in breach of Article 9 of the European Convention on Human Rights. As you will recall from Chapter 10, this Article protects religious belief but, as on other occasions involving Christians, it did not help him. The nub of the judge's decision was that 'Article 9 of the ECHR guarantees only absolute entitlement to hold religious views. It does not guarantee absolute protection to the manifestation of them.' In any event, the paper which Dr Raabe wrote could not fairly be called a manifestation of religious beliefs and thus did not come within the protection offered to religious beliefs by Article 9. In addition, the judge distinguished between acts that were a manifestation of religious belief and acts which were motivated by it: writing a public political lobbying document which presented itself as 'medical opinion' did not fall within the scope of Article 9.1 because it could only be said to be motivated by religious belief.

Thus Dr Raabe was dismissed from a public position not because of any wrongdoing on his part but through no more than a suspicion that he might be influenced in his work by views, in themselves perfectly legal, that he had expressed some years previously. This looks like a witch-hunt against Christians who disapprove of homosexuality and it is noteworthy that Dr Raabe received support from a surprising quarter: the former Liberal Democrat MP, Dr Evan Harris who, when in Parliament, was noteworthy for this secularist stance on many issues. He is now director of the Campaign for Evidence Based Policy and was reported as saying in relation to this case: 'No advisor should be dismissed purely for holding and expressing entirely lawful views on another subject, no matter how objectionable.'

Conclusion

Lord Neuberger, the President of the Supreme Court, giving the Rainbow Lecture on Diversity at the House of Commons on 12 March 2014, referred to a 'creeping liberal censoriousness' in Britain where, for instance, criticism of abortion or same-sex relationships, is regarded as unacceptable. He referred to:

> a censoriousness about what views people can publicly air as to the merits of diversity or other issues which indirectly relate to diversity. As has been said on more than one occasion, freedom only to speak inoffensively is a freedom not worth having. The more that arguments and views are shut out as unacceptable the less diverse we risk becoming in terms of outlook. And the less diverse we become in terms of outlook, the more we risk not valuing diversity and the more we therefore risk losing diversity in practice.

These are wise words and those who would restrict the freedom of Christians to speak on matters of concern to them should ponder them carefully. For when the freedom of speech of one section of society is attacked it is an attack on that freedom for us all. The German pastor Martin Niemöller, in a celebrated poem, put it thus:

> First they came for the Socialists,
> and I did not speak out –
> Because I was not a Socialist.
> Then they came for the Trade Unionists,
> and I did not speak out –
> Because I was not a Trade Unionist.
> Then they came for the Jews,
> and I did not speak out –
> Because I was not a Jew.
> Then they came for me –
> and there was no one left to speak for me.

Notes

1 For a treatment of the current position of Christians and members of other religions vis-à-vis the law in areas such as access to goods and services and children and the family, which are not covered in this book, see C. Dwyer, *Religion and the Law, the Current Position in England* (Chichester: Otter Memorial Paper Number 30, University of Chichester, 2012).

2 The case is known as *Beatty v. Gillbanks*.

3 This case is known as *Hammond v. DPP*.

4 See, for example, Ahdar and Leigh, *Religious Freedom in the Liberal State* (Oxford: Oxford University Press, 2013), pp. 446–447.

5 See www.theguardian.com, 14 January 2013 (accessed 20 February 2014).

6 This test is contained in s. 2 of the Act.

7 There is, interestingly, no contemporary account of his words.

8 See also the discussion in Chapter 3 on the extent to which Christianity was regarded as part of the law of England.

9 It is interesting, in view of the problems which the use of the word 'insulting' in this area has caused in other cases that, although this legislation did originally include insulting or abusive words or behaviour, a campaign in the House of Lords to limit it to 'threatening' succeeded. Say, for example, that I quote a biblical text. That could in some cases be regarded as insulting but not threatening.

10 Readers might care to consider this topic in the light of the discussion caused by the massacre at the offices of the magazine *Charlie Hebdo* in Paris on 7 January 2015.

11 A point well made by N. Doe and R. Sandberg in 'The Changing Criminal Law of Religion', in *Law and Justice*, 161 (2008), pp. 88–97.

12 You can read the judgement in what was known as *Smith v. Trafford Housing Trust* at [2012] EWHC 3221.

Chapter 12

Christians and the Law

'I appeal to Caesar' *(Acts 25:12)*

Introduction

Christians throughout history have rightly availed themselves of the protection of the law just at St Paul did in appealing from the Roman Governor, Festus, to Caesar in Rome. However, in recent years Christians have often felt themselves in conflict with the law and we have seen some examples of this in the previous chapter.

We now turn in this chapter to look at particular cases where Christians and Christian bodies have recently come into conflict with the law in the area of discrimination, and at the impact of these claims on the protection of religious freedom granted by Article 9 of the European Convention on Human Rights. In each of these cases, Christians must ask themselves whether the claim by the Christian concerned was justified or whether the State had a legitimate interest in the matter which overrode that claim.

It is worth emphasising that here we are dealing with civil law. Thus any breach of the law is likely to result in monetary compensation and, in addition, a tribunal can recommend that the employer follows a course of action so that the discrimination does not re-occur. However, no punishment, in the form of imprisonment, fines or other criminal sanctions, will result. The extent to which the law can and should promote equality and the Christian viewpoint on this were considered in Chapter 10. Here we are concerned with the law in practice.

The Claims under Discrimination Law

In recent years there have been a number of cases in which Christians have claimed that their right not to be subjected to discrimination on the ground of their religion had been infringed by their employer. In a number of these, the issue was the relationship between their rights and the parallel provisions outlawing discrimination on the grounds of sexual orientation. In order to understand these claims, it is necessary to know something about how our laws prohibiting discrimination work.

Laws introducing legislation against discrimination were passed at intervals in the last century, with Labour Governments responsible for those prohibiting discrimination on the grounds of sex and race, and with legislation dealing with disability being introduced by a Conservative Government. The Council of the European Community then introduced a general Framework Directive (2000/78) prohibiting discrimination on the grounds of religion or belief, disability, age or sexual orientation. This meant that, for the first time in the UK, discrimination on the grounds of religion or belief and sexual orientation was prohibited by regulations that came into force in 2003, with those prohibiting discrimination on the grounds of age coming into force in 2006. Meanwhile, existing disability discrimination was amended to comply with the Directive by regulations that came into force in 2003.

The Equality Act 2010 consolidated all of these regulations, making changes also, so that the present law is now contained in this Act. As we pointed out in Chapter 10, the title 'Equality Act' is a misnomer as the law does not in general promote equality as such but, instead, works to remedy discrimination. It does this by allowing those who have been discriminated against to claim remedies through the civil courts, as discrimination is a civil and not a criminal matter. The remedy sought is normally compensation. The law works by first defining the areas where discrimination is prohibited and then by defining exactly what discrimination is. The effect is that not all discrimination is unlawful. It is, for example, sometimes lawful to discriminate on the ground of a person's political beliefs.

What Discrimination is Prohibited? The Protected Characteristics

Under the Equality Act 2010, discrimination in employment is prohibited against those who have certain protected characteristics. These are set out in s. 14 and are: age, disability, gender reassignment, marriage and civil partnership, pregnancy and maternity, race, religion or belief, sex and sexual orientation. Thus there must be no discrimination in recruitment and selection, determining pay, training and development, selection for promotion, discipline and grievances and in taking action against bullying and harassment.

What is Meant by 'Religion or Belief'?

The Act does not only prohibit discrimination on the grounds of religion but also on the grounds of belief, which leaves us with two questions: what is a religion and what is a belief? S. 10 of the Act gives us the answer although it does not take us very far. It provides that religion means any religion and a reference to religion includes a reference to a lack of religion, so enabling an atheist to claim as well as a believer. Thus it will include all major religions and we can use the definition in s. 3 of the Charities Act 2011 which provides that the term 'religion' includes a religion which involves belief in more than one god, and also one which does not involve belief in a god. Although this legislation applies specifically to applications for charitable status,[1] this extension of the term 'religion' is used in cases of discrimination so that, for instance, Hinduism and Buddhism are religions.

The way in which the meaning of religion has changed is shown by the decision of the Supreme Court in *R (on the application of Hodkin and another) v. Registrar General of Births, Deaths and Marriages* in 2013. Two members of the Church of Scientology, Louisa Hodkin and Alessandro Calcioli, wished to be married in a Scientologists Church, but this is only possible where the building is a place of religious worship within the meaning of s. 2 of the Places of Worship Registration Act 1855 so that ceremonies of marriage can be conducted there. In an earlier case, that of *R v. Registrar General, ex p Segerdal* (1970), it had been held that a Scientologists Church was not a place of religious worship. In the words of Lord Denning, a place of meeting for religious worship means 'a place of which the principal use is as a place where people come together as a congregation or assembly to do reverence to God. It need not be the God which the Christians worship. It may be another god, or an unknown god, but it must be reverence to a deity.' He found that in the case of Scientology: 'When I look through the ceremonies and the affidavits, I am left with the feeling that there is nothing in it of reverence for God or a deity, but simply instruction in a philosophy. There may be belief in a spirit of man, but there is no belief in a spirit of God.'

The Supreme Court held that by 2013 times had changed and that, as Lord Toulson observed: 'Unless there is some compelling contextual reason for holding otherwise, religion should not be confined to religions which recognise a supreme deity. First and foremost, to do so would be a form of religious discrimination unacceptable in today's society.' This is, of course, true and so the judge was led on to attempt a legal definition of religion which ran thus:

> a spiritual or non-secular belief system, held by a group of adherents, which claims to explain mankind's place in the universe and relationship with the infinite, and to teach its adherents how they are to live their lives in conformity with the spiritual understanding associated with the belief system. By spiritual or non-secular I mean a belief system which goes beyond that which can be perceived by the senses or ascertained by the application of science.

Although this definition strictly applies only to whether a building is a place of religious worship for the purpose of the Places of Worship Registration Act 1855, it is likely to be used in other cases.

Let us now turn to the term 'belief' used in the Equality Act. This is important for Christians because, as the Act treats both religion and belief in the same way, the level of respect for belief will inevitably affect that accorded to religion. Whether this is right is another matter which we will consider later.

S. 10 of the Act defines it as: 'any religious or philosophical belief and a reference to belief includes a reference to a lack of belief' but further guidance was provided by Mr Justice Burton in the first major case on the meaning of belief, *Grainger v. Nicholson* in 2009, where he identified the following characteristics of a belief:

(i)   The belief must be genuinely held.
(ii) It must be a belief and not an opinion or viewpoint based on the present state of information available.
(iii) It must be a belief as to a weighty and substantial aspect of human life and behaviour.
(iv) It must attain a certain level of cogency, seriousness, cohesion and importance.
(v)   It must be worthy of respect in a democratic society, be not incompatible with human dignity and not conflict with the fundamental rights of others.

This has been given a wide meaning to include a belief that fox hunting is wrong, a belief in man-made climate change and humanism. In the latter case the matter arose in the case of *Streatfield v. London Philharmonic Orchestra* in 2012. Here the claimant was a humanist and also first violinist in the London Philharmonic Orchestra. She had placed her name on a letter of protest published in the *Independent* which opposed an invitation extended to the Israel Philharmonic Orchestra to play at the 2011 Proms. The Board of the Orchestra concluded that this had caused serious damage to the organisation and suspended her without pay for six months. She argued that she had suffered discrimination on the grounds of her humanist beliefs. The Employment Tribunal agreed, although in fact her claim failed, one reason being that she had not raised the issue of her humanist beliefs until she brought the claim to the tribunal. Thus the Orchestra could not have discriminated against her because of these beliefs as they did not know that she held them.

Lord Justice Sedley in the Nadia Eweida case, which will be discussed shortly, having referred to the 'protected characteristics' where discrimination is prohibited (see above) observed that, 'One cannot help observing that all of these apart from religion or belief are objective characteristics of individuals; religion and belief alone are matters of choice.' This has echoes of the remarks made by Lord Justice Laws in another case that 'religious faith is necessarily subjective'.[2]

The remarks of Lord Justice Laws are true of belief but not, I suggest, of religion. However, not all would agree and would claim that a belief that, for instance, fox hunting is wrong is just the same as, for example, the belief of Christians that Jesus Christ is God.

Christians would disagree but how to make this distinction? There is a pressing need to do so and to separate 'religion' from 'belief' because otherwise protection of religious belief will suffer by being considered subjective in the way that matters of belief are. I suggest that we base the distinction on the fact that, as Volf says: 'Christians have traditionally understood their faith not as a religious add-on to life but as itself constituting an integrated way of life. Correspondingly, Christian wisdom in one sense is that faith itself – an overarching interpretation of reality, a set of convictions, attitudes, and practices that direct people in living their lives well'.[3] One could, I suggest, say the same for most other religions as well and here we have the contrast with a particular belief. For a belief in, say, the wrongness of fox

hunting is a belief in itself: it is not *ipso facto* part of any system
of belief by which a person lives their lives.

Thus a distinction can be drawn between religion and belief
and I suggest that, if and when the law on discrimination is
revised, Christians should campaign for religion and belief to be
dealt with separately so that religion is not downgraded to sit
alongside beliefs which, although worthy in themselves, are not
in the same category as religious beliefs. This is especially vital in
view of the increasing recognition that there ought to be a duty
on employers and others to give reasonable accommodation to
religious beliefs. The problem is that if religion and belief are
dealt together there will be many who, whilst content for religious beliefs to be given reasonable accommodation would not
be prepared to accord the same degree of recognition to other
beliefs.

We shall return to this issue when we have looked in more detail
at how Christians have fared in court cases where their beliefs have
come into conflict with the law.

How is Discrimination on These Grounds Prohibited?

The broad definition is that of less favourable treatment and in
most cases the law requires what is called a comparator against
whom that less favourable treatment can be measured. Thus the
Act provides that: 'A person (A) discriminates against another (B)
if, because of a protected characteristic, A treats B less favourably
than A treats or would treat others.'

What does this mean? The simple case is, of course where a
person is not given a job because they are, for example, a
Christian. This would be less favourable treatment on the grounds
of religion. However, in most cases any discrimination is much less
overt than this and so the law often needs to probe further. Thus
the Act divides discrimination into different types:

(a) Direct discrimination. This is defined as less favourable
treatment of a person because of any of the protected characteristics set out above. The test is objective and intention to
discriminate or motive is irrelevant. Therefore the above example
of a person being denied a job expressly on grounds of religion
would be a case of direct discrimination.

However, the Equality Act recognised that, in some cases, it may
be necessary for someone with a protected characteristic to do a

particular job where this is an occupational requirement and the application of the requirement is a proportionate means of achieving a legitimate aim. An obvious example is where a rape crisis centre advertises only for women to perform counselling services. Thus even though this discriminates against men it is highly likely that it would be allowed by the Act.

There are also two specific exemptions which are relevant to religions and we shall look at them below. However, apart from this, direct discrimination can never be justified except in the case of age discrimination.

(b) Indirect discrimination. This is more subtle and is often known as 'adverse impact'. It has been used to attack rules that disadvantage particular groups of workers. A good example, although it does not concern religious discrimination, is the case of *Price v. Civil Service Commission* (1978). Here the issue was a rule of the civil service that applicants for executive officer grade posts had to be between the ages of 17 and 27. There is nothing discriminatory on the face of this and so no question of direct discrimination arises, but if you consider further you may well conclude that it does indirectly discriminate against women, as many women are taking a career break at these ages in order to start a family. Thus the practical effect of this rule was that by the time women came to apply for a job in the civil service it would be too late. The result is that this rule was held to be indirect discrimination against women.

There is one vital difference between direct and indirect discrimination: as we saw above, apart from some specified exceptions, direct discrimination is never lawful unless it is based on a genuine occupational requirement or in narrowly defined exceptions. However, indirect discrimination can be justified if it is a proportionate means of achieving a legitimate aim. In simple terms this means that it is possible for the courts to say that, even though there has been indirect discrimination, it was justified in the circumstances. As we shall shortly see, this has become important in cases involving Christians and this area of the law. It is also important to note that harassment is prohibited by the Equality Act. This is defined by s. 26 as where a person engages in unwanted conduct related to a relevant protected characteristic which has the purpose or effect of violating the dignity of the person against whom it is aimed or of creating an intimidating, hostile, degrading, humiliating or offensive environment for that person. A claim for harassment can be made as well as one for direct or indirect discrimination, an example of this being in the case of Lilian Ladele, which is discussed below.

Cases Involving Christians and Discrimination Law

Cases involving Christians and discrimination law have often turned on the specific examples set out in the Equality Act where discrimination on the grounds of religion may be lawful and so we need to look at these in detail.

The first is set out in Schedule 9, paragraph 3 of the Equality Act. This provides that it can be lawful to have a requirement that a person shall be of a particular religion or belief where the employer has an ethos based on religion or belief and, having regard to that ethos and to the nature or context of the work, this is a genuine occupational requirement and the application of the requirement is a proportionate means of achieving a legitimate aim. This could obviously apply where, for example, a school with a Christian ethos advertises for a chaplain, but what of other posts in Christian organisations which are not so specifically religious?

One example of is the case of *Muhammad v. the Leprosy Mission International* (2009) where an Employment Tribunal found that a Christian charity could restrict the post of finance administrator to Christians because of the Charity's emphasis on the importance of prayer in achieving its goals.

The second way in which some element of discrimination is allowed to religious bodies is where the law prohibiting discrimination on the ground of sex, sexual orientation or marriage may conflict with religious beliefs of that body. This is set out in Schedule 9, paragraph 2 of the Equality Act and applies to employment for the purposes of 'an organised religion'. This is a restricted phrase and would not cover, for example, a medical practice with a Christian ethos. If the employment is indeed for the purposes of an organised religion then the employer may discriminate provided that three conditions are met:

(i)   The requirement is applied so as to comply with the doctrines of the religion.
(ii) Because of the nature or context of the employment, the requirement is applied so as to avoid conflicting with the strongly held religious convictions of a significant number of the religion's followers.

(iii) The person to whom the requirement applies does not meet it, or the employer has reasonable grounds for not being satisfied that the person meets it.

How does this apply in practice? The case of *Reaney v. Hereford Diocesan Board of Finance* (2007) is a good example, and a detailed study of the facts illustrates how this complicated piece of legislation works.

Mr Reaney, who had previous experience as a Diocesan Youth Officer, applied for the position of Youth Officer for the Diocese of Hereford. He made it clear in his application that he was homosexual and that the fact that he was in a relationship had led to his premature departure from a previous post; however, he stated that this relationship had ended a few weeks before he applied for the Hereford post. When he was asked in a private 'pre-interview' about his sexuality, he replied that he was not in a relationship and that he did not intend to enter into one. The interview panel decided unanimously that he should be appointed, subject to the agreement of the Bishop of Hereford. When Reaney met the Bishop, he assured him that he would stay celibate and when the Bishop asked, 'What would you do if you met someone?' he replied that, if a relationship might develop in the future, he would discuss it with the Bishop.

The Bishop decided not to appoint Reaney; in a subsequent letter he explained that the issue was not about sexual orientation but rather about practice, lifestyle and evidence of a sufficient period of stability. The Bishop was particularly concerned that Reaney's attitudes might be affected by his raw emotion following the end of his previous relationship.

Mr Reaney brought a claim in an Employment Tribunal, claiming discrimination on the grounds of sexual orientation. His claim was brought under the Employment Equality (Sexual Orientation) Regulations 2003 but, as we have seen, the law is now contained in the Equality Act 2010. The first issue was whether he had been treated less favourably on account of his homosexuality and it was held that he had because it was precisely because of his homosexuality that he was required, in effect, to convince the Bishop of his future intentions.

That being so, the Tribunal moved to the possible application of the exception stated above and accepted that the appointment was for the purposes of an organised religion even though the holder of the post of Diocesan Youth Officer need not be an ordained minister.

In relation to point (i) the tribunal accepted that the requirement that Reaney should remain celibate was to comply with the doctrines of the Church of England and in relation to point (ii) it was accepted that a significant number of people within the Church of England had strong feelings against homosexual practice.

However, the Diocese fell down on point (iii) as it was held that the Bishop did not have reasonable grounds to believe that Mr Reaney did not meet the requirements of the post which were in effect, in his case to remain celibate. He had indicated that he was happy to remain celibate for the duration of the post, his referees had testified to his good character and the Bishop had no evidence to suggest that Reaney was not telling the truth when he said he did not have any present relationship. It was not, therefore, reasonable for the Bishop to take the view that Reaney did not meet the requirements of the post. Thus as there had been discrimination and the exception allowing this in certain cases did not apply, the Diocese of Hereford was liable and was ordered to pay compensation to Mr Reaney of over £47,000.

Many Christians will regard this case as extremely unsatisfactory. Julian Rivers points out[4] that the courts are not willing to accept an argument that religious organisations should be able to foster a community spirit by ensuring that all jobs are limited to those of the same religion. He remarks that 'the law is thus forcing an "instrumental" or "functional" view of work on religious bodies', where the emphasis is on the employee's function in the organisation, 'as opposed to a view that the work is organic (i.e. part of the religious organisation's whole activity) or vocational (i.e. part of a person's whole identity).'

The European Convention on Human Rights

The Convention is part of UK law by the provisions of the Human Rights Act 1998 and, as with the law on discrimination, is part of the civil law so that most successful claims result in an award of compensation to the injured party. It must be stressed that the European Convention on Human Rights (ECHR) and the European Court of Human Rights (ECtHR), are entirely distinct from the European Community although as pan-European institutions there is clearly a good deal of recognition between them.

Under the Human Rights Act all courts and tribunals must take account, where relevant to proceedings before them, of decisions of the ECtHR and, so far as is possible, all legislation, whether existing or future, must be read and given effect to in a way which is consistent with the rights in the Convention. The Human Rights Act applies directly to all public bodies—bodies that exercise public functions—which is not enlightening, but it is clear that central and local government are public bodies and, therefore, when acting as employers will be directly subject to the ECHR. However, the ECHR does not apply directly to private bodies. This is most important in practice. Take the example of the private day centre mentioned in Chapter 10. Suppose that it subjects someone to inhuman and degrading treatment. Their relatives, as we saw, may have no avenue of complaint and under previous law it appeared that the day centre could be outside the Human Rights Act. This was because it was not a public body. Now, as we saw, under the Care Act 2014 it is declared that such homes are exercising public functions.

An important provision, especially in the context of this book, is that when considering whether a state is in breach of the Convention, the courts allow it a 'margin of appreciation' with the result that the court gives a certain amount of discretion to the state in achieving its particular policy goals. Here is an example. In Chapter 4 we examined the decision in the *Lautsi* case from the point of view of reason as a concept and the argument in the first court in *Lautsi I* that the display of religious symbols could be emotionally disturbing. In the final hearing (*Lautsi II*) before the Grand Chamber, this view was rejected and the Court held that the decision about the presence of religious symbols in public schools falls within the State margin of appreciation. The Court did not express agreement (or disagreement) with the Italian government on the question of the display of crucifixes in public schools. Its only function was to decide if there had been a violation of religious freedom and it concluded that Italy was entitled to choose its own symbols and that, in the absence of coercion, intolerance or indoctrination of persons thinking differently, the Court cannot interfere with choices legitimately adopted in accordance with the Italian democratic legislative process. Not only was the decision important in the context of the margin of appreciation but also in the context of religious freedom.

The ECHR covers a wide range of social and political rights such as the Right to life (Article 2), Prohibition of torture (Article 3), Right to a fair trial (Article 6), Right to respect for private and family life (Article 8), Freedom of thought, conscience and religion (Article 9), Freedom of expression (Article 10), and Freedom of assembly and association (Article 11).

A striking feature is the extent to which the articles reflect the prevailing ethos of the post-war period, given that the ECHR came into force in 1950, and so the emphasis is on political rights, with the need to protect from tyranny very much in mind. What is missing is any clear statement of social and economic rights, such as a right to work, for example. In 2000, the European Union at the Council of Nice solemnly proclaimed the EU Charter of Fundamental Rights. This covers workers' social rights, data protection, bioethics and the right to good administration, as well as civil and political rights. The United Kingdom, Poland and the Czech Republic have secured an opt-out from the application of the Charter and it may be thought that, in practice, it adds little to existing legal protections, but this is a matter for debate among Christians.

There have been a number of well-publicised cases where Christians have claimed the protection of the ECHR and in particular of Article 9, which guarantees freedom of thought, conscience and religion and it is worth looking at some of these in detail.

The right in Article 9 to actually hold a religious belief is absolute, but the freedom to manifest that belief is not.[5] Instead, there is the question of whether any interference with the manifestation of religious belief is justified. This is decided by Article 9 (2) which allows for interference in three cases provided that the interference is prescribed by law, which means that there must be some legal basis for it. The three cases are:

(a)   In the interests of public safety,
(b)   For the protection of public order, health or morals,
(c)   For the protection of the rights and freedoms of others.

However, even if the interference does come within any of these headings it must be necessary in a democratic society. Cases heard by the ECtHR have established that this means that the interference with the manifestation of religious belief will only be held valid if it corresponds to a pressing social need and is proportionate to the legitimate aim pursued. As Gwyneth Pitt points out,

The main areas where manifestation of religion or belief may cause problems at work are: first, where workers want time off for religious

observance during normal working hours; secondly, where manifestation of belief involves a conflict with the employer's dress code;
and, thirdly, where workers seek a modification of their duties in
order to comply with the requirements of their religion or belief.[6]

Protection of Freedom of Thought, Conscience and Religion

It will be noted that Article 9 protects not only freedom of religion
but also that of thought and conscience. This chapter naturally
looks at freedom of religion and the extent to which Article 9
protects this but, in fact, freedom of conscience for the religious
believer is difficult to disentangle from freedom of religion. This
was seen in the recent case of *Greater Glasgow Health Board v. Doogan
and Another* (2014)[7] where the Supreme Court considered the
application of the 'conscience clause' in s. 4 of the Abortion Act,
and Lady Hale, who gave the leading judgement, also noted the
possible relevance of Article 9. We shall return to this towards the
end of this chapter.

The Right to Manifest One's Religious Belief under Article 9

The vital word here is often *manifest*: what does it mean to manifest
one's religion? It would certainly include taking part in the
worship of that religion but what about wearing religious symbols
such as a crucifix? In the case of *Eweida & Others v. United Kingdom*
(2013), the details of which will be examined below, the ECtHR
said that: 'it cannot be said that every act which is in some way
inspired, motivated or influenced by it constitutes a "manifestation" of the belief. Thus, for example, acts or omissions which do
not directly express the belief concerned or which are only
remotely connected to a precept of faith fall outside the protection
of Article 9'.

A restrictive application of the term 'manifest' is provided by the
case of *R. (on the Application of Playfoot (a child)) v. Millais School
Governing Body* (2007) where a school was held entitled to prevent
a pupil from wearing a 'purity' ring at school. The pupil argued
that the ring was a symbol of her commitment to celibacy before
marriage and she contended that the decision not to let her wear

the ring was in breach of Article 9 since, although the school had a uniform policy which banned all jewellery apart from a pair of plain 'stud' earrings, exceptions had been allowed to enable, *inter alia*, Muslim girls to wear Islamic headscarves and Sikh girls to wear the Kara bangle. However, the High Court held that although she held a 'religious belief', in that she had made a decision to remain a virgin until marriage because she was a Christian, the wearing of the ring was not a manifestation of that belief. Wearing a ring is not 'intimately linked' to the belief in chastity before marriage and she was under no obligation, by reason of her faith, to wear the ring.

The approach of the court in this case was unfortunate as it would require courts to conduct detailed investigations into what was, and what was not, required by, or intimately linked to, the religion of the claimant. It also gives the impression that followers of a religion which places greater demands on its followers to wear particular religious dress and symbols are being treated more favourably than members of religions that do not place such demands, such as Christianity. It was therefore welcome that in *Eweida & Others v. United Kingdom* the ECtHR went on to say that in order for a person to succeed in a claim that an act was manifested by one's religion it was not necessary to establish that the act was mandated by the religion in question. Thus in *Eweida & Others v. United Kingdom* it was accepted that the wearing of a crucifix did amount to a manifestation of one's Christian religion and so in principle was protected by Article 9.

The Specific Situation Rule

Another troublesome area has been what is known as the 'specific situation rule'. This has recently been modified, as we shall see, but the principle behind it is that if one has voluntarily accepted employment in a specific situation where there is a restriction on one's freedom of religion then one cannot complain and freedom of religion is protected by being able to move to another job. Thus in *Copsey v. WWB Devon Clays Ltd* (2005), an employee who complained that his employer's requirement on him to work on Sundays interfered with his freedom of religion and was in breach of Article 9, lost his case on the grounds that his freedom was protected as he could move to another job. He had accepted the 'specific situation' of that particular employment and that was that.

This rule was applied to school uniforms in *R (on the application of Begum) v. Headteacher and Governors of Denbigh High School* (2006). Here Shabina Begum, a Muslim born in the United Kingdom to parents of Bangladeshi origin, attended Denbigh High School, a mixed-sex secondary community school for pupils aged eleven to sixteen. The school offered girls three uniform options: navy-blue trousers, knee-length skirt or *shalwarkameez* (a sleeveless smock-like dress worn to between knee and mid-calf length). On the first day of term in September 2002, Ms Begum went to the school wearing a *jilbab* (which has been judicially described as 'a long shapeless dress ending at the ankle and designed to conceal the shape of the wearer's arms and legs') and was told to go home, change, and return wearing a school uniform. She did not return to the school; and a solicitor's letter later contended that she had been 'excluded/suspended' from the school in breach, *inter alia*, of Articles 9 of the ECHR. Lord Bingham held that there was no interference with her right to manifest her belief as the 'specific situation' applied: in this case Shabina Begum's family had chosen the school from outside their catchment area and there was no evidence of any real difficulty in her attending another school.[8]

The specific situation rule has been strongly criticised. Ahdar and Leigh point out that instead of the State being required to demonstrate that a restriction on religious liberty is necessary it makes the applicant have to show that: 'she could not have found another way of exercising her belief so that no clash arose'.[9]

In fact, as with the manifestation requirement, this rule has been relaxed in the decisions of the ECtHR in *Eweida & Others v. United Kingdom* (2013), which involved four separate claims that encompassed discrimination law as well as human rights law. The Court said that, where an individual complains of a restriction on freedom of religion in the workplace, the fact that they could just change their job and take another was not the point, and so the specific situation rule is no longer an absolute principle. Instead, the possibility of leaving and taking another job was one factor to be considered in deciding if the restriction on freedom of religion was proportionate for the purposes of Article 9 (2). This is a welcome development and opens up the possibility of a Christian arguing, for example, that they could not easily find another job and so, as they have to stay in their present post, the restriction on freedom of religion imposed by their present employers is in breach of Article 9.

We now turn to these four cases.

The Ewieda, Chaplin, Ladele and McFarlane Cases[10]

These four cases were all heard together in 2013 and to some extent can be considered together. In the first, Ms Eweida was a check-in clerk employed by BA plc (formerly British Airways) and had been suspended from work for wearing a visible cross on a chain in contravention of the company's uniform policy, but had later been reinstated after BA had decided to allow the display of authorised religious symbols, including the cross. However, BA had refused to compensate her for loss of earnings during her suspension. The issue in the UK courts had been indirect discrimination on the ground of religion, but the Court of Appeal had held that BA's refusal to allow her to wear her cross had not been indirect discrimination because inconvenience to a single individual did not constitute a disadvantage that 'puts or would put *persons* of the same religion or belief ... at a particular disadvantage when compared with other persons' for the purposes of the Regulations.

However, the ECtHR held that her claim succeeded under Article 9 as BA's refusal to allow her to wear a cross was in breach of her right to freedom of religion. The court said that: 'Ms Eweida's cross was discreet and cannot have detracted from her professional appearance. There was no evidence that the wearing of other, previously authorised, items of religious clothing, such as turbans and *hijabs*, by other employees, had any negative impact on British Airways' brand or image.' Moreover BA had clearly undermined its own case by amending its own uniform policy before the hearing.

The second case concerned Shirley Chaplin, a nursing sister, who had refused on religious grounds to stop wearing a crucifix necklace with her uniform, contrary to the Devon and Exeter Health NHS Foundation Trust's health and safety policy (based on Department of Health guidance) that, 'No necklaces will be worn to reduce the risk of injury when handling patients' and was therefore redeployed in a post in which she was not subject to the same restrictions. The Trust had offered her the alternative of wearing her crucifix as a brooch rather than on a chain around her neck but she had refused.

Here the employer's case was much stronger and Ms Chaplin lost. The management felt that there was a risk that a disturbed patient might seize and pull the chain, thereby injuring the patient or Ms Chaplin, or that a swinging cross on a chain might come into contact with an open wound. Moreover, another Christian nurse had been requested to remove a cross and chain, two Sikh nurses had been told they could not wear a *kara* bangle or *kirpan*, and flowing *hijabs* were prohibited – again on health and safety grounds. Furthermore, Ms Chaplin had been offered the alternative of wearing a cross as a brooch or under a high-necked top under her tunic, but she did not consider that this would be sufficient to comply with her religious convictions. In legal terms, the interference with her Article 9 rights had not been disproportionate and had been 'necessary in a democratic society'.

The third case involved Lilian Ladele, a registrar employed by Islington Borough Council, who had refused on religious grounds to conduct civil partnership ceremonies. The issue in the UK had been indirect discrimination but the Court of Appeal had held that she had neither been directly nor indirectly discriminated against nor harassed. The Court accepted that Islington Council's requirement that all registrars be designated as civil partnership registrars had had a particularly detrimental impact on her because of her religious beliefs, especially as she had worked for the council in this capacity since 2002, before civil partnerships were introduced by the Civil Partnerships Act 2004, and so there was no question of her waiving her right to take part in these ceremonies when she entered employment. The consequences of her refusal had been very serious: given the strength of her religious convictions, she had felt that she had no choice but to face disciplinary action rather than be designated a civil partnership registrar and she had lost her job as a result. On the other hand, Islington Council had a 'Dignity for All' equality and diversity policy, which stated, *inter alia,* that 'The council will promote community cohesion and equality for all groups but will especially target discrimination based on age, disability, gender, race, religion and sexuality.'

In this case, unlike the others above, there was, in effect, a clash between two rights protected under the ECHR: the right not to be discriminated against on grounds of religion and the right not to be discriminated against on grounds of sexual orientation. There were two factors that militated against Lilian Ladele: the ECtHR has held that any differences in treatment based on sexual orientation require particularly serious reasons by way of justification and the fact that, where there is a conflict between different rights, the ECHR accords individual states a wide margin of appreciation. Thus Lilian Ladele lost.

The final case was that of Gary McFarlane who had been employed as a counsellor by Relate Avon. He had refused on religious grounds to offer psychosexual counselling to same-sex couples and been dismissed. His case was weakened as he had enrolled voluntarily on Relate's postgraduate training programme in psychosexual counselling, even though he knew that, because of Relate's policy of providing its service without discrimination, he would not be able to filter out clients on the grounds of their sexual orientation. The ECtHR held that states have a wide margin of appreciation in deciding where to strike the balance between Mr McFarlane's right to manifest his religious belief and Relate's interest in securing the rights of others and, though the loss of his job was a severe sanction with grave consequences, in the circumstances, that margin of appreciation had not been exceeded.

Of all these case, one may feel that, whilst Nancy Ewieda won, of the others Lilian Ladele was dealt with especially harshly, as there was no shortage of other registrars to conduct civil partnerships, and that the Council's Dignity for All Policy rode roughshod over her rights. Shirley Chaplin had not been treated differently from other religious believers and Gary McFarlane had enrolled in a course to enable to do the very thing to which he objected.

Since these cases, there have been others, such as that of *Bull v. Hall* (2013) where the UK Supreme Court held that a hotel's policy of only letting married heterosexual couples share a double-bedded room amounted to direct discrimination against a homosexual couple in a civil partnership. The requirement to be married, imposed by the hotel owners because of their religious beliefs, was discriminatory because gay people could not, at that date, get married.

Reasonable Accommodation of Religious Beliefs?

These cases will no doubt continue but what should our response as Christians be? One solution is to argue for a duty to give reasonable accommodation to religious beliefs. The precedent here is the duty to give reasonable accommodation to disabled persons at work. If this existed then would, for example, Mr Copsey have succeeded in his claim (see above) not to work on Sundays? Not necessarily because of the word 'reasonable'. Lucy Vickers[11] points out that, although the idea of reasonable accommodation is open to the objection that it might provide too much protection for religious interests, there would need to be a threshold for justifying a refusal to accommodate religious beliefs. She mentions the principle adopted in the USA that a duty to accommodate religion does not apply where, to do so, would cause undue hardship which has been interpreted as anything more than *de minimis* hardship and has included matters such as economic cost and inconvenience. It might still not have helped Mr Copsey in his case, but then one might argue that here the employer was in fact right. What such a duty would do is to force employers to make an attempt to accommodate religious beliefs, and the burden of proof would be on employers who would have to show that they would suffer some identified hardship if they accommodated the employee's religious beliefs. By contrast, Gwyneth Pitt argues that to impose a positive duty to accommodate religious belief would be to privilege religion or belief over other protected characteristics and, in the case of disability, some accommodation is widely recognised as essential in order to deal with the problems caused by the fact that disabilities vary enormously in kind and degree.[12]

Very recently the argument for some degree of accommodation of religious belief has been given support by Lady Hale, the Vice President of the Supreme Court, who has asked: 'would it not be a great deal simpler if we required the providers of employment, goods and services to make reasonable accommodation for the religious beliefs of others?'[13] Here is a door that is opening for Christians. If we are prepared to put our case reasonably, and avoid the doctrinaire shouting that has unfortunately characterised too many Christian interventions in this area, then we may make progress. It is incidentally noteworthy that, as mentioned in Chapter 6, she advised the Glasgow midwives who failed in their attempt to invoke the protection of s. 4 of the Abortion Act, that they 'may still claim that, either under the Human Rights Act or under the Equality Act, their employers should have made reasonable adjustments to the requirements of the job in order to cater for their religious beliefs'. This might have been a better route in the first place and it is to be hoped that it will be pursued.

In fact, the concept of reasonable accommodation of religious belief does exist in Canada under the Canadian Charter of Rights and Freedoms (1982) and the Canadian Human Rights Act (1985). It is for the employer to justify the discriminatory measure, and the question is whether it is impossible to accommodate individual employees without undue hardship on the part of the employer. Factors to be taken into account in assessing 'undue hardship' include: financial cost, any disruption of a collective agreement, morale problems for other employees, the interchangeability of workforce and facilities, the size of the employer, and safety considerations. This test sets a high standard for the employer but, if society feels that religious belief is a value worthy of protection, then I suggest that it is an appropriate one.

A recent UK case, *Mba v. London Borough of Merton* (2013), was a partial victory for Christians in the workplace. A care home worker claimed that a Sunday working requirement indirectly discriminated against her. The court held that it was not necessary for her to show that a whole group of people (i.e. Christians) could be affected by a requirement. What mattered was that her own beliefs meant that she was affected by it. This is important as some Christians are prepared to work on Sundays and if 'group' disadvantage was required this would have resulted in her losing. However, the court went on to hold that the Sunday working requirement was justified in a care home. This was doubtless correct, but it was a pity that the court did not base its decision on the question of whether the employers had a duty to make reasonable accommodation of her religious beliefs.

Catholic Adoption Agencies

Another area where religious views have come into conflict with discrimination law is that of adoption agencies. It was the practice of Catholic adoption agencies to exclude same-sex couples from consideration as adoptive parents, in accordance with Roman Catholic teaching, and it appeared that this was of little if any importance in practice as same-sex couples wishing to adopt did not apply to these agencies. Despite this, the Equality Act (Sexual Orientation) Regulations 2007 made the policy of Catholic adoption agencies unlawful although, as a minor concession, they were given a year's grace to comply. The matter was complicated by the fact that Catholic adoption agencies operate as Roman Catholic charities but they felt that if they made their services available to same-sex couples they could not, as a matter of Roman Catholic canon law, operate as Roman Catholic charities. They would have to sever their links with the Church, lose Church funding and close. Naturally they did not wish to do so and in a number of cases challenged the legislation, but with very little success.

For instance Catholic Care, of the Diocese of Leeds, whilst accepting that religious conviction alone could not in law justify the denial of its adoption services to same-sex couples, argued that the proposed discrimination was proportionate to achieving a legitimate aim[14] because same-sex couples would be able to access services from other voluntary adoption agencies and local authorities. In addition, unless it was permitted to discriminate, it would no longer be able to raise the voluntary income needed to run its adoption service – and if it had to close, that would of itself reduce the overall provision of adoption services and the number of children placed with adoptive families. The court rejected this and held that, although same-sex couples could seek access to adoption services elsewhere, that would not stop them from feeling discriminated against nor remove the harm to the general promotion of equality of treatment for heterosexuals and homosexuals.[15]

However, in Scotland, a Roman Catholic charity, St Margaret's, has fared better, but here the charity was not solely an adoption charity and it did allow adoption by couples in civil partnerships, although they were given lower priority than married couples. It was held that as St Margaret's was a religious organisation, all its activities had to be considered and so the Office of the Scottish Charity Regulator should have considered all the activities of the charity – including those unrelated to adoption – then weighed the benefit to the public from these with the disbenefit from its policy of preferring married couples.[16]

How unnecessary all of this was! No Christian can condone discrimination on the grounds of sexual orientation but, equally, all Christians must insist that they have a right not to be discriminated against on the grounds of their beliefs. The matter could easily have been solved by giving charities who had a strongly-felt objection to adoption by same-sex couples an exemption from these provisions and, if necessary, made this subject to review after a certain period to ensure that there was no actual discrimination against same-sex couples, as they could go to other agencies. Thus there would have been a reasonable accommodation of religious belief with no actual detriment suffered by anyone.

Although the above discussion has been concerned with the detailed impact of discrimination law on Christians it is impossible not to note in conclusion the profound impact that the advent of discrimination law has had on the place of Christianity in this country. As Sir Terence Etherton has said: 'What is clear, however, is the extraordinary distance that the law has travelled in barely half a century. It has moved from a Christian-centred body of law with no anti-discrimination legislation to one of neutrality towards all religions or beliefs and a complex framework of civil and criminal anti-discrimination legislation'.[17]

Charity Law

In 1962, a case came before the courts (*Neville Estates v. Madden*) involving a synagogue at Catford in South East London. There were several issues but the one which concerns us was the question of whether the synagogue was set up for charitable purposes. Charitable status has always been important to religious, as well as other bodies, as it confers various tax advantages, such as, today, the right to take advantage of the gift-aid plan, and it confers a degree of public recognition. Religious charities (of which there are 32,000) received 14% of the total money given to charity by the public in the UK, amounting to nearly £1.5 billion in 2014, ahead of medical causes – accounting for 13% of money donated – children's charities (12%), and overseas causes (12%).[18]

In order for an organization to be considered a 'Charity', it must be established for charitable purposes and there must be some degree of public benefit. The problem with the Catford synagogue was that there were few members and so where was the public benefit? This did not trouble the court as the judge, Mr Justice Cross, observed that: '... the court is, I think, entitled to assume that some benefit accrues to the public from the attendance at places of worship of persons who live in this world and mix with their fellow citizens. As between different religions the law stands neutral, but it assumes that any religion is at least likely to be better than none.' Here then, in 1962, is a striking statement of the value of religion.

In fact, the members of the Catford synagogue were more fortunate than the nuns of the Carmelite Priory at St. Charles Square in London. In the well-known case of *Gilmour v. Coats* in 1949, the court had to consider a gift by will to the nuns, and the legal issue was whether the activities of the Priory were charitable, as only then could it be valid. The problem was that this was a contemplative order where the nuns engaged in no works outside the convent. But surely their prayers were for the public benefit? Perhaps so, but how could this be proved? The answer was that one cannot prove in court that prayers have been answered. One of the judges, Lord Simonds, put it this way: 'The faithful must embrace their faith believing what they cannot prove. The court can only act on proof'. Here was the difference from the members of the Catford synagogue: they went out into the world, one assumes edifying it by their presence; the nuns, in effect, stayed at home. Nevertheless it does seem that the nuns were harshly treated.

These two cases show that the courts did recognise religion *in itself* as a valid object of charity but that attempting to evaluate the extent to which religion promoted any measurable public benefit was fraught with difficulties.

The law had been clear until the Charities Act of 2006[19] when problems began to appear, caused by:

(a) Muddled drafting of that part of the Charities Act which concerned public benefit.
(b) What seemed to many to be an unsympathetic attitude on the part of the Charity Commission, especially to religious charities.

The muddled drafting was simply this: in the 2006 Act, Parliament declared that there was no longer any presumption that any purpose, including of course religious purposes, were for the public benefit. This by itself seemed to annul the approach of Mr Justice Cross in the case of the Catford synagogue where he assumed 'that any religion is at least likely to be better than none.' However, the Act then went on to say that all previous case law, including the cases mentioned above, was not affected. This meant that there was still a presumption, based on these cases, that religion was presumed to be for the public benefit.

The Charity Commission took the line that religions now had to prove that they existed for the public benefit and issued detailed guidance[20] on how this could be shown. In most cases churches will not find the question of public benefit a problem as they are willing to admit all to their services, and the performance of baptisms, weddings and funerals surely counts as beneficial to the public. However, some small religious groups could fall foul of this requirement, and one that did so was the Preston Down Trust, which runs meeting halls for the Exclusive Brethren in Torquay, Paignton and Newton Abbot. The 'Exclusive Brethren' is a Christian denomination who have no fellowship with those outside. They affix a small sign to their meeting hall stating that it is a place of public worship to satisfy the law, but little else gives its function as a church away. Thus they are not involved in the community at large, keeping themselves as separate as they can from the world.

The Charity Commission refused to grant the Trust charitable status on the ground that there was insufficient evidence of public benefit, as the Exclusive Brethren's practice of 'separation from evil' resulted in a moral and physical separation from the wider community. The Commission's decision document said that it had heard allegations of harsh disciplinary practices for minor transgressions and people being cut off from the community, and there had been claims that threats of legal action were made against people who spoke out against the Brethren, and those who leave 'are ostracised and consequently treated differently from other members of the public'.

This decision was seen by some as an attempt by the Charity Commission to use the notion of public benefit to advance a left-wing, secularist anti-religion agenda. Speaking in the House of Commons on 13 November 2012, Fiona Bruce, MP, said: 'It would be wrong of me to try to divine what is in the minds of the charity commissioners in that way, but we are perhaps seeing a clash between what we might call a secular liberal society and the traditional society that we have seen in our country up until now, which has respected the role of religions, particularly the Christian Church, over many centuries.' There was also a feeling among some that this secularist line was pursued by the then Chair, Dame Suzi Leather.

However, the Charity Commission then changed its mind, apparently as a result of evidence that the trust had 'demonstrated a willingness to make amends and to do what it could as a Christian organisation to ensure, as far as it was consistent with its religious beliefs, that it would act with Christian compassion in the future', particularly in respect of its disciplinary practices and in its relations with former members of the Brethren.[21]

What does this episode tell us about the relations of Christians with the State?

First, by drawing the attention of churches to the fact that they need to have an element of reaching out to the public, one could say that the Commission has actually done religion a service by reminding us all that we must not close our doors on the world. All mainstream churches do show this degree of openness anyway and so will have nothing to fear from this approach. However, although many Christians will find the attitude of the Exclusive Brethren unacceptable to say the least, what does give cause for concern is another change in attitudes: from that of Mr Justice Cross in the case of *Neville Estates v. Madden* in 1962 to that of the Charity Commission today. Here the Commission did not start from the premise that religion by itself is beneficial to the public and instead, both in the Preston Down case and in its guidance, has attempted to define what many Christians would say was indefinable: how can a religion be of benefit to the public? It is really nonsense to try to do this. Instead the Charity Commission would have been on firmer ground if it had rested its decision to refuse charitable status to the Preston Down Trust simply on its particular practices.

The Government did not accept the recommendation of the House of Commons Public Administration Committee that there should be a statutory definition of public benefit: this is regrettable as any ensuing debate would have enabled Christians to argue for the reinstatement of the principle of Mr Justice Cross that at least: 'any religion is at least likely to be better than none' and that religious charities should be presumed to be for the public benefit. If not, then the secularists will have won another victory.

As a footnote to this discussion, one wonders what the implications are of the decision of the Supreme Court mentioned above that one of the chapels of the Church of Scientology was a place of religious worship. The Charity Commission had, in 1999, rejected the application for charitable status of this Church on the grounds that it was not a religion and did not advance the public benefit.

The Charity Commission has now said that the Supreme Court decision could affect the meaning of religion and religious worship in the context of charity law and said it was considering the ruling: 'Although this Supreme Court judgment did not directly concern the meaning of charity, it affects the legal meaning of religion and religious worship. These have the potential to affect their meaning in charity law. The Commission is considering the impact of the judgment in that context.'[22] One might ask though: now that the Commission has agreed to register the Preston Down Trust, can it say no to the scientologists?

Notes

1   See later in this chapter.
2   See Chapter 3 for his remarks in full.
3   M. Volf, *A Public Faith* (Grand Rapids: Brazos Press, 2011), p. 101.
4   In the *Law of Religious Organisations* (Oxford: Oxford University Press, 2011), pp. 133–134.
5   See remarks of Sir Terence Etherton, Chancellor of the High Court in 'Religion, the Rule of Law and Discrimination' in the *Ecclesiastical Law Journal*, 16, 3 (2014) at p. 272.
6   G. Pitt, 'Taking Religion Seriously', *Industrial Law Journal*, 42, 4 (2013), pp. 398–408.
7   This is considered in detail in Chapter 6.
8   See the detailed critique of this decision by R. Sandberg, *Law and Religion* (Cambridge: Cambridge University Press, 2011), pp. 90–94.
9   R. Ahdar and I. Leigh, *Religious Freedom and the Liberal State* (Oxford: Oxford University Press, 2013), p. 171.
10 See F. Cranmer, 'Accommodating Religion in the Workplace – or Maybe Not? A Note on Chaplin, Eweida, Ladale and McFarlane', *Law and Justice*, 170 (2013), pp. 67–76, for a full account of these decisions.
11 In *Religious Freedom, Religious Discrimination and the Workplace* (Oxford: Hart Publishing, 2008), especially pp. 220–225.
12 G. Pitt, 'Taking Religion Seriously', *Industrial Law Journal*, 42(4), (2013), pp. 398–408.
13 In a lecture entitled 'Religion and Sexual Orientation' delivered at Yale Law School on 7 March 2014 and available on the website of the Supreme Court at http://supremecourt.uk/news/speeches.html
14 Note the terminology here: the issue was one of indirect discrimination and so could be justified.
15 This case is known as *Catholic Care (Diocese of Leeds) v. Charity Commission for England and Wales* (2012).
16 This case is known as *St Margaret's Children and Family Care Society v. Office of the Scottish Charity Regulator* (2014).
17 Sir Terence Etherton in 'Religion, the Rule of Law and Discrimination', in the *Ecclesiastical Law Journal*, 16 (3), (2014), pp. 265–282, at p. 282. The criminal aspect of anti-discrimination legislation is relevant in areas such as freedom of speech and was considered in Chapter 11.
18 *Annual UK Giving Report*, published each year by the Charities Aid Foundation (CAF) and the National Council for Voluntary Organisations, based on figures supplied by the Office for National Statistics.
19 The Act is now the Charities Act 2011 but this merely replaces the provisions of the 2006 Act with regard to the matters under discussion. It was the 2006 Act which made the changes.
20 This detailed guidance is, at the time of writing (August 2015) under review.
21 The decision of the Charity Commission is available on its website at www.charitycommission.gov.uk
22 See Third Sector: www.thirdsector.co.uk/news/1Note 2224712? (accessed 2 February 2014).

Chapter 13

Conclusion:
A Future for Religion in Public Life?

'And we, shall we be faithless?
Shall hearts fail, hands hang down?
Shall we evade the conflict,
and cast away our crown?'

(Edward Plumptre 1821–1891)

Introduction

The rousing words quoted above, the opening of the fifth verse of
the hymn 'Thy Hand O God Has Guided', were written by a
Kentish vicar, later Dean of Wells, in 1889, at a time when the
Christian view of the world held a dominant place in the life of this
country. Of course it does not do so now but, as this book has tried
to show, this is no reason to be downhearted or tentative in the
promotion of our faith in the public life of our country. Many
Christians do unfortunately give the impression of hands 'hanging
down' and 'evading the conflict'. Instead we must argue for the
continuing relevance of Christian teaching and point out how
much of our law is in fact built on the precepts of Christ. In particular we must stress the place of reason, not secular reason but
reason linked to faith, as well as the natural law as the touchstone
against which the validity of secular law is to be measured. In this
way we shall indeed reach that 'better grace' to which this hymn
goes on to refer.

Is Christianity in Danger?

At the conclusion of this book, we need to answer, if we can, the
question of whether Christianity is indeed in danger. George

Carey, the former Archbishop of Canterbury, and his son Andrew, in their book *We Don't Do God,*[1] refer to the contention of the Scottish theologian Lesslie Newbigin that, although the churches can accept plurality, they cannot accept pluralism. Thus, although there is nothing wrong in a society where there is a plurality of beliefs, and indeed many would say that Christianity is healthier in that situation, where there is pluralism there is a society where all truth is subjective and there is no right and wrong. This Christians cannot accept. Not only this but Newbigin also saw what lay behind the call to 'secularisation': the stated aim not to grant privileges to any religion can be simply a front for an attempt to do away with religion altogether, and we have seen in Chapter 9 of this book how there are suggestions that religious faith of any kind should not have its voice heard in public but be confined to private devotions.

Are Christians Persecuted in Britain Today?

Rupert Shortt in his book *Christianophobia, How the Global Oppression of Christians is Being Ignored,*[2] argues that, by comparison with other countries where there is real persecution and Christians are, for instance, tortured for their beliefs, Christians in Britain are not persecuted. On this basis, that is certainly true. George and Andrew Carey, in their book, agree but they do point to the fact that: 'Christians feel hemmed in as never before by often well-meaning legislation which they believe has had the unintended consequence of restricting liberties that have been taken for granted for centuries'.[3] We have seen examples of this in this book and, although the word 'persecution' might be thought too strong for what happens in this country, what other term would we apply to, for example, Lilian Ladele who, as we saw in Chapter 12, can no longer practise her profession as a civil registrar because of her religious beliefs? The same could be said of many others mentioned in this book. Whether or not we use the term 'persecution' in relation to Christians, there is no doubt that a rebalancing exercise is needed to assert Christian values in relation to the law and so in relation to the State.

This is a book on the theme of Christians and the State. How, then, shall Christianity ensure that its mission of preaching the Gospel can be carried out in a world where, certainly in Western Europe, this seems to be beset with increasing challenges? This is what we turn to consider in these concluding reflections.

A Three-Point Programme

I propose a three-point programme of action to deal with the place of religion in the public sphere.

The first is for the churches to campaign vigorously to establish their right not only to be heard in debates in the public sphere, but also for their right to seek to influence the content of legislation. The Catholic Bishops Conference in their recent document, *Choosing the Common Good*, put it well: 'The right to religious freedom means the right to live by faith, within the reasonableness of the common good, and to act by faith in the common forum'.[4]

In many areas, acting by faith in the common forum will accord with what many non-believers would agree with. For example in debates on the environment, the continuing scandal of avoidable poverty and the role of peace-making initiatives in conflicts, the churches often reflect what thoughtful non-believers say. In other cases it can be argued that the language of debate is enriched by the religious contribution. One thinks of the use of the word 'sacred' in debates on the beginning and end of life as distinct from the more secular word 'dignity'. But, and here is the awkward point, there are areas where the religious voice may conflict with the prevailing secular one. This is not only in obvious areas such as abortion and euthanasia but in, for example, the debate on the treatment of newly-arrived immigrant minorities. It is at precisely this point that we need to insist on our right to seek to influence the actual content of legislation with our distinctive contribution based not only on our beliefs but on the fact that faith values are group values in contrast to the individualism which characterises so much of secularism.

Secondly, there needs to be recognition that churches should be granted the right, under general principles of law including the Human Rights Act, to have their own personal legal systems in some areas. This is not quite what the Archbishop of Canterbury may have been arguing for in his lecture on 7 February 2008, 'Law in England: a religious perspective',[5] but to a much more limited degree.

The recognition which I am arguing for already exists to some extent. For example, under the Divorce (Religious Marriages) Act 2002, where a marriage has been entered into under Jewish religious usages and under British law, the courts may refuse to issue a decree of divorce unless the parties have co-operated in ensuring that the marriage will also be dissolved according to

Jewish religious usages. By contrast the Government is persisting in attempts to impose employment status on all clergy of all denominations despite objections from many of them. A system of personal law would mean that such matters were left to the churches themselves. However, as I argued in Chapter 2, it would be unhealthy for the State and religious bodies if this became a wholesale opting out of national law, and religious bodies retreated into themselves and amongst their followers, and used their own laws in areas such as family and inheritance disputes. What needs to be looked at are the precise ways in which some limited opting-out by religious bodies from the legal system could work.

The final item should be the conclusion of what would be, in effect, a concordat between all religious groups and the State setting out the respective rights and duties of each other. Thus it would deal with, for example, the rights of churches and other faith groups to manifest their beliefs, engage in evangelisation, and to run their own schools, hospitals and so forth, without interference from the State. It may be objected that the Human Rights Act already deals with some of these matters but it does so only by means of one article in the European Convention, whereas I propose a comprehensive settlement of all questions affecting the relationship between Church and State.

The danger here is, of course, obvious and is precisely that which the Catholic Church fell into when it concluded the concordat with Hitler's Germany in 1933. In return for the grant of certain rights to the Church, the Catholic Centre party in Germany agreed to dissolve itself and, as Michael Burleigh puts it in '*The Third Reich*': Hitler viewed the Catholic Church as restricted to 'cultic and caritative functions'. Any accommodation between the State and the churches must expressly guarantee the rights of the churches to take part in, and influence, public debate on the lines indicated above.

But where would this leave Establishment? On a personal view, but speaking, I suspect, for many Catholics, I greatly value the contribution made by the Church of England to national life and debate and would be loath to see its special position go. There would, in fact, be no need for dis-establishment to be a consequence of a new settlement along the lines I propose, as the guarantees to be given to all churches and faith groups would not affect the position of the Church of England in our constitution. However there is no doubt that the very existence of establishment is a stick used by secularists to beat us all and, if the end of establishment is the price to pay for a settlement which would guarantee the place of religion in both public and private life in this country then I, for one, would, with reluctance, pay it.

There would be one incidental but, I suggest, great benefit. Parties to the 'concordat' would not, of course be only the Catholic Church nor even just Christian Churches but non- Christian ones too. This would naturally include Islam and could remove that sense of isolation from the mainstream of religious and political life felt by Muslims. Surely no government could ignore such an opportunity and thus, the tide of militant secularism would be neatly turned.

In conclusion, what above all is vital is that Christians have both the courage to challenge popular ideas and the discernment to recognise when in fact those popular ideas are in fact right. What we must not do is to adopt some easygoing attitude and merely shrug our shoulders when confronted with some challenge to Christian belief and say in a comfortable manner: 'Oh well, that's the way it is' and pass on. In Robert Bolt's play *'A Man for All Seasons'*, Will Roper, Thomas More's son-in-law, changes his religious beliefs in the opposite direction to the way that the religious wind is blowing. Thomas More resignedly remarks that this is a characteristic of the Roper family and says: 'Now let him swim with the current and he'll turn round and start swimming in the other direction'.[6] There is no need for Christians to be Ropers and automatically go against the tide but we have too many anti-Ropers in the Christian camp who cannot bear not to be *with* the tide. It is never the place of Christians to seek an easy life and when our fundamental beliefs are under threat by a rising tide of secularism, then our task is even more difficult, but we must use our faith and our reason to ensure a visible expression of our beliefs.

As it happens, these final lines are being written on the Feast of Pope St Gregory the Great who sent St Augustine of Canterbury to England on a mission to convert the Anglo-Saxons. It can be claimed that it was St Augustine, inspired by St Gregory, who was the first person to link Church and State in this country when he baptised King Ethelbert of Kent in 597. Through all the years since, Christianity has played a major role in the public life of this country, shaping its laws and institutions and putting forth a Christian view of how the State should behave. We too must constantly put forward the view that the Christian message, as applied to public life, is one that is not only valid in this country but also enriches societies in all places and in all nations, in all cultures and in all climes. Nor should we be fainthearted in our task for, as the final verse of the hymn quoted at the head of this chapter puts it:

> 'Thy mercy will not fail us,
> nor leave thy work undone;
> with thy right hand to help us,
> the victory shall be won.'

Notes

1   A. Carey and G. Carey (Oxford: Monarch Books, 2012), pp.143–144.
2   London: Rider Books, 2012.
3   P. 17.
4   Catholic Bishops Conference of England and Wales, *Choosing the Common Good* (Stoke-on-Trent: Alive Publishing, 2010), p. 19.
5   See Chapter 2.
6   This story does not seem to be historical although Roper certainly did change from Lutheranism back to Catholicism. See W. Roper and N. Harpsfield (ed. E. Reynolds), *Lives of St. Thomas More* (London and New York: J.M. Dent & Sons, 1963), pp. 100–103.

Bibliography

Ahdar, R. and Leigh, I., *Religious Freedom and the Liberal State* (Oxford: Oxford University Press, 2013).

Allen, C.K., *Law in the Making*, 7th ed. (Oxford: Oxford University Press, 1964).

Allison, S., 'Stair and Natural Law', *Law and Justice*, 169 (2012), pp. 189–209.

Annual UK Giving Report, published each year by the Charities Aid Foundation (CAF) and the National Council for Voluntary Organisations.

Aquinas T., *Summa theologiae* (Rome: Leonine ed., 1882–1948).

Aristotle, *Nicomachean Ethics*, trans. D. Ross (Oxford: Oxford University Press, 1925).

Aristotle, *Politics*, trans. B. Jowett (Oxford: Oxford University Press, 1905).

Ashley, J., 'Cardinals, back off from this war with women and state', *The Guardian*, June 4, 2007.

Augustine (Saint), *The City of God* (London: Penguin Books 1972).

Avis, P., *Church, State and Establishment* (London: SPCK, 2001).

Baker, J., *A History of English Law*, 4th ed. (Oxford: Oxford University Press, 2002).

Bano, S., 'In Pursuit of Religious Diversity', in *Ecclesiastical Law Journal*, 10 (2008), pp. 283–309.

Bingham, T., *The Rule of Law* (London: Penguin Books, 2011).

Bishop, J., 'Natural law and ethics: some second thoughts', *New Blackfriars*, September 1996, pp. 381–389.

Bishop, J., 'A Question of Torture', *Law and Justice*, 159 (2007), pp. 103–113.

Blanche, N., (ed.), *A Time for Triumphs, Scottish Movers and Shakers of the Twentieth Century* (Edinburgh: Saint Andrew Press, 2005).

British Humanist Associations, *'Right to Object? Conscientious*

Objection and Religious Conviction' (London: BHA, 2011).

British Medical Journal, 5 July 2014 (vol. 349, issue 7965).

Brownlie, K., *Conscience and Conviction: The Case for Civil Disobedience* (Oxford: Oxford University Press, 2012).

Butterfield, H., *Christianity and History* (London: Collins, 1949).

Capland, A. and McIlroy, D., ' "Speaking Up" – Defending and Delivering Access to Justice', (London: Theos, 2015).

Carey, A. and Carey, G., *We Don't Do God* (Oxford: Monarch Books, 2012).

Cargill Thompson, W., *The Political Thought of Martin Luther* (Brighton: The Harvester Press, 1984).

Cartabia, M. and Simoncin, A., (eds), *Pope Benedict's Legal Thought* (Cambridge: Cambridge University Press, 2015).

Catechism of the Catholic Church, English translation for the United Kingdom (London: Geoffrey Chapman, 1994).

Catholic Bishops Conference of England and Wales, *The Common Good and the Catholic Church's Social Teaching* (1996). together-forthecommongood.co.uk/.../whats-the-common-good.html?

Catholic Bishops Conference of England and Wales, *Choosing the Common Good* (Stoke-on-Trent: Alive Publishing, 2010).

Chadwick, O., *The Early Church,* Vol. One of the *Penguin History of the Church* (London: Penguin Books, 1967).

Chaplin, J. and Spencer, N., (eds), *God and Government* (London: SPCK, 2009).

Chaplin, J., 'The Place of Religious Arguments for Law Reform in a Secular State' in *Law and Justice,* 162 (2009), pp. 18–35.

Chaplin, J., *Talking God, the Legitimacy of Religious Public Reasoning* (London: Theos Report, 2008).

Compendium of the Social Doctrine of the Church (Vatican: Pontifical Council for Justice and Peace, 2004).

Coplestone, F., *Aquinas* (London: Pelican Books, 1955).

Cranmer, F., Accommodating Religion in the Workplace – or Maybe Not? A Note on Chaplin, Eweida, Ladale and McFarlane, *Law and Justice,* 170 (2013), pp. 67–76.

Cranmer, F. and Oliva, J., 'Church-State Relationships: An Overview' in *Law and Justice,* 162 (2009), pp. 4–17.

Dante, *Purgatorio,* trans. A. Mandelbaum (London: Everyman's Library, 1995).

Davie, G., *Religion in Britain since 1945: Believing without Belonging* (Oxford: Blackwell, 1994).

D'Costa, D., Evans, M., Modood, T., Rivers, J., (eds), *Religion in a Liberal State* (Cambridge: Cambridge University Press, 2013).

D'Entrèves, A., *Natural Law*, 2nd ed. (London: Hutchinson University Library, 1970).

de Silva, A., (ed.), *The Last Letters of Thomas More* (Grand Rapids, Michigan and Cambridge, UK: Eerdmans Publishing Co, 2000).

Devlin, P. (Lord Devlin), *The Enforcement of Morals* (Oxford: Oxford University Press, 1965).

Dicey, A., *Introduction to the Study of the Law of the Constitution*, 10th ed. (London: Macmillan, 1959).

Dicey, A., *Law and Public Opinion in England*, 2nd. ed. (London: Macmillan,1963).

Doe, N. and Sandberg, R., 'The Changing Criminal Law of Religion' in *Law and Justice*, 161 (2008), pp. 88–97.

Doe, N., *Fundamental Authority in Late Medieval English Law* (Cambridge: Cambridge University Press, 1990).

Doe, N., *Law and Religion in Europe* (Oxford: Oxford University Press, 2011).

Doe, N., 'The Notion of a National Church: A Juridical Framework' in *Law and Justice*, 149 (2002), pp. 77–91.

Duddington, J., 'The Employment Status of the Clergy: Preston Starts to Unravel' in *Law and Justice*, 171 (2013), pp. 79–94.

Duddington, J., 'God, Caesar and the Employment Status of Ministers of Religion' in *Law and Justice*, 159 (2007), pp. 129–135.

Duffy, E., *Saints and Sinners: A History of the Popes* (New Haven and London: Yale University Press, 1997).

Dwyer, C., *Religion and the Law, the Current Position in England* (Chichester: Otter Memorial Paper Number 30, University of Chichester, 2012).

Early Christian Writings: the Apostolic Fathers, M. Staniforth, (trans.) (London: Penguin Books, 1968).

Eberle, E., *Church and State in Western Europe* (Aldershot: Ashgate, 2011).

Esau, A., 'Islands of Exclusivity: Religious Organisations and Employment Discrimination', *UBC L Rev*, 33 (2000), pp. 719–827.

Etherton, T., 'Religion, the Rule of Law and Discrimination' *Ecclesiastical Law Journal*, 16 (3) (2014), pp. 265–282.

Fair Employment Monitoring Report (Belfast: Equality Commission for Northern Ireland, 2004).

Finnis, J., *Human Rights and the Common Good,* Vol. III of the *Collected Essays of John Finnis* (Oxford: Oxford University Press, 2011).

Finnis, J., *Natural Law and Natural Rights,* 2nd ed. (Oxford: Oxford University Press, 2011).

Finnis, J., 'Natural Law', *Reason in Action,* Vol. I of the *Collected Essays of John Finnis* (Oxford: Oxford University Press, 2011).

Finnis, J., *Religion and Public Reasons,* Vol. V of the *Collected Essays of John Finnis* (Oxford: Oxford University Press, 2011).

Flannery, A., *The Basic Sixteen Documents; Vatican Council II* (Dublin: Dominican Publications, 1995).

Gardner, S. and Davidson, K., 'The Supreme Court on Family Homes', *Law Quarterly Review,* 128 (2012), pp.178–183.

Gollwitzer, H. K., Kuhn, K. and Schnieder, S., (eds), *Dying We Live: Letters written by prisoners in Germany on the verge of execution* (London: Fontana Books, 1958).

Grudem, W., *Politics According to the Bible* (Grand Rapids: Zondervan, 2010).

Hailsham, Lord, *A Sparrow's Flight* (London: Fontana 1990).

Hale, B. (Lady Hale), *'Religion and Sexual Orientation'* delivered at Yale Law School on 7 March 2014. http://supremecourt.uk/news/speeches.html

Hart, H., *Law Liberty and Morality* (Oxford: Oxford University Press, 1963).

International Theological Commission, *In Search of a Universal Ethic: A New Look at the Natural Law* (London: CTS, 2012).

Helmholz, R., 'Natural Law in the Trial of Thomas More' in *Thomas More's Trial by Jury* (Woodbridge, Suffolk: The Boydell Press, 2011).

HM Government, *The Governance of Britain,* Cm 7170 (London: TSO, 2007).

Jennings, J., (ed.), *Benedict XVI and Blessed John Henry Newman, The State Visit September 2010, The Official Record* (London: CTS, 2010).

Jones, D., *The Soul of the Embryo* (London: Continuum, 2004).

Kelly, J., *Dictionary of the Popes* (Oxford: Oxford University Press, 1986).

Kirwan, M., *Political Theology* (London: Darton, Longman and Todd, 2008).

Krieg, R., Catholic *Theologians in Nazi Germany* (New York: Continuum Publishing, 2004).

Laing, J. and Wilcox, R., (eds), *A Natural Law Reader* (Oxford: Blackwells, 2013).

Lawrence, T., (ed.), *Good News for the Public Square* (London; Lawyers Christian Fellowship, 2014).

Leigh, I., The European Court of Human Rights and Religious Neutrality in *Religion in a Liberal State* (D. D'Costa, M. Evans, T. Modood, J. Rivers, eds, Cambridge: Cambridge University Press, 2013).

Livingstone, T., *George Pell, Defender of the Faith Down Under* (San Francisco: Ignatius Press, 2002).

Llewelyn, R., *Julian Then and Now*, Annual Julian Lecture (Norwich: The Julian Centre, 1997).

Locke, J., *An Essay Concerning Human Understanding* (London: Penguin Books, 1997).

Locke, J., *Two Treatises on Government*, ed. M. Goldie (London: Dent, 1993).

Longley, B., Archbishop of Birmingham, 'Secularism can help, spread of the Gospel, says Archbishop' *The Tablet*, 11 February 2012, p. 33.

Mackay, J. (Lord Mackay), 'Does Establishment have a Future?' *Law and Justice*, 170 (2013), pp. 7–18.

MacCulloch, D., *Reformation, Europe's House Divided* (London: Penguin Books, 2004).

Macquarrie, J., *Principles of Christian Theology* (London: SCM Press, 1966).

Malatry, J., *Faith Through Reason* (Leominster: Gracewing, 2006).

Malatry, J., *When Might Becomes Human Right* (Leominster: Gracewing, 2007).

Martinez-Touron, J., 'Institutional Religious Symbols, State Neutrality and Protection of Minorities in Europe', Law *and Justice*, 171 (2013), pp. 21–51.

McCabe, H., *God Still Matters* (London and New York: Continuum, 2005).

McIlroy, D., *A Biblical View of Law and Justice* (Milton Keynes: Paternoster Press, 2004).

McIlroy, D., '*A Christian Understanding of Human Rights*', a lecture delivered at Swansea University on 20 March 2013 and available at https://lawcf.org/resources/.../Christian-understandings-of-human-rights

McIlroy, D., 'Does the law need a moral basis?' in *Religion and Law* (London: Theos, 2012).

McIlroy, D., 'Human Rights Theory: Fit For Purpose, Fundamentally Flawed or Reformable?', *Law and Justice*, 173 (2014), pp. 129–144.

Menski, W., Hindu Law, *Law and Justice*, 164 (2013), p. 64.

Meyendorf, J., *The Byzantine Legacy and the Orthodox Church* (New York: SVS Press, 2001).

Micklem, N., *Law and the Laws, being the marginal comments of a theologian* (London: Sweet and Maxwell, 1952).

Micklem, N., 'The Theology of Law', *Law and Justice*, 172 (2014), pp. 4–9.

Nazir-Ali, M., *Triple Jeopardy for the West* (London: Bloomsbury Publishing, 2012).

Newbigin, L., 'The Welfare State: a Christian Perspective', *Theology*, 87 (May 1995).

Nichols, A., *From Hermes to Benedict XVI: Faith and Reason in Modern Catholic Thought* (Leominster: Gracewing, 2009).

Nichols, A., *The Realm: An Unfashionable Essay on the Conversion of England* (Oxford: Family Publications, 2008).

Nichols, A., *The Thought of Benedict XVI, An Introduction to the Theology of Joseph* Ratzinger (London: Burns and Oates, 2007).

Norman, J., *Edmund Burke* (London: William Collins, 2013).

Norwich, J., *A Short History of Byzantium* (London: Penguin Books, 1988).

O'Donovan, O., *The Ways of Judgment* (Grand Rapids: Eerdmans, 2005).

Parker, G., *Empire, War and Faith in Early Modern Europe* (London: Penguin Books, 2002).

Passalecq, G. and Suchecky, B., *The Hidden Encyclical of Pius XI* (New York: Harcourt Brace, 1997).

Patriarch Kirill of Moscow, *Freedom and Responsibility* (London: Darton, Longman and Todd, 2011).

Pitt, G., 'Taking Religion Seriously', *Industrial Law Journal* 42 (4) (2013), pp. 398–408.

Plato, *The Republic*, trans. H.D.P. Lee (Harmondsworth: Penguin Classics, 1955).

Plunkett, T., *A Concise History of the Common Law* (London: Butterworths, 1929).

Pollock, F., The History of the Law of Nature, an essay reprinted in *Jurisprudence and Legal Essays* (London: Macmillan, 1961).

Pope Benedict XVI, *Address of 18 April 2008 before the General Assembly of the United Nations Organisation in New York* (AAS 100, 2008).

Pope Benedict XVI, *Caritas in Veritate*.

Pope Benedict XVI, *Deus Caritas Est*.

Pope Benedict XVI, *The Fathers of the Church* (London: CTS 2008).

Pope Benedict XVI, *Jesus of Nazareth* (San Francisco: Ignatius Press 2011).

Pope Francis, *Evangelii Gaudium.*

Pope Gregory XVI, *In Supremo Apostalatus.*

Pope St John Paul II, *Dignities Humanae.*

Pope St John Paul II, *Dives et Misercordia.*

Pope St John Paul II, *Evangelium Vitae.*

Pope Leo XIII, *Immortale Dei.*

Pope Paul III, *Sublimis Deus.*

Pope Pius X1, *Quadragesimo Anno.*

Ratzinger, J., *Values in a Time of Upheaval* (San Francisco: Ignatius Press, 2006).

Rawls, J., *Theory of Justice,* revised edition (Oxford: Oxford University Press, 1999).

Rawls, J., *Political Liberalism* (New York: Columbia University Press 1993).

Report of the Committee on Homosexual Offence and Prostitution (the Wolfenden Committee), Cmnd. 247 (London: HMSO, 1957).

Rivers, J., *The Law of Organised Religions* (Oxford: Oxford University Press, 2010).

Robertson, G., 'We should be ashamed that this has happened', *The Guardian,* 22 August 2009.

Roper, W. and Harpsfield, N., (ed. E. Reynolds), *Lives of St. Thomas More* (London and New York: J.M. Dent & Sons, 1963).

Ross, J., 'A History of Torture' in *Torture,* K. Roth and M. Worden, eds (New York: The New Press, 2005).

Roth, K. and others, (eds), *Torture: A Human Rights Perspective* (New York: Human Rights Watch, 2005).

Sagovsky, N., *Christian Tradition and the Practice of Justice* (London: SPCK, 2008).

Sandberg, R. and Doe, N., 'Church-State Relations in Europe', *Religion Compass,* 1/5 (2007), pp. 561–578.

Sandberg, R., *Law and Religion* (Cambridge: Cambridge University Press, 2011).

Sandel, M., *Justice: What's the Right Thing to Do?* (London: Penguin, 2010).

Schnall, J., *The Regensburg Lecture* (South Bend, Indiana: St. Augustine's Press, 2007).

Schmidt, A., *How Christianity Changed the World* (Grand Rapids: Zondervan, 2004).

Scholder, K., *A Requiem for Hitler and Other New Perspectives on the*

German Church Struggle (London and Philadelphia: SCM Press, 1989).

Sewell, D., 'I was wrong: OFSTED is a real menace', *Catholic Herald*, 30, January 2015.

Shachar, A., *Multicultural Jurisdictions: Cultural Differences and Women's Rights* (Cambridge: Cambridge University Press, 2002).

Shorrt, R., *Christianophobia, How the Global oppression of Christians is being ignored* (London: Rider Books, 2012).

Sophocles, *Antigone*, E. F. Watling, (trans.) (Harmondsworth: Penguin, 1974).

Spencer, N., *Freedom and Order* (London: Hodder and Stoughton, 2011).

Spencer, N., (ed.), *Religion and Law*, (London: Theos, 2012).

Stenton, F., *Anglo-Saxon England* (Oxford: Clarendon Press, 1943).

Thompson, J., *Introducing Catholic Social Thought* (New York: Orbis Books. 2010).

Twomey, V., *Pope Benedict, the Conscience of our Age* (San Francisco: Ignatius Press 2007).

Uppsala Speaks, Section Reports of the World Council of Churches (Geneva: World Council of Churches, 1968).

Vallelly, P., The London Newman Lecture, *The Newman*, 74, May 2008, pp. 2–11.

Vickers, L., *Freedom, Religious Discrimination and the Workplace* (Portland, Oregon and Oxford: Hart Publishing, 2008).

Walsh, A., (trans.), *The Revelations of Divine Love of Julian of Norwich* (Wheathampstead: Antony Clarke Books, 1980).

Waltman, J., *Religious Free Exercise and Contemporary American Politics* (London and New York: Continuum, 2011).

Walvin. J., *A Short History of Slavery* (London: Penguin, 2007).

Ware, T., (Bishop Kallistos of Diokleia), *The Orthodox Church* (London: Penguin Books, 1997).

Warnock, M., *Dishonest to God: On Keeping Religion out of Politics* (London: Continuum, 2010).

Washington, J. M., (ed.), *A Testament of Hope: The Essential Writings of Martin Luther King, Jr.* (San Francisco: Harper and Row, 1986).

Williams, G., *Textbook of Criminal Law* (London: Stevens and Sons, 1983).

Williams, R., 'Civil and Religious Law in Perspective', *Ecclesiastical Law Journal*, 10 (3) (2008), pp. 262–282.

Williams, R., *Faith in the Public Square* (London: Bloomsbury Publishing, 2012).

Williams, S., *God and Caesar: Personal Reflections on Politics and Religion* (London: Continuum, 2003).

Wortley, B., (ed.), *The Spirit of the Common Law, a collection of the papers of Richard O'Sullivan* (Tenbury Wells: Fowler Wright Books, 1965).

Index of Cases

Alekseyev v. Russia (2010) Appl. nos. 4916/07, 25924/08 and 14599/09: 168–169

Beatty v. Gillbanks (1882) 9 QBD 308: 165

Bowman v. Secular Society (1917) AC 406: 50

Bull v. Hall (2013) UKSC 73: 194

Burns v. Burns (1983) EWCA Civ 4: 77–78

Christian Education SA v. Minister of Education (2000) (4) SA 757: 86

Copsey v. WWB Devon Clays Ltd (2005) EWCA Civ 932: 190

Engel v. Vitale (1962) 370 U.S. 421: 37

Eweida & Others v. United Kingdom: 181, 189–194

Forbes v. Eden (1867) Law Reports 1 Sc&D 568: 31

Gilmour v. Coats (1949) AC 426: 198–199

Goodridge v. Dept. of Public Health (2003) 798 N.E.2d 941 (Mass.): 130

Grainger v. Nicholson (2010) ICR 360: 180–181

Greater Glasgow Health Board v. Doogan and Another (2014) UKSC 68: 86–87, 92, 95, 189

Green v. City of Westminster Magistrates Court (2007) EWHC 2785 (Admin): 171

Hales v. Petit (1562) Pl Com 253: 69

Hammond v DPP (2004) EWHC 69 (Admin): 165–166

Heglibiston Establishment v. Heyman and Others (1977) 36 P&CR 351: 111

Inwards v. Baker (1965) 2 QB 29: 103

Janaway v. Salford Health Authority (1989) AC 537: 86

Jones v. Kernott [2011] UKSC 53: 84

Kohn v. Wagschal & Others (2007) All ER (D) 366: 53

Lautsi v. Italy (2011) Appl. no. 30814/06: 30, 61–63, 187

Leyla Sahin v. Turkey (2007) ECHR 819: 63

Marsh v. Chambers (1983) 463 U.S. 783: 37

Mba v. Mayor and Burgesses of the London Borough of Merton (2013) EWCA Civ 1562: 196

McFarlane v. Relate Avon Limited (2010) EWCA Civ 880: 50

Mouvement laïque québécois v. Saguenay (City) (2015) SCC 16: 37–38

Muhammad v. the Leprosy Mission International (2009) ET Case No. 2303459/09: 184

National Secular Society v. Bideford Town Council (2012) 2 All ER 1175: 38

Neville Estates v. Madden (1962) Ch. 832: 198, 201

Percy v. Church of Scotland Board of

National Mission (2005) UKHL
  73: 31
*President of the Methodist Conference v.
  Preston* (2013) UKSC 29: 32
Price v. Civil Service Commission (1978)
  1 All ER 1228: 183
R v. Brown (1993) 2 All ER 75: 115
R v. Chief Rabbi ex. p. Wachman (1993)
  2 All ER 249: 31
*R (on the application of Begum) v.
  Headteacher and Governors of
  Denbigh High School* (2007) 1 AC
  100: 191
*R (on the Application of Playfoot (a
  child)) v. Millais School Governing
  Body* (2007) EWHC 1698:
  189–190
*R (on the application of Nicklinson and
  another) v. Ministry of Justice*
  (2014) UKSC 38: 117–118
*R (on the application of Hodkin and
  another) v. Registrar General of
  Births, Deaths and Marriages*
  (2013) UKSC 77: 179–180
R v. Penguin Books (1961) Crim. LR
  176: 112
R v. Registrar General, ex. p. Segerdal
  (1970) 3 All ER 886: 179
R v. Taylor (1676) 1 Vent 293: 170
R v. Hetherington (1841) 4 St Tr (NS)
  563: 171
Reaney v. Hereford Diocesan Board of

Finance (2007) ET Case
  No.1602844/2006: 185–186
Redmond Bate v. DPP (2000) HRLR
  249: 165, 169–170
*Refah Partisi (The Welfare Party) and
  Others v. Turkey* (2003) 37 EHRR
  1: 132–133
Rogers v. Booth (1937) 2 All ER 751:
  37
*School District of Abington Township v.
  Schempp* (1963) 374 U.S. 203: 37
*Sharpe v. Worcester Diocesan Board of
  Finance Ltd and The Bishop of
  Worcester* (2015) EWCA Civ 399:
  32
Shaw v. Director of Public Prosecutions
  (1962) AC 220: 112
Shergill & others v. Khaira & others
  (2014) UKSC 33: 31
Smith v. Trafford Housing Trust (2012)
  EWHC 3221: 173
Stack v. Dowden (2007) UKHL 17: 50
*Streatfield v. London Philharmonic
  Orchestra* (2011) ET Case no.
  2390772/2011: 181
Town of Greece v. Galloway (2014)
  572 U.S. ___ (2014): 37
Upfill v. Wright (1911) 1 KB 506:
  110–111
Whitehouse v. Gay News Ltd, R v. Lemon
  (1979) AC 617: 170

Index of Statutes

Abortion Act 1967 3, 70, 79, 86, 91–92, 112, 124,135
Act in Restraint of Appeals 1532 48
Act of Supremacy 1535 16, 96
Arbitration Act 1996 52, 54

Care Act 2014 157, 187
Charities Act 2006 199
Charities Act 2011 75, 179
Church of Scotland Act 1921 31
Constitutional Reform Act 2005 55
Crime and Courts Act 2013 167
Criminal Justice and Immigration Act 2008 171

Employment Act 1989 91
Equality Act 2010 72, 86, 95, 141–142, 145, 173, 178, 182–185, 195

Human Fertilisation and Embryology Act 1990 70, 91, 135
Human Rights Act 1998 51, 146, 151, 156, 186

Legal Aid Sentencing and Punishment of Offenders Act 2012 107

Local Government Act 1972 38
Local Government (Religious etc. Observances) Act 2015 38

Marriage Law Amendment Act 1995 (Malta) 24–25
Methodist Church Act 1976 36
Methodist Church Union Act 1929 36
Military Service Act 1916 91
Minimum Wage Act 1998 71
Modern Slavery Act 2015 159
National Health Service (Family Planning) Act 1967 112

Places of Worship Registration Act 1855 180
Public Order Act 1986 166, 171
Racial and Religious Hatred Act 2006 171
Road Traffic Act 1988 91

Salvation Army Act 1931 36
Same-Sex Marriage Act 2013 133
Sexual Offences Act 1967 112
Suicide Act 1961 70–71, 116–117

Wills Act 1837 53

Index

Abortion 3, 10, 33, 60, 70–71, 79,
    85–86, 91–93, 95, 112, 119, 124,
    128–129, 135, 154, 175, 189, 195,
    205
Acacius, Patriarch of Constantinople
    11
Ahdar, Prof. Rex 136–137, 191
Althaus, Paul 9
Ambrose, St., Bishop of Milan 11
Anastasius, Emperor 12
Aquinas, Thomas, St.
    Conscience 88
    Human law 121
    Justice 100, 103
    Natural Law 60, 65–67, 69
    Reason 59
Ashley, Jackie 124
Atkinson, Rowan 167
Augustine of Canterbury, St. 207
Augustine of Hippo, St. 11
Austin, John 78
Autonomy
    Autonomy v. Communitarianism
      76–78
    Common Good 119
    Euthanasia 116, 118
    Human rights 155
    Medical ethics 76
    Morality 120
    Islamic principles 54
    Justice 101
    Personal autonomy 73, 100

    Reason 58
    Same-sex marriage 130
    State bodies 75
Avis, Paul 41

Baptist tradition 67
Becket, Thomas, Archbishop of
    Canterbury 16
Bede, The Venerable 45
Benedict VIII, Pope 13
Benedict XVI, Pope, on
    Conscience 60, 87–90
    Faith and Reason 56–61, 78
    Human rights 154–155
    Justice 59, 99–101, 126, 154
    Natural law 60, 78, 154
    Relativism 144
    Religion and politics 1, 9, 24, 27,
      126
    Subsidiarity 75
Bernard of Clairvaux, St. 15
Bland, Tony 119
Bonhoeffer, Dietrich 87
Bracton, Henry 46, 48, 54
Brown, Gordon 52, 128
Bruce, Fiona, MP 200
Burke, Edmund 73
Burleigh, Prof. Michael 57, 206

Caesaropapism 12–13
Calvin, John 17, 19–20, 26
Campbell-Savours, Lord Dale 61

Carey, Andrew 204
Carey, George, Bishop 203–204
Chadwick, Rev. Prof. Owen 11
Chalcedon, Council of 12
Charity Commission 199–201
Church and State relations in
  Denmark 18, 25–26, 34
  France 28, 39–40
  Germany 26–27, 206
  Iran 26
  Ireland, Republic of 25–26, 28
  Malta 24
  Scotland 31, 33, 35–36
  Turkey 28, 40
  USA 28, 38–39
Church of Scientology 179, 201
Common Good 8, 57, 69, 71–74, 76,
  78, 94, 100, 110, 119–121, 131,
  136, 144, 149, 155–156, 205
Conscience
  Aquinas, Thomas, St., on 88
  Catholic notion of 3
  Christian view of 8, 85–98
  Conscientious objection to a law
    85–87, 90–93
  Equity and 49, 95
  Human rights and freedom of 149
  McCabe, Rev. Herbert, on 87
  Natural law and 66
  Pope Benedict XVI, on 60, 87–90
  Protection of freedom of
    conscience under the
    European Convention on
    Human Rights 39, 62, 86,
    93–95, 151, 168, 188–189
  Universal Declaration of Human
    Rights and 151
Conti, Archbishop Mario 73
Coplestone, Frederick 60, 66
Cranmer, Frank 36, 40

Dante 58
Davis, David 167
Death Penalty 73–74
Devlin, Lord 113, 114
Dicey, Albert Venn 51, 108

Doe, Prof. Norman 29, 32
Doogan, Mary 85, 87
Dworkin, Prof. Ronald 119

Equity, as a system of law 49, 97, 102,
  103, 109
Erastian system 25
Establishment (of the Church of
  England) 30, 33–36, 40–41, 45,
  206–207
Ethelbert, King of Kent 207
Exclusive Brethren, The 199–200

Faulkner, Lord Charles 76, 118
Finnis, John 66, 69, 72, 87
Francis, Pope, on
  Christians in Public Debate 27,
    123,
  Death Penalty 74
  Natural Law 127
  Subjective truth 133

Gelasius I, Pope 14–15, 20
General Medical Council (GMC) 92,
  117
General Pharmaceutical Council 92
Glanvil, Ranulf de 46
Greene, Sir Wilfrid 49
Gregory the Great, St., Pope 207
Gregory V, Pope 15
Gregory VII, Pope 16
Gregory XVI, Pope 158
Grosch, Paul 146

Hailsham, Lord 105
Hale, Lady 195
Harris, Dr Evan 172, 175
Hart, Prof. Herbert 113–114, 122
Harris of Pentregarth, Lord 27
Henry II, King of England 16
Henry VII, King of England 48
Henry VIII, King of England 16,
  34–35, 48, 96
Henry IV, King of Germany 16
Hooker, Richard 32
Human Dignity 69–71, 74, 76, 121,

137, 144, 146, 153–154, 156, 159, 180
Human Rights
Conscience 91
Christian view of human rights 147–157
European Convention 3, 30, 39–40, 61–63, 86, 93–95, 117–118, 132, 140, 145, 151, 156, 168–170, 174, 177, 186–196
Human Dignity 14, 61,
Human Rights Act 1998 51, 54, 146, 151, 156, 186–187, 205
Justice 100–101, 106
Natural Law 49, 81, 149
Protestantism 149
Quebec Charter of Human Rights and Freedoms 38
Universal Declaration of Human Rights 150–152
Hume, Cardinal Basil 69

Innitzer, Cardinal Theodor, Archbishop of Vienna 125
Islam 190, 207
Ivan the Terrible, Tsar of Russia 14–15

Jackson, Robert 46
John XXIII, Pope 72, 140, 150, 152, 155, 162
Jones, Prof. David 12
Julian of Norwich 104–105
Justice
Access to justice 106–108
Aquinas, on 100–101, 103
Aristotle, on 102–103
Christian justice 47, 98–108, 153
Equity and justice 49, 102–103
Human and divine justice 19
Human rights and justice 100–101
McIlroy, David, on 102, 105
Mercy and justice 35, 104–106
Natural justice 159
Natural law and justice 46, 63, 66–67, 79–81, 89, 127, 149

Plato, on 100
Pope Benedict XVI, on 59, 99–101, 126, 154
Pope Francis, on 127
Pope John XXIII, on 72
Pope John Paul II, on 146
Rawls, John, on 101–102
Justinian, Emperor 12–13.

Kirill, Patriarch 14, 15, 21–22
Knowles, David 15

Langton, Stephen, Archbishop of Canterbury 47
Leather, Dame Suzi 200
Legal Positivism 78–80
Leigh, Prof. Ian 29–30, 136–137, 191
Leo X, Pope 35
Leo XIII, Pope 159
Liberalism 136–137
Llewelyn, Rev. Robert 104
Locke, John 57, 149
Luther, Martin 5, 17–19
Lutheran Church of Denmark 18
Lutheran States 18
Lyons, Michael 94

MacCulloch, Prof. Sir Diarmaid 23
Macdonald of River Glaven, Lord 168
Mackay, John 150
Mackay, Lord 35, 133
Macquarrie, John 68
McCabe Rev. Herbert 87
McIlroy, David 67, 72, 81, 105, 110, 120, 146, 149, 156
Marklow, Wendolyn 105
May, Theresa 167
Methodist Church 25, 36
Micklem, Rev. Nathaniel 79
Milan, Edict of 9
More, Thomas, St.
Conscience 87, 96
Christians and the State 16, 207
Faith and reason 48, 57–58
Natural law 48
Montesimo, Anton 147–148

Munby, Sir James 44, 45, 110, 114
Murphy-O'Connor, Cormac 71

Natural Law
  Aquinas 60, 65–67, 69
  Common Good 71–73, 131
  Conscience 60, 88–89
  Contraception 133–134
  Human Dignity 70–71
  Human Rights 51, 81, 146–147, 149, 154
  Pope Benedict XVI 60, 154
  Reason 48, 60, 63, 78, 203
  Relationships 74–76
  Theory 3, 10–11, 46–49, 54, 65–81, 119, 127, 137
Newbigin, Lesslie 128, 136, 204
Nichols, Aidan 9, 59
Nicklinson, Tony 117, 119–120
Niemöller, Martin 175
Norman, Rev. Dr Edward 124–125
Nurser, John 150, 152

Odone, Christina 124
Oliva, Javier 36, 40
O'Sullivan, Richard 21, 46, 55, 57, 82
Otto III, Emperor 15

Pavia, Synod of 13
Pell, George, Cardinal 88
Pitt, Gwyneth 188–198, 195
Pius XI, Pope 75, 153
Pius XII, Pope 150, 152
Porteous Wood, Keith 167
Powell, Enoch 61
Presbyterian Church of Scotland 20
Preston Down Trust 199, 201

Raabe, Dr Hans-Christian 173–174
Radbach, Gustav 80
Richard III, King of England 48
Rivers, Prof. Julian 42, 139, 186
Roper, William 207

Robertson, Geoffrey 106
Russian Orthodox Church 14, 21–22

Sagovsky, Nicholas 100–101, 103
Salvation Army, The 36, 37, 165
Sandberg, Russell 29
Sandel, Michael 101, 130
Schmidt, Alvin 10
Secularism 27–28, 40, 129, 205, 207
Sharia Law 51–52
Shortt, Rupert 204
Simonds, Lord 112, 199
Smith, Adrian 172–173
Societas perfecta 125
Spencer, Nick 6, 20, 22, 45, 122
St. German, Nicholas 47
Strange, Rev. Roderick 74
Sylvester II, Pope 15

Tatchell, Peter 167
Temple, William, Archbishop of Canterbury 150
Theodosius I, Emperor 11
Two Kingdoms Theory 5, 17–19

Vallely, Paul 134
Vardy, Peter 146
Vickers, Prof. Lucy 61, 194
Voluntarism 78

War Crimes Trials 46, 81
Welby, Justin, Archbishop of Canterbury 114
Westphalia, Peace of 18
Williams Prof. Glanville 119
Williams, Rowan, Bishop 18, 41, 51–53, 146
Williams, Shirley 159, 162
Wood, Concepta 85, 87
Wulfstan, St., Bishop of Worcester 147

Zeno, Emperor 11